Nobody Here But Us Chickens

Nobody
Here
But Us
Chickens

by MARVIN MUDRICK

NEW HAVEN AND NEW YORK

TICKNOR & FIELDS

1981

Designed by Sally Harris / Summer Hill Books

Library of Congress Cataloging in Publication Data

Mudrick, Marvin.
    Nobody here but us chickens.

    1. Characters and characteristics in literature.
2. Biography. I. Title.
PN56.4.M8   809'.927   81-4408
ISBN 0-89919-042-1   AACR2

Printed in the United States of America

    V   10   9   8   7   6   5   4   3   2   1

I am grateful to Fred Morgan and Paula Deitz for permission to reprint in this book chapters that appeared
originally in *The Hudson Review*.

To Suzanne

Contents

Preface

The people I write about in this book come from history and fiction, i.e. from books. Nevertheless they speak for themselves in their own words, they live their own lives, they look to the mind's eye just like you and me and give the impression of being just as free to choose, hence I needn't pretend they're only an historian's abstracts or a novelist's inventions. They often come in pairs, not matched but braced, making their competitive and complementary choices: for instance the historical King Philip II of Spain grandly chooses greatness over goodness, but his foster brother Prince William of Orange makes the grander choice of greatness and goodness together and so at Philip's command pays for it with his life ("great power and moral virtue are seldom seen in one person together," says Chaucer's fictitious Criseyde, thinking of the great and good Prince Hector, whom she reveres as she would have revered William if she had met him in a book); or the fictitious Prince Troilus is chivalrously keen to choose love over life, but in fear and sorrow his lady-love Criseyde has no choice except to nullify his choice by choosing life over love though she would rather choose both. Life is real, life is earnest, and because (with apologies to Longfellow) the grave is unambiguously its end if not its goal some of the loveliest and best of us, Criseyde for example, can't resist the choice of lingering a while among even its lesser pleasures; life is full of choices, not necessarily right versus wrong; life is plural and defines itself against life; life is too emphatic to get lost in the words on a page.

Critics worry about the distance between reality (life, truth, experience) and mere bookish (historical or fictitious) approximations of it. Aristotle supposed the approximations should be rated in accordance with exactly how proximate they are—which of the two, history or fiction, is truer to life?—and in his role as the first literary critic he led the way for all his dreary successors by swinging late on a fast ball and deciding, now you see it now you don't! that in fact fiction is truer than history because fact is stranger than fiction, which is "more philosophical than history and of graver import, because *its* statements are of the nature of universals whereas those of history are singulars"; but Thucydides might have countered that history is really less fictitious than philosophy (or literary criticism), and that anyhow, if philosophers are truly lovers of wisdom, they won't be less happy contemplating historical choices than fictitious ones.

Or maybe, if nothing else works, history ought to be called a public mode and fiction a private: but Schiller's or Verdi's fictitious Grand Inquisitor has purged himself of every private feeling in order to serve after his fashion the public good; and the historical William of Orange, reproached for having dared to make his private choice of a lovable but publicly inappropriate wife, ringingly justifies it in the very terms in which he justifies his public burdens which, because he will always bear them, seem to leave him no private choice.

I write about the people in this book from the angle (with the bias) of certain at least theoretical choices of my own: either over neither, both over either/or, live-and-let-live over stand-or-die, high spirits over low, energy over apathy, wit over dullness, jokes over homilies, good humor over jokes, good nature over bad, feeling over sentiment, truth over poetry, consciousness over explanations, tragedy over pathos, comedy over tragedy, entertainment over art, private over public, generosity over meanness, charity over murder, love over charity, irreplaceable over interchangeable, divergence over concurrence, principle over interest, people over principle.

Life is wherever it turns up, in life and books, in history and fiction, in public and private, in Aristotle's appetite for universals and Thucydides' eyewitness account of people and events in Periclean Athens and during the last years of the Athenian Empire. Readers take for granted the obvious differences between history and fiction (nobody but a critic would try to settle which of the two is truer to life) and rejoice to notice signs of life in either. Writing about Philip, William, Solzhenitsyn, Trotsky, Criseyde, Troilus, Alcibiades, the Grand Inquisitor, Chaucer, Jane Austen, Shakespeare, Jesus, Boccaccio, and a cast of thousands, I'll be absolutely delighted to notice and record enough signs of life to keep readers from suspecting they'd be better off reading for themselves a good book of history or fiction.

PART I

HISTORY, POLITICS, AND RELIGION

History, politics, and religion are all bigger than both of us, but size is no guarantee of quality or power, and the bigger they are the harder they fall. For instance here are a number of people—doers, iconoclasts, loners, heroes—who don't just take as they find them history, politics, or religion but go out of their way to break or even make them, as if to prove that people matter.

The
Unsung
Hero Who
Baffled Poets
and Put History
in Its Place

Fiction has to get its characters from somewhere, and why not from history? which teems with characters but tends to make them look redundant and instrumental and morally indefinite, a host of supers and spear-carriers, neither good nor bad but available. History likes to give the impression of having a mind of its own. It's easy, for instance, to think of Europe in the sixteenth century as a train of events, incentives, pressures, configurations, the inexorabilities of Providence or historical process with names sitting here and there along the corridors like labels on suitcases: a guided tour; a rattling big show starring whoever happens to be on the spot at the moment (you can't tell the players without a program). Luther says the word and presto! the Church Indivisible starts to shudder and split; but if Luther didn't say it somebody else would. Henry VIII happens to have one wife already (daughter of Ferdinand and Isabella, that serviceable couple who a generation earlier had done God's still undivided work by defeating the Moors, banishing the Jews, uncorking the Spanish Inquisition, and sending Columbus to convert the heathen), randy King Henry is restive because he has noticed that monogamy is the state of having one wife too many and one wife too few, so against the Church's apoplectic opposition he sets his heart on a divorce because he won't do the decent thing and just sleep with his new girl, he insists on marrying her—what a romantic!—but after all it's too late to keep the faith, it isn't Henry's foolish heart or Anne Boleyn's pretty head on her shoulders but universal erosion and division, the drift of things

(God, Providence, history), that forces the possessive old Church to fumble away its millennial grip on England. Toward the middle of the century the German states have accomplished on their own what seems a free-wheeling man-sized miracle by sorting themselves out, with the unenthusiastic consent of their Catholic overlord the Holy Roman Emperor Charles V, as Lutheran or Catholic; but you can bet they haven't circumvented old mother history, who lightly postpones till the next century the religious war that will lay Germany low before the Reformation is accommodated into the bosom of history. The Netherlands are in rebellion, the liveliest and most cosmopolitan country in Europe, which prodigies of dynastic matchmaking have placed under the heel of the last feudal despotism in Europe, but which at the end of many years of desperate contention will surely win through because otherwise where's the march of progress or the triumph of the masses that vindicates the general drift of things? History is so plausible all by itself that it seems to deny its characters the freedom of fiction; yet as a matter of fact the revolt of the Netherlands has a villain and a hero both of whom are as free as fiction, take off on their own, don't hesitate to buck trends and tendencies as flagrantly as characters in epics, novels, plays, operas. So the characters of history have been known to burst out of history, notwithstanding our suspicion that they're labels on suitcases or plaster busts or reflections in funhouse mirrors, unfit for life or fiction.

King Philip II of Spain was the last medieval villain (autocrat and executioner, benighted, bigoted, more Catholic than the Pope, cleaving to the dead letter); Prince William of Orange was the first modern hero (advocate and moderator, worried, tolerant, less Calvinist than Calvin, honoring the spirit by letting it alone); and for twenty-five years, till Philip managed to bring off William's assassination, they opposed each other like darkness and light and gave history a chance to be as modest as it seldom is.

(Of course as between any pair of adversaries—say, St. George and the dragon—it's possible not only to affirm the white and black but to argue that white is black and vice is versa, e.g. to dispute the account in Schiller's *Secession of the Netherlands* or Motley's *Rise of the Dutch Republic* by explaining that Philip was the last-ditch defender of the Faith against Prince William the Apostate

and Luther the Arch-Fiend and worse: W. T. Walsh's *Philip II*,
a manic exhumation of the "Most Catholic King" from his last
ditch that was published by a U. S. Catholic press during Hitler's
heyday and even got a rave review in the *Times-Lit-Sup*, traced
both the revolt of the Netherlands and the coming of Protestantism
to a worldwide Jewish conspiracy aided and abetted by at least
two Popes. Then there are those who like to think that give or
take a little here or there and now or then people are pretty much
the same anytime and everywhere, that things get blown up out
of proportion, that the Spanish Inquisition was probably a weekend
birdwatchers' club and Philip its recording secretary and that in
any case he was merely as isn't the worst or best of us a reflection—
in a funhouse mirror?—of his age. This hypothesis, which is a
tad more depressing than Walsh's, resembles in its condescension
a recent mealy-mouthed anthropological hypothesis concerning the
practice of cannibalism: that there wasn't any, that there wasn't
ever an extended or nuclear family anywhere that ate people day
in and day out, it was nothing but loose talk by tribes on the
other side of the mountain, who didn't eat people either. Well,
once in a while they ate people, but only at Easter and Thanksgiving.)

Philip of Spain and William of the Netherlands were in their
separate ways sons of the same father. Philip inherited the Netherlands (much larger than the present Netherlands—it included
modern Belgium and parts of modern France) as well as Spain,
Naples, Sicily, and half the Western Hemisphere from his natural
father, the Emperor Charles V (and would have had Germany and
Austria also if Charles's brother Ferdinand hadn't declined to surrender his claim on the Imperial succession), but, born and brought
up in Spain, he knew his father mainly by mail and his father's
Court in Brussels not at all; whereas William, the preëminent
noble of the Netherlands, had passed his childhood and youth at
the Imperial Court as the Emperor's precocious confidant and counselor and in all but law his adoptive son: the good brother armed
with love and favor, the bad brother armed with powers and
principalities. When Charles had to appoint a commander-in-chief
for his army in France he chose the twenty-two-year-old William,
not from any sign of military talent but because he trusted him
as he didn't trust any of his experienced commanders; the same

year he appointed him to the Council of State; when he decided
to abdicate, he chose William to convey the Imperial crown (which
Philip had coveted) to the new Emperor; at the assembly of the
States-General in Brussels at which he turned the Netherlands over
to Philip, who was among the dignitaries in the audience, the old
Emperor supported himself with one hand on a crutch and the
other on the shoulder of William of Orange. Philip hated William
from the outset, no doubt jealous of his father's partiality; but for
a few years the two men maintained the semblance of a personal
connection because the Emperor had wanted them at least friends
if not brothers: Philip was godfather to William's first child (Philip
William); when William's wife died suddenly, Philip sent a conventional message of condolence and William may even have star-
tled the young King into momentary sympathy by answering it
with a burst of anguish—"I am the unhappiest man in the world."

Personal affairs mattered; but neither the Emperor's trust nor
Philip's hatred made William miss the opportunity that the change
of sovereigns offered to his country. The seventeen provinces forming the Netherlands, which Charles picked up as residuary legatee
to various late-fifteenth-century royal marriages, had special rights
and privileges spelled out in ancient charters and a habit of religious
toleration and a tradition of self-government that no autocrat could
be comfortable with and that slippery Charles never subscribed
to or repudiated. Now, though, William and the other nobles
insisted that, taking the oath, Philip bind himself expressly to
what it only suited his father not to brush aside: "I, Philip, do
vow and swear . . . that I will well and truly hold, and cause to
be held, the privileges and liberties of all the nobles, towns,
commons, and subjects which have been conferred upon them by
my predecessors, and also the customs, usages, and rights which
they now have and enjoy, jointly and severally, and moreover, that
I will do all that by law and right pertains to a good and just
prince and lord, so help me God and all His Saints." Further, on
the eve of Philip's return to Spain the States-General wouldn't vote
him an appropriation until he agreed to withdraw all Spanish
troops stationed in the Netherlands. He agreed, and the money
was voted; but at the harbor, while William sped the parting
guest and waited for the royal party to embark, Philip began to

complain about this insult to him of having a condition attached. William replied that the decision to attach it was the States-General's, but Philip broke in angrily, "Not the States but you, you, you!"

They never saw each other again. Once back in Spain Philip never left it for the remainder of his long life and never faltered in his aim of reducing the Netherlands to a captive colony by a policy of terror: the six-year military dictatorship of the Duke of Alba, whose "Council of Blood" had 18,000 persons put to death, "not counting men slain in battle and executed after victory" (by the latter phrase he meant his hanging of prisoners taken in battle and his massacres of the entire populations of captured cities); the burying alive or burning of "heretics" (i.e. Lutherans, Calvinists, Anabaptists); the public beheading or private strangling or poisoning of political leaders—till the Pope himself was moved to recommend some show of mercy: Pius V, not known for shows of mercy, who before his election had been the implacable "Grand Inquisitor for all Christendom." (The specific figure of 18,000 civil executions by Alba—a bagatelle in comparison with credible estimates of the number of deaths under other rubrics of the Netherlands bloodbath—is interesting because it's attributed contemporaneously, though by Netherlands authorities, to a statement made by Alba himself when he left the country in 1573. A Spanish document of 1574 sets it at 6000.) From being under the Emperor Charles the richest source of revenues—richer than the New World with its Aztec and Inca gold—for the Crown, the Netherlands became a bottomless pit into which Philip had to pour revenues from everywhere else to keep the endless war going; its bustling mercantile cities were sacked and huge numbers of the citizens who weren't murdered emigrated to England, as many as half a million out of a total population of three million, until even Alba (though not Philip) began to conjecture that razing the country and driving out those among its inhabitants who hadn't yet been exterminated mightn't be the best possible solution.

Philip could work on a smaller scale too. While his policy was becoming clear but before he despatched Alba to emphasize it, the Netherlands nobles sent two envoys, the Marquis of Berghen and the Baron of Montigny, to Philip to plead with him to ease up a little. (A certain monk, a spiritual adviser to Philip, had already informed him that Berghen was a heretic who deserved death because he had asked the Dean of St. Gudule's Cathedral: "Where in the Scriptures do you find that heretics ought to be burned or suffer the penalty of death?" It may have been an earnest question: Berghen was a Catholic.) Philip treated them with affability and banquets, but once their mission was over they discovered with alarm that he wouldn't let them leave. Berghen had the decency to pine away promptly and die; but because Montigny didn't he was clapped into a dungeon where he moldered for three years while Philip debated with his Council whether to execute him publicly or poison or strangle him on the q.t.; and when at length the decision to strangle him was arrived at (by Philip; the Council preferred poison) and carried out, Philip announced to the world that he had died of fever. Finally, a dozen years after Philip had secretly ordered William's assassination, he publicly proclaimed him an outlaw and promised wealth and glory to his murderer ("we will give him and his heirs in lands or ready money as he wishes, immediately after the deed, the sum of twenty-five thousand crowns in gold"); and when, twenty-five years after their last sight of each other, he learned that the deed had been done, his comment was "Better late than never" (but, tightwad about everything except his sepulchral palaces and his wars against the heretics, he stalled four years till he paid off not with gold but with a patent of nobility and a piece of William's confiscated property). He himself lived another fourteen years and died in his bed—one might say "peacefully and in the odor of sanctity" if it wouldn't sound like a grisly joke, because for the last two months of his life his body was a mass of suppurating and stinking open sores (out of which, according to one report, crawled maggots by the thousands), he suffered hellishly, bore everything with unshakable orthodoxy and calm, and said he was able to die with a good conscience because "never in his whole life had he wittingly wronged a single human being."

Fiction, phlegmatic suitor, doesn't break the doors down to take advantage of history. It wasn't till two centuries later that the first notable literary works were written about these events: Schiller's *Don Carlos* and Goethe's *Egmont*: both completed in the same year by the two most notable German poets, who hadn't yet become acquainted and didn't know they had both undertaken historical dramas on the same subject. The coincidence is surprising enough; but the time was ripe and almost overripe, it was 1787, at the zenith of the Enlightenment, two years before the storming of the Bastille, and history could still though not for long be relied on to contribute steadily and serenely toward the liberation of the human spirit: the revolt of the Netherlands looked like the blood-red sunrise (Schiller was inspired to write not only his play but concurrently the opening volume of his projected comprehensive history of the revolt), its villains were the horrid past, its heroes the men of the dawning day. The other coincidence is that in neither play is William of Orange the hero or even a prominent character. In *Don Carlos* he is mentioned a few times but doesn't appear at all. In *Egmont* he appears in a single scene, trying to talk the hero into getting out while the getting is good; and the leaden dialogue makes him even duller than Goethe intends him to be as the prudent and calculating foil to a second speechmaker who Goethe hopes will sound like a high-spirited, loyal, generous hero:

> EGMONT: Has the King any more loyal servants than we?
>
> ORANGE: We serve him in our way; and among ourselves we can admit that we know quite well how to balance the King's rights against our own.
>
> E: Who but does likewise? We submit to him and are ready to serve him in all that is his due.
>
> O: But what if he should claim that *more* was due to him, and term disloyalty what we call standing up for our rights?
>
> E: We shall know how to defend ourselves. Let him assemble the Knights of the Golden Fleece; we will submit ourselves to their judgment.
>
> O: And what if the judgment should precede the investigation, punishment the judgment?
>
> E: That would be an injustice of which Philip would never be guilty, and a piece of folly of which I do not believe him or his councillors capable.

Schiller wrote a review of *Egmont* in which he complained that the hero, lacking any qualities of greatness, seems only a feckless cavalier in the fell clutch of circumstance; and maybe while writing it Goethe began to fear that Egmont would dwindle out of sight altogether unless he cut William back. But the violation of history is egregious. In the first place historians agree with rare unanimity about Egmont, whom the Dutch historian P. J. Blok sums up as "a finished courtier and valiant soldier, but otherwise . . . of little significance, vain, and without any political penetration." Insofar as he played a part in the revolt he played it as a subordinate to William, and insofar as he differed with him showed what the world might have called prudence if it had saved him but was right to call stupidity because it didn't. When Philip, having already made up his mind to unleash Alba and authorize a reign of terror, commanded his vassals in the Netherlands to take a new and slavelike loyalty oath ("to serve His Majesty, and to act toward and against all and every, as shall be ordered me on his behalf without limitation or restriction"), Egmont tamely took it and so did most of the other nobles except William, who refused on the grounds that he had already taken the regular oath, and that the new one was "unprecedented and general, against my conscience, and to the injury of the King and the country, and contrary to my allegiance as feudal lord, and subject of this land"; and he forthwith resigned all his offices. Philip's half-sister Margaret, Duchess of Parma, Regent of the Netherlands (till Alba took her place), begged him to reconsider, but he refused again, adding that "the new oath might compel him to act against the Provinces of which he was hereditary chief, against the Emperor, or even to kill his own wife since she was a Lutheran." He had correctly inferred that the new oath was the harbinger of the fatal crackdown, that, for instance, the concessions to religious toleration he had wrung out of Margaret would be annulled; his efforts to unite the nobles in resistance and to recruit help from Germany had failed; Alba was coming, and the nobles who stayed to greet him would be his first victims; the only prudent (unsuicidal) course was flight until the day when resistance became possible.

Meanwhile brush-fire hostilities were already flaring up: Antwerp, center of world trade and the richest city in the world, was on the verge of ruin and pillage by religious rioting—the Calvinists were threatening revenge against the Catholics, whose loyalist troops had just routed and slaughtered a Calvinist force outside the city. Margaret asked William to do what he could to restore peace; and because, though no longer in the King's service, he was hereditary burgrave of the city, he went at once and on his arrival appeared alone before a mob of ten thousand enraged Calvinists armed with everything from pikes and sledgehammers to pieces of artillery (who screamed insults and threats at the Most Catholic King's lackey: "Die, treacherous villain!" shouted one of them, shoving an arquebus into his face but it was struck aside by somebody else), he carefully explained to them that their military force had been chewed up and that a mob on the same errand would be unlikely to do better. Having cooled them down a few degrees and gained time, he spent the next three days negotiating with the other factions in the city, then met again with the mob that was gathered in still greater numbers in the enormous market-square, explained to them the truce he had got the others to accept, and persuaded them they would be wise to accept it themselves. At the end he cried out for the last time in his life, "Vive le Roi!" and in response "the crowd of Calvinists raised one tremendous shout of 'Vive le Roi!' "

The city was spared, and William returned to his preparations for leaving the Netherlands. At Margaret's request he had one more meeting with Egmont, but neither could budge the other: William said that Philip intended to wreck the country, and "You will be the bridge across which the Spanish will enter this land"; he embraced Egmont and "both weeping, they took a last farewell" (William was abandoning his wealth and property and turning toward years of harried and comfortless exile: one account has Egmont saying, "Goodbye, landless Prince" and William retorting, "Goodbye, headless Count"; but they give the impression of having been too fond of each other to part on such an exchange). William left for Germany a step ahead of the hangman Alba, who came with secret orders from Philip "to seize the Prince first and foremost and bring him to execution within twenty-four hours," and then at his leisure dispose of such small fry as Egmont: when Cardinal Granvelle, one of Philip's advisers, learned that Egmont was caught but William had escaped, "What's the use of catching minnows," he exclaimed, "when the salmon jumps free?" (Alba, incidentally, was quite a phrase-maker himself. When Egmont welcomed him at the border, Alba turned to an aide and said loudly enough to be overheard, "Here is the great heretic"—in fact Egmont was Catholic, it was one of his reasons for remaining loyal—but then threw his arm round Egmont's shoulder as if he had been making a joke. After the sentence of death had been pronounced Egmont's wife came to plead for him, and Alba assured her that the next day her husband would "go free"—as no doubt, from a good Christian's point of view, could be said to have happened when the next day Egmont's head was chopped off.) Egmont is an ordinary man caught in a trap, William is one of the bravest and most magnanimous men who ever lived; Goethe's attempt to balance them off is an unhistorical nuisance; and though Philip's polemicists called William sly, crafty, uncandid, even a coward, Goethe doesn't do himself proud by allowing their poison pens the shadow of a justification.

But the play is claptrap from start to finish, most of it not just pompous and inaccurate but so persistently simple-minded that it begins to look like a deliberate travesty—Schiller isn't the only reader who asks himself why Goethe transformed Egmont from history's middle-aged, respectably married man with eleven children to the play's bachelor gallant with a sentimental bourgeois mistress:

> CLARA: Let me be silent! Let me hold you. Let me look into your eyes, find everything there—comfort and hope and joy and grief. (*She embraces him and gazes at him.*) Tell me! Speak! I do not understand. Are you Egmont? Count Egmont? the great Egmont who is so famous, about whom they write in the newspapers, to whom the Provinces cling?
>
> EGMONT: No, dear Clara, that is not who I am.
>
> C: What do you mean?
>
> E: Listen, Clara.—Let me sit down!—(*He sits, she kneels before him on a footstool, rests her arms on his lap, and looks at him.*) *That* Egmont is a bad-tempered, stiff, cold Egmont, who has to keep a firm grip on himself, put on now one expression, now another; harassed, misjudged, involved, while

everyone thinks him light-hearted and gay; loved by a people that does not know what it wants; honored and praised by a mob with which nothing can be done; surrounded by friends to whom he cannot trust himself; watched by men who would use any means to get the better of him; working and striving, often to no purpose, usually without any reward—oh! how he fares and feels is better left unspoken! But *this* Egmont, my Clara, *this* Egmont is at peace, free to speak, happy, is loved and known by the best of hearts, which he too knows and presses to his own in perfect love and trust. (*Embraces her*) This is *your* Egmont!

    C: Let me die so! The world has no joys after this!

(Holy liverwurst!) And Schiller also dared to find unworthy—"operatic"—the final scene, in the dungeon where Egmont has a vision: "*Music. . . . He falls asleep; the music continues . . . the wall seems to open, and a shining vision appears.* FREEDOM, *in celestial raiment, surrounded by a halo of light, rests on a cloud. She has* CLARA'S *features, and bends toward the sleeping hero. . . .*" Clara, by the way, has prepared for this apotheosis by perishing in the previous scene from an attack of hyperbole ("O fetter me, that I may not despair, cast me into the deepest dungeon, that I may beat my head against oozing walls . . ."), going down for the count so to speak; but don't leave yet, because, back in his cell, the count with comparable fervor hails the beating of the drums that signals his imminent deliverance from this vale of tears ("Hark, hark! How often has that tone led my free steps to the field of combat and victory!"), and soon he'll be winging like a big-assed bird in the direction of that celestial sugarplum awaiting him on Cloud Nine: "*Drums. As he advances toward the guards and the door rear, the curtain falls; the orchestra strikes up and ends the play with a symphony of victory.*" In this climactic tactic Goethe is soliciting from the organ-grinders of the world some traveling music to match his daydreams, and one hopes that when the play was put on he got what he deserved (sixty-nine variations on "Ach, du lieber Augustin"); but years later along came Beethoven who was impolite enough, without asking Goethe's permission, to compose the "incidental music" which is the only surviving work of art called *Egmont* (though

Goethe would never know, because his ear for music was no better than his ear for death-cell heroics: Mozart's *Abduction from the Seraglio* "did not appeal to me"; he didn't care for Beethoven— who went all out one evening at the piano to demonstrate his art for the great poet, who after it was over bowed like the courtier he was and remarked that Beethoven had "played charmingly"— nor did he take to Schubert's settings of his poems; oh no, not he, for the composer he positively madly doted on was Karl Friedrich Zelter).

As for Schiller's *Don Carlos*, like Goethe's *Egmont* it's first of all an historical drama about people who never existed. True, Philip is one of the major characters, not the villain as in Schiller's own history of the revolt and not the hero, but more like a hero than like the historical villain. Nor is William the hero or even on stage at all. The hero isn't even singular but a sort of Damon-and-Pythias duumvirate—one of them, Don Carlo, a romantic falsification of his historical namesake; the other, Rodrigo, Marquis of Posa, a wholly fictitious character. (Both come directly from Schiller's source, which wasn't history but an "historical novel" written by a seventeenth-century French romancer named Saint-Réal. Everybody agrees that there is no historical basis for Posa; but I'm pleased to have noticed in a seventeenth-century Spanish biography of Philip a "Marqués de Poza," President of Philip's Council of Finance, about whom no personal information is given but whose name Saint-Réal may have found there and borrowed.)

The historical Don Carlos is an odd armature on which to model a romantic hero. Some of the facts of his life look very promising if they are presented in a kind of shorthand: he was quick to anger and action; he hated his father, the wicked King Philip; he adored his beautiful stepmother, Elizabeth de Valois, to whom he had been betrothed before she was married off to his father; he was so fixed on going as Regent to the Netherlands that when Alba, who had been designated, came to say goodbye Carlos tried to murder him; he was finally imprisoned—and, some (including William) said, murdered—by his father; he died in prison at the romantic age of twenty-three, and two months later his stepmother died at the same age. These are the facts on which Schiller (following his source) bases his love-sick, mettlesome, liberty-loving

prince. But the historical Carlos was also a physically and emo-
tionally unattractive young man who seems to have had little
interest in women except to insult and beat them for sport on the
streets; who adored his stepmother not from amorous inclinations
(they were both only fourteen during their brief betrothal, which
seems to have been strictly a matter of State) but because the good-
hearted young Queen showed motherly affection toward her husband's ungovernable and neglected heir; whose motive for hating
his father (bitterly enough to confess to a priest that he intended
to kill him), wanting to be off to the Netherlands, and trying to
kill Alba was more likely thwarted ambition than political idealism. The official Spanish version of his imprisonment and death
was that the risk he posed to the stability of the throne had become
intolerable; he was therefore confined; during his imprisonment
his rage and wilfulness—he went on a hunger strike, he indulged
in monstrous gluttonies—forced his always fragile health to give
way and he died. It's not beyond the limits of the probable that
Philip killed him or ordered him killed, because Philip had a
rather extreme view of autocratic responsibility; yet it must also
be granted that Philip was a good family man who for example
wrote loving and playful letters to his (other) children.

But in *Don Carlos* what interests Schiller isn't historical truth
(which belongs to the volume of history he wrote about these same
events), it's the extravagance and grandeur of the feelings that
might or should have been associated with it. In Schiller's play
Carlos's love for the Queen is so high and nice that when at last
they can talk a bit she needs only a few moments to convince him
to deflect it toward serving and liberating his nation ("Elizabeth
was your first love. Now let your second love be Spain"); in the
interview between the Grand Inquisitor and the King, the power
of the Church and the power of the State hurl warnings and
denunciations at each other like thunderbolts from rival moun-
taintops ("If I did not now stand before you—by the living God!
you would have stood before me thus tomorrow"); in the interview
between Philip and Posa, the boundlessly idealistic Marquis compares the King to God Himself as he adjures him to "give us
freedom of thought" and thus emulate God Himself—

> *The rustling of a leaf*
> *Strikes terror in the lord of Christendom—*
> *You must fear every virtue. He—lest Freedom's*
> *Delightful presence be disturbed—He sooner*
> *Allows the entire ghastly host of Evil*
> *To rage throughout His universe . . .*

(not the most delightful prospect to propose to "Philip" if he were the order-at-any-cost tyrant that the historical Philip in fact was); when Schiller's Philip in an Othello-like frenzy accuses the Queen of adultery, she defends herself from an altitude of indignation and courage that recalls by contrast the marshmallow helplessness of Shakespeare's heroines in similar crises—

> *I am not accustomed*
> *To being questioned in the presence of courtiers*
> *As if I were a criminal . . .*

—so that when Philip "thrusts . . . [his terrified little daughter, who has been a witness to the scene] roughly away," the Queen embraces her and, addressing herself to the child because the infuriated King is no longer worthy of being talked to directly, reminds whoever happens to be listening that the Queen is not only Philip's consort but a French princess still: "if the King refuses / To know you any longer I must send / Beyond the Pyrenees and have defenders / Come to take up our cause." The most concentrated instance occurs when Posa pays his farewell visit to the Queen: she discovers that he has served Carlos's hopeless love of her only because he expects it to incite Carlos to great deeds (e.g. the liberation of the Netherlands), and she suddenly understands that Posa, champion of freedom, bound in blood-brotherhood to Carlos and in unavowable love to her, committed to a glorious act of self-immolation, has accomplished his utterly private goal of tying together and experiencing all the great feelings at once—

> QUEEN: *You go, Marquis—*
> *And yet you have not told me when we shall—*
> *How soon we meet again.*

MARQUIS: (comes back again, his face averted.)
                            We certainly
   Shall meet again!
Q: *I understand you, Posa—*
   I understand you very well—Why did
   You do this to me?
M: *He or I.*
Q: *No! No!*
   You plunged into this action which you term
   Sublime. Do not deny it. I know you,
   You have been thirsting for it this long time . . .

—and she appeals to him to let her try to rescue him, she is brave,
she has friends in France; but he will not yield:

Q: *There is no rescue?*
M: *None at all.*
Q: (leaves him and covers her face.) *Then go!*
   I shall esteem no man again.
M: (throwing himself at her feet in the most vehement
emotion)
                            My Queen!
   —My God! but life is beautiful!
   (He leaps up and walks rapidly away.
   The Queen retires to the inner chamber.)

The talismanic name in Posa's pursuit of sublimity is William
of Orange. To save Carlos and sacrifice himself, Posa writes a letter
to William that he makes sure will be intercepted and read by
the King's agents. Posa (like William) is assassinated at the King's
command; and Carlos, confronting Philip, taunts him for his inferiority to the man he wished to befriend and could only murder:

                    the letter
   To Orange he composed to rescue me—
   My God! It was the first lie in his life! . . .
                    The splinters
   From his mind would have made a god of you.
   You have robbed yourself—

What will you offer to replace a soul
The like of this?
            (A profound silence. Many of the grandees look
            away or cover their faces with their mantles.)
O you who stand assembled here all mute with horror
And with astonishment—do not condemn
The young man who has used such language to
His father and his King—Behold this sight!
He gave his life for me! Do you have tears?

—and the distraught King, when at last he is able to speak his feelings, says: "Give me back this dead man. I must have him back."

It's a play full of archaic voices, written by an uncompromising young man (he was in his twenties) who goes on and on at unconscionable length and is never less than exalted, is in love with goodness and greatness and has the confident intention of reconciling them, borrows gigantically from Shakespeare and improves on what he borrows from—indeed the jealousy plot is just stolen from *Othello* and then redone in the right way: there's a bad-as-bad-can-be Iago (divided into two characters, so that he can convincingly talk to himself: the King's confessor plus none other than the Duke of Alba) whom the King handles with so much authority and shrewdness that one never has the sense as in *Othello* of watching the slow murder of a helpless animal; the bright and beautiful Queen stands up so intrepidly against the horn-mad King that one never has the sense as in *Othello* of watching etc. Though Schiller dismissed the Birth-of-Freedom scene in Goethe's *Egmont* as "operatic," by which of course he meant that it tried to cover up its lack of brains with a patch of grandiosity, still there's another meaning of the word according to which no play in the world is more operatic than *Don Carlos*: it isn't grandiosity but grandeur that's in question: it's what Rossini meant when, having attended the premiere of Verdi's opera derived from Schiller's play, he declared that the new work "proved that Verdi was the only man alive capable of writing Grand Opera."

The nineteenth-century composers of opera had the good sense to direct their librettists often to Schiller's plays, which for example were the sources of four of Verdi's operas, one of them *Don Carlo*. (Verdi composed his opera to a French libretto, by Joseph Méry and Camille du Locle, with the title *Don Carlos*. I use the Italian title partly because, after its premiere over a century ago, the opera has almost always been sung in Italian and the arias are generally known by their Italian first lines, partly because the Italian title permits one to discuss the opera without having to keep telling the reader that it isn't the play. The version of the opera I'll be talking about is the one that incorporates most of Verdi's late revisions and restores the first act; the recorded performance I'm most familiar with is the one conducted by Solti, with a cast including Bergonzi, Tebaldi, Fischer-Dieskau, Ghiaurov, Bumbry, and Talvela.) It's customary to jeer at opera libretti, but the libretto of *Don Carlo* preserves the contours and momentum of the play, prunes back many of Schiller's exaltations only to clear a space for Verdi's, and as a matter of fact is responsible for changes and additions that make one wonder why Schiller didn't think of them himself.

The two conspicuous changes in the plot both involve Posa. In *Don Carlos* it's the King who commands Posa's death; and, in the splendid scene between Philip and the Grand Inquisitor which follows the assassination, it's this very command which the Grand Inquisitor singles out as he denounces the King for usurping the prerogatives of the Holy Office, which has planned to do the job itself. In *Don Carlo*, however, not only does the King (as in the play) solicitously warn Posa that if he doesn't watch his language the Grand Inquisitor will get him ("Ti guarda dal Grande Inquisitor!"); but in the scene between Philip and the Grand Inquisitor, which here *precedes* and foreshadows Posa's death, the King defends his friendship with Posa while the Grand Inquisitor demands that "the innovator" be handed over to him; and it's not the King but the Grand Inquisitor whose agents murder Posa— so that this aspect of the libretto has a symmetry that Schiller misses and that alters the sense of Philip's mourning over Posa's body from a rather contorted sort of remorse to a simple gesture of loss and grief ("Who will give me back this man?"). There are two conspicuous additions: the entire first act, a kind of prologue in which Elizabeth and Carlos at Fontainebleau meet and fall in love and almost at once learn their desolating fate; and the grand-opera scene with a cast of thousands at the auto-da-fé where heretics are marched in to be burned at the stake (Spanish-type historians irritably point out that *no* executions happened at an auto-da-fé, they happened *later* and *outside!*): both, especially the latter, provide Verdi with wonderful occasions for the sound and spectacle of individual and massed voices on a packed stage. And even the change to a "happy ending"—Carlos not under arrest as in Schiller but whisked away from the King and the Grand Inquisitor by the timely materialization of that *deus ex machina* the Emperor Charles V, or his revenant, in full regalia—makes for a spectacular operatic conclusion which at least doesn't feature a Goethean charade of heavenly cuties, and which besides has the advantage of Verdi's grandest and most somber concluding orchestral flourishes.

Less than a century after the Enlightenment, Europe was being washed by another wave of political optimism, and the last romantic idealists had their day. Verdi, like Schiller, hated tyranny and priestcraft; he eagerly applauded the diplomatic and military actions by Cavour and Garibaldi in behalf of liberating and unifying Italy (he was even ready to do some gun-running!); he composed operas with plots that the government censorship mangled because they suggested too nearly his political hopes, and with rousing arias that became patriotic rallying-cries for all Italians. So it was time for Philip and his invisible antagonist to take the stage again; and one pauses wistfully to try to imagine a duet by Verdi for Egmont and William at their last meeting or for Philip and William at any meeting or a great stage full of singers in gorgeous period costumes when William shows up at the Red Gate in Antwerp to quiet and convince the raging mob, because Verdi like Schiller can be trusted with such moments, he has the imagination for the true sublime and not, like Shakespeare, for the petulant-pathetic or the bloody-awful pretending to the sublime. (But we settle blissfully for what, accepting the text his librettists give him, Verdi enlivens it with: e.g. the marvelously transfiguring music of the soliloquy-arias—"Ella giammai m'amò," most affecting of all arias of unrequited love, as Philip despairingly muses that "she never loved me"; "O don fatale," the Countess Eboli's vehement lamentation on the curse of beauty; "Tu che le vanità," as Elizabeth, kneeling at the Emperor's tomb, sadly renounces the world.)

Moreover evil can be as sublime as virtue. Schiller's and Verdi's Grand Inquisitor doesn't after all say, "Oh fudge! I wish I hadn't" or "Evil, be thou my good." For Shakespeare evil is misbehavior up to a point and repentance at leisure (Claudius and Macbeth) or mustache-twirling and melodrama: Edmund or Iago is thrilled by his own wickedness: even in the opera that Verdi and Boito made from *Othello* Iago can't restrain himself from bawling out his self-conscious "Credo" in case anybody in the audience still hasn't guessed he's a double-dipped dirtball from blackest hell (because even Verdi's genius for sublimity can't find a basis in Shakespeare's pygmy villains); for Shakespeare virtue is an old lecher's *mea culpa*: Never trust a boy's love or a whore's oath, don't paddle in a lady's palm or twiddle with her placket, support your local king, and if you're lucky Iago won't come slithering your way, and just maybe you'll stop feeling so rotten most of the time. But for Schiller and Verdi evil is more virtuous than Shakespeare's virtue and most terrifying by its resemblance not only to good but to the best: their Grand Inquisitor is ninety years old, feeble, blind, and so strong in the assurance of his possession of the truth that he can disregard all human connections and outface all the kings and favorites of the earth; Schiller and Verdi understand that such men are sublime and the terrors of the earth, "a type" (as W. E. H. Lecky describes them in his *History of Rationalism in Europe*)

that is singularly well defined, and is in many respects exceedingly noble, but which is continually marked by a total absence of mere natural affection. In zeal, in courage, in perseverance, in self-sacrifice, they towered far above the average of mankind; but they were always as ready to inflict as to endure suffering. These were the men who chanted their Te Deums over the massacre of the Albigenses or of St. Bartholomew, who fanned and stimulated the Crusades and the religious wars, who exulted over the carnage, and strained every nerve to prolong the struggle, and, when the zeal of the warrior had begun to flag, mourned over the languor of

faith, and contemplated the sufferings they had caused with a
satisfaction that was as pitiless as it was unselfish. These were
the men who were at once the instigators and the agents of that
horrible detailed persecution that stained almost every province
of Europe with the blood of Jews and heretics . . .

—and anybody who listens to the deep-as-a-well duet of the two
basses, Philip and the Grand Inquisitor, in *Don Carlo* can feel in
his bones what Lecky (whose *History* is contemporaneous with
Verdi's opera) is talking about. But then *Don Carlo* is the last and
sublimest of all romantic masterpieces, so it may not be accidental
that its subject is the sublimest episode in the history of Europe.
William, though, never got to sing or be sung to. (Unless one
counts the patriotic tune that began to be heard in the Netherlands
during Alba's terror, "Wilhelmus van Nassouwe," in which William is represented as singing a song of himself:

> *My life and all that is my own*
> *I to your cause confide;*
> *My brothers, loyal gentlemen,*
> *Stand faithful at my side.*
> *Count Adolf we left lying there*
> *In Friesland's woeful fray,*
> *His soul in the eternal life*
> *Awaits the Judgement Day.*)

He was too important, he blocked out the others, he did too
much, it went on too long, there was too much geography between
him and his royal assassin. Schiller chose Madrid and the heart
of King Philip, assuming he had one. Goethe chose Brussels and
Egmont, because visions of sugarplums danced in the riggish poet's
head and William was too busy a man to be conceived of even
by Goethe as spending his Saturday afternoons making speeches
to sugarplums. For poets and composers William is the big man
who wasn't there.

Among the numerous Williams of Orange he is the one whom
because of a silly mistranslation history knows as William the
Silent. A henchman of Philip's, either Cardinal Granvelle or the

Inquisitor Peter Titelmann, called him "sluwe" ("sly"), and the Dutch was mistranslated into Latin as "taciturnus," which in turn was retranslated literally into the European vernaculars—a strange epithet for a man who was genial, approachable, and loquacious all his life. Later it was supposed, reasonably enough, to have derived from his behavior at the turning point of his life. In 1559 the French and the Spanish had concluded a peace treaty, and Philip sent three envoys to Paris to help the French celebrate it: Alba, Egmont, and William. The French king, Henri II, taking for granted that all the envoys were in Philip's confidence, brought up in a private chat with William the plans he and Philip had been working out to exterminate all the Protestants in Europe, beginning with that heretical pesthole the Netherlands. William not only kept his counsel but led the king on to disclose more and more: so "the Silent" because he knew when to keep his mouth shut; and it was at this moment, as he wrote many years later, that he came to understand that Philip was the enemy and that there would have to be a resistance to the death. Think of the duet that Verdi would have made of this scene!

There is a portrait of him painted during this year (the year also when he paid his respects to Philip at the harbor in Antwerp). He is twenty-six years old: a soberly handsome young man without shyness or ostentation: standing, in armor, his left hand on his helmet which rests on a table at waist level, his right grasping what seems to be a lance; his head long but not narrow with close-cropped brown hair; the face is three-quarters profile with the dark, contemplative eyes directed at the painter, a straight fine nose, the chin strong and with a cleft unconcealed by a wisp of beard, the wide firm mouth slightly downturned; and there is something in the face which, as one commentator remarked, "makes the observer forget William is a young man." But the portrait by no means exhausts the man. Before he went into exile he was one of the richest lords in Europe, he had a personal retinue of twenty-four nobles and eighteen pages, at his various palatial residences it snowed (as Chaucer says about his Franklin's hospitality) meat and drink: he kept open house, the magnificence of his table was the talk of Europe, he maintained a huge staff of cooks and servants (once as an economy measure he discharged in a single day twenty-eight of his cooks), great nobles throughout Europe sent their cooks to school with William's, on one occasion Philip wrote from Spain begging William for a particular master chef of his. (During the worst years of his exile, unaccompanied and on the run just one step ahead of Philip's hit-men, he coped quite well with reduced circumstances that obliged him to scrape along with occasional homely help from his brother John: "I beg you to send by the bearer of this, the little hackney given me by the Admiral, in case he is in good condition. Send me also two pairs of trunk hose. Your tailor has one that Nuenar gave him to mend; the other pair please have taken from the things I recently used at Dillenburg, which are on the table with my accoutrements. If the little hackney is out of condition, please send me the gray drudge with the cropped ears. . . . Pray forgive me for troubling you with my affairs. I hope to repay you some time.") He was a social man and a lavish host, he loved dancing, masquerades, courtly entertainments, hawking and hunting and knightly tournaments, he was gracious without loftiness, he spoke candidly and unaffectedly with everyone he met whether at court or in the streets. Once, during William's last years, the English poet-diplomat Fulke Greville came upon him ("Vader Willem": already Father of His Country and much more than any other a parlor-and-kitchen paterfamilias) sitting among the citizens of Delft, "so fellow-like encompassed with them as—had I not known his face—no exterior sign of degree, or reservedness, could have discovered the inequality of his worth or estate from that multitude. Notwithstanding I no sooner came to his presence, but it pleased him to take knowledge of me. And even upon that—as if it had been a signal to make a change—his respect of a stranger instantly begot respect to himself in all about him: an outward passage of inward greatness which, in a popular estate [i.e. a democratic country], I thought worth the observing. Because there, no pedigree but worth could possibly make a man prince, and no prince, in a moment, at his own pleasure." According to Pontus Payen, a contemporary of William's, a loyalist historian hostile to him, "He is the most courteous and most agreeable man alive; he has made himself beloved of the people by his humility and liberality, and by his eloquence and vivacity has made himself admired by the highest;

in brief it seems that God has endowed him with all the gifts of nature one can wish for to gain the hearts of men." Pontus noted that even the Catholic clergy—from prelates to priests—of the Netherlands, his lifelong opponents, "bore him a very good affection, especially those who had some intimacy or talk with him at the States-General; and had nothing in their mouths but his modesty, his courtesy, his generosity, so unlike the haughtiness, pride, and ambition of the other lords of the country." And Pontus also noted, disapprovingly, that "It was his custom to say that in matters of religion God alone should inflict punishment."

He may well have been the first man in the history of Europe, perhaps in the history of the world, who advocated complete freedom of conscience, not only for himself but for everybody else; and he never stopped advocating and trying to legislate it through every political vicissitude till his death, often against the harsh and distrustful opposition of his own associates (indeed of his own brother John) in the struggle against Philip, often at mortal risk to what he always considered the first order of business—the restoration of political autonomy and representative government in the Netherlands (so much for his "slyness" and "opportunism"). "In the clash of . . . competing bigotries [as Frederic Harrison summarizes these efforts in *William the Silent*] William of Orange strove to enforce mutual toleration by stirring appeals, by indignant rebuke, and by vigorous action. Time after time he drew up and obtained assent to a scheme of religious compromise or peace, on the basis of each party being free to exercise their own worship, subject to conditions to secure public order, and to avoid offence to their opponents. Both Catholic and Reformed communions were to have equal liberty, where either were in sufficient numbers to form a congregation, and were to have separate churches assigned to them. The rites, ornaments, and property of all religious bodies were to be held free from interference, attack, or insult by word or deed. Open-air and tumultuous preaching was forbidden, and everything which could invite strife or wound the conscience of believers in any creed. William now extended this toleration even to Anabaptists, by which his own chief agent was much scandalised. . . . In his zeal for real and complete toleration of creed William of Orange was in advance of his age by many centuries.

And in this he stood absolutely alone." Because, as it's necessary
to recall, the Calvinists wanted freedom of conscience for themselves
and so did the Lutherans and so too, wherever they were in the
minority, did the Catholics but none of them wanted it for anybody
else even in the same sect if he differed on what could be interpreted
as a point of doctrine. In matters of religion, said William, God
alone should inflict punishment. He had been born into a Lutheran
family, he was raised (at Charles's Court) a Catholic, he returned
to Lutheranism while in exile, he became ultimately a very gentle
Calvinist ("calvus et calvinista"—bald and Calvinist—as he liked
to joke, balancing a loss and a gain of his middle age); and there
is evidence in his letters, not to mention his moral nature, that
the two changes when he was a grown man were heartfelt, made
after serious self-instruction and consultation, and of no political
usefulness. His enemies called him a cynic and a weathervane,
ready to veer into whatever wind promised advantage, and no
doubt they said so because if an attitude like his were to take over
they would soon find their fun and games—murdering men,
women, and children in the name of God—spoiled or, God forbid,
prohibited forever.

   He was multifarious and flexible in all things except conscience,
so that he could puzzle his friends by maintaining at the same
time, and in fact for a lifetime, positions that seemed wildly
contradictory. For instance, he supported both legitimacy—the
continuity of tradition, human relations, lordly responsibility, the
community of Europe that under Charles the Empire had stood
for—and representative government: a double commitment that
caused him to cling for many years to the absurd fiction, as others
regarded it, of contending against Philip in the name of Philip.
He would gladly have consented to the sort of dispensation that
Charles in his best days had allowed more than the appearance
of—a republic under the benign supervision of the Imperial Crown.
When Philip's unsuitability as the emblem of what Philip was so
wholeheartedly trying to smash became at length clear enough,
William to the mystification of his partisans refused to surrender
his hope of turning up an alternative, steadfastly refused to accept
the sovereignty for himself (he was not a "legitimate" candidate),

expended substance and energy over many years on candidates whose incapacity (which often he himself felt obliged to acknowledge) mattered less to him than their pretensions to European legitimacy as well of course as the pledge they might bring of assistance from outside—Queen Elizabeth of England; relatives of the reigning Emperor; the despicable Duke of Anjou, French and Catholic, who later had to be driven out of the country after attempting a *coup d'état*, but who when England and Germany had been unresponsive seemed to William the only remaining hope, as a few months before his death he wrote to his brother John:

> Your theologians and others say that this is contrary to the will of God, but mark well—the minority only is Protestant in the Netherlands, and among the minority the greater part, although strong in their zeal against Anjou and the Catholics, are, when it comes to action, weak and uncertain, as has been repeatedly proven. Moreover, there is no evangel to prevent obedience to a prince of a different creed, or to an alliance with one. The histories of the patriarchs, of David and of Solomon, of the Swiss and Poles, of the German princes in the days of Maurice of Saxony, were all proofs of this. Freedom of religious service could always be guaranteed. And still you write me that there are those who are presumptuous enough to accuse my conscience and my honor, which I would find very strange if I did not recognize the ingratitude inherent in men and the unbridled desire to speak ill.
>
> Who in this world is sufficiently courageous to touch another's conscience? And as regards honor—I can say to a brother without hesitation, is there anyone who has worked more, suffered more, lost more in order to establish, aid, and maintain the church than I? Let them who criticize me do more and better than I. I will serve them and, so far as I can, honor them. Continue, brother, to aid me with your advice for the defense of the good cause wherein, God giving me grace, I am determined to end my days and never to come to an accommodation with Spain, knowing that with such would come the ruin of the churches, of the country, and

of many people, a general tyranny over all inhabitants of this land and particularly [because John, the homebody and conservative of the Nassau family, was always moved by this irrefutable argument] the destruction of our whole house.

And he reassured John that he would continue to do his utmost to defend country, religion, and freedom, "hoping that God by some means will not abandon me in a quarrel so just and so necessary, for which I implore him from the bottom of my heart."

He was a legitimist and a monarchist, he was also unbending on the right of states to govern themselves, also unbending on the principle of representative government, also something like the first democrat in the history of Europe. During the last decade of the many years he spent conducting the defense against Philip, he was de facto king, president, prime minister, chief justice, commander-in-chief; yet in accordance with his stipulations all issues were discussed openly and often acrimoniously in the representative body the States-General, who made all the binding decisions, could and on occasion did overrule him, had the authority to dismiss him and made clear that given the right conditions they wouldn't hesitate to use it. When he was considering new policies and actions it was his custom to travel around the country discussing and arguing them with people of every rank in the cities and villages. Meanwhile he was fighting a war of survival against the most formidable political and military power in the history of Europe.

Nor did he have the usual primary qualification of the successful rebel: though he was a brave and intelligent soldier, he was not a great or at any rate lucky military leader. A year after Alba's occupation of the country, William mustered a mixed army of Netherlanders and German mercenaries with what money he had remaining of his own and all he could beg and borrow from adherents inside the Netherlands and fellow-exiles, crossed the border, and tried to force an engagement with Alba, who however was too skillful a soldier to be drawn in; and after a few months William's army, out of money and provisions, was falling apart and retreating to the French border:

And so at last [according to C. V. Wedgwood's biography of William], "tired and worn out and half dead with hunger" they reached France, William himself having tasted neither bread nor wine for nine days. But his troubles were not over; indeed barely begun, for the French government indignantly ordered him to take his troops away and he struggled back at length in the New Year of 1569 to an inhospitable Strasbourg. He was so ill by this time that he could no longer ride, and his haggard and desperate condition provoked pity in all who met him, except his mercenary captains who stormed his lodging at Strasbourg threatening to make an end of him if he would not meet their wages. Abandoning all hope of retaining his troops, he sold what remained of the artillery to pay the men, left his plate, tapestries, and household stuffs in pawn to the merchants of Strasbourg and escaped one dark night down the Rhine, traveling in a covered barge, almost alone.

The disaster was total. He had thrown in all the resources he had, his entire fortune, the gifts and loans of a trusting and faithful people, and he had lost everything, money, men, credit, and reputation. "We may regard the Prince of Orange as a dead man," wrote Alba with satisfaction.

William thought differently however; as he wrote to John (Schiller himself couldn't have imagined it better, and William didn't have the benefit of a poet's hindsight), "With God's help, I shall go on."

It was at this time that his second wife, Anne of Saxony, was multiplying his public miseries by all the private ones she could inflict. She had been a fault-finding and difficult woman from the first—early in their marriage, before William's exile, Cardinal Granvelle characterized her as "the Prince's Xantippe"—but during the exile she appears to have done everything in her power to embarrass and humiliate him personally and even if possible destroy him politically: she told visitors she had always warned William against getting embroiled with the Spaniards and now that he was she had no sympathy for him, she demanded he abase himself

before Alba and return to the Netherlands, she wrote to Philip
pleading for the reversion to her of all of William's property because
by his failure to return at the King's summons he was legally a
dead man; asserted she couldn't abide William's not royal enough
family (she was, after all, a German princess, daughter of the
renowned Maurice of Saxony), eventually while William was away
betook herself to Cologne to set up an independent household
there because there she had people to talk to and wasn't stuck out
in the boondocks with her husband's family, nor would she come
back at his request: "Do you not see, my wife, that you who are
my spouse leave me to find consolation in trouble from others who
are not so near me?" In Cologne she became involved in a liaison
with a lawyer named Rubens (father of the painter), who told all
to William, but at first Anne denied all: "If you fell into the
hands of the Duke of Alba, which God forbid, you too would
confess that white was black. So he cannot be too severely blamed
for what he said nor should my honor be suspected from it, for
usually unfair questions receive false answers, as has just happened
to you." Soon afterward, however, she wrote to John asking him
to forgive her and to use his good offices with William in her
behalf; but, though she came back to William's family, her mind
and spirits kept deteriorating, she grew so violent that her maids
were in danger of their lives, and at last she was returned to her
family in Germany, where a few years later she died insane.

Meanwhile William had met another woman whom he wished
to marry. She was Charlotte de Bourbon, daughter of the French
Duke of Montpensier. Almost from birth she was raised at a
convent by her aunt the Abbess there, whom by the quaint high-
born-Catholic custom of disposing of spare daughters she was
intended to succeed; and at the age of twelve, despite her formal
declaration that "she was about to take her vows under compulsion,
against her will, and at the command of her parents whom she
feared to disobey," her aunt having died Charlotte took the veil
and became Abbess of Jouarre. For years she kept making plans
to escape, and at the age of twenty-five carried them out by
managing to reach Germany, where she was given refuge by the
Count Palatine of the Rhine. William met her, and soon proposed
marriage ("She must bear in mind," he advised an intermediary,

"that we are in the midst of a war whose issue is uncertain, and that I am deep in debt for this cause, to princes and other gentlemen, captains, and men-at-arms. She must remember, too, that I am beginning to grow old, being forty-two years of age"); but the problem was that Anne, though out of her mind, was still alive in Germany. William requested opinions from a number of Calvinist clergymen in France and the Netherlands, all of whom agreed that Anne's behavior had released him from his conjugal ties and that he was therefore free to marry. Of course the episode was a scandal throughout Europe, political repercussions were anticipated even to the breaking of connections with friendly neighbors (the Landgrave of Hesse: "for his circumstances he ought rather to wish, if he were in his senses, that he had neither wife nor child. . . . If it's beauty he's after, you can hardly believe he was charmed by that, since no one can look at the bride without being frightened rather than pleased"), and solemn John expressed his shocked and anxious remonstrances, which William put an end to with some plain speaking:

> my method has always been . . . not to trouble myself about objections to anything I could conscientiously do without wrong to my neighbors. If I had heeded the remonstrances of princes and others, would I ever have embarked on the enterprise I have undertaken? As soon as I was convinced that neither prayers nor exhortations would have any effect, I saw that active resistance was the sole course open.
>
> It is the same thing now with my marriage. It is something I do with a clear conscience before God and without just cause for reproach from men. Indeed I consider that I am bound to this procedure by God's holy ordinance and that there is really no need to answer men, because the matter is so clear. . . . There is nothing that checks evil suspicions so quickly or that is in such good taste as a quiet and rapid mode of procedure, as though one's self were the most competent judge of one's own behavior, rather than to blazon matters abroad with the sound of the trumpet and then to invite criticism from those who must necessarily be only partially informed as to details.

In regard to the difficulties you raise, of dowry and of provision for children who may be born to me, pray consider that no delay till the next Diet [the Imperial Congress], or the next century, so to say, would have solved them. . . . I have made a frank statement about my duties to my older children . . . and there was no further reason for my being longer in the state of widowerhood to which I have been condemned for so long. . . . I firmly believe that I have taken the right course, not only for myself, but for the public weal.

Charlotte was a loving, affectionate, protective, devoted wife during the seven years they had together (even John was won over, saying that his brother had found in her "a wife distinguished by her virtue, her piety, her great intelligence, in sum as perfect as he could desire her"): she died a few weeks after the first assassination attempt on William, having worn herself out in those weeks of constant attendance on her apparently dying husband. On March 18, 1582 William had been shot through the face by a young man named Jean Jaureguy, hired by a Spanish merchant living in Antwerp who wanted Philip's bounty money. One of the witnesses was an English envoy, who sent this account to Lord Burghley:

suddenly a person of small stature and less representation (of the age of three or four and twenty years, ill clad, and of face pale, drawing to a black melancholick colour, shaven, saving the upper lip, whence a thin black hair began to issue) presented himself as though he had some request to exhibit and once being put back by a halberder, still persisted and suddenly discharged a pistol (that he held unseen) at the Prince, which by reason of overcharging recoiled in his hand and made the piece and bullet to mount upwards from his level, taking the Prince between the ear and the end of the jaw of the right side, passing clean through the left cheek, without offence to the arterye, the jaw, tongue, or tooth (as yet hitherunter is said) saving that it grated upon one tooth, whereat the Prince neither staggering, nor astonyed, beheld the fellow, till he, amazed with his own fact, and bound as it were to the place with a divine power, let his dagger fall to have made away, whereat one Bonnyvet stabbed him in the breast, and then he was presently slain in furie by the company much against the Prince's will, who cried still to save him, but in vain, for he had in less than a moment no less than thirty-three mortal wounds given him.

William had said, as soon as he caught his breath, "Do not kill him. I forgive him my death"; but the revenge had already been taken. For weeks William was thought to be past help, but when Jaureguy's accomplices were put on trial he was able to send a note saying that he believed they should be pardoned, but that if the decision were otherwise "I beg you to ask the magistrates not to inflict torture," and at least his latter wish was honored. He had no need for revenge; he is the only person of the time to be on record against torture as an instrument of justice; and his moral superiority, even at the brink of death, begins to be insufferable. He recovered, however, and continued his work for the two years left to him. On July 10, 1584 he was shot to death in his home by Balthasar Gérard, a young Frenchman who before he undertook the deed had consulted with a Jesuit, a Grey Friar, and Philip's latest Regent the Duke of Parma, and who had bought the pistol with money William had given him in charity. He fired three shots at pointblank range into William's body; William said, "My God, have pity on my soul, I am grievously wounded; my God, have pity on this poor people!" and fell. He was fifty-one years old. His last word, in answer to his sister's question as she knelt beside him, "Do you commend your soul to Jesus Christ?" was "Yes."

Out
Among
the Heathen

William was a European figure; but Philip was a world figure who must have believed that with God's help and a little luck he might any day now be master of the world, for already he not only cast the longest shadow over the Continent and was master of the Americas but sent trading vessels and evangelizing priests out as far as the Philippines (named after Philip when he was heir-apparent by the Spanish sea-captain who had claimed them for the Emperor Charles). The Pope as Universal Proprietor had quite a while back divided all the not-yet-Christianized parts of the globe between Spain and Portugal; and, when in 1580 Philip of Spain became King of Portugal too, he took over completely the Church's sanction for picking up whatever in the whole wide world hadn't yet been nailed down. The gold and spices would go to Madrid and Lisbon, the converted souls to Rome.

Japan was one of the early targets in Asia, and probably the most promising. It had just begun to pull itself together after generations of political disorder and continual petty warfare among the various feudal baronies: the new national leaders were ready to try diplomacy and foreign trade; besides they had no love for Buddhism, whose monks during the time of civil wars had organized themselves into aggressive military enclaves that would take as much subduing as the provincial barons. Thus when the first missionaries, Portuguese Jesuits, arrived in Japan, they got a friendly reception (St. Francis Xavier, who led the first group, was so enthusiastic about the politeness and tractability of the Japanese that he declared that "among unbelievers no people can be found to excel them"); and for decades they did their work with spectacular results and without opposition, indeed they had official encouragement and even grants of land and money from the authorities.

Nothing seemed likely to prevent the Christianization of Japan, converts were being made by the tens of thousands under the instruction of a few dozen Jesuits. Oda Nobunaga (in Japanese names the surname takes precedence as in Chinese and Hungarian: Liszt Franz) had begun to tame the barons and to develop a central government in association with which the Emperor, hitherto for generations powerless and often out of pocket, would serve as constitutional monarch or at least venerated secular symbol: Nobunaga had no religion himself, but if any religion seemed to stand in the way of his ambitions it was militant Buddhism; so he was hostile to the Buddhists, many of whom he slaughtered while storming and destroying their strongholds, and cheerfully hospitable to the ingratiating foreigners. His chief lieutenant was Toyotomi Hideyoshi (Japanese names, at any rate in days of yore, were metamorphic and mysterious—this wasn't his name *now,* but became his *final* name later, and he had had still others before): when in 1582 Nobunaga was assassinated Hideyoshi succeeded him and maintained the same policies toward the Buddhists and the missionaries. Everything was coming up roses.

Until, from out of the blue, in 1587 Hideyoshi issued an edict denouncing the missionaries and commanding them to leave the country within twenty days. He gave no explanation, but it appears he had become concerned about the implications of countenancing a contingent of foreigners who had been turning huge numbers of Japanese (by 1587 estimated at 200,000) into what amounted to a political base for a foreign king. The edict remained unenforced, however, while the Jesuits argued there were no ships to transport them and gradually though much more discreetly resumed their activities, conducted Mass in private homes, made no appearances in public, did their traveling by night, and continued to make converts. The track seemed safe and sure again, if hubris hadn't crossed it in the form of overzealous Spanish Franciscans from the Philippines. Disregarding the Jesuits' Papally-established monopoly of evangelization in Japan, by 1593 Franciscans had moved in and begun propagating the faith as openly and energetically as if Hideyoshi's edict were a dead letter. Still, for a few years, there was no crackdown. In 1596 a Spanish ship ran aground on the Japanese coast and was salvaged by the local ruler over the angry protests of the captain, who came to Osaka to insist to the Minister of Works that his cargo be returned. The captain tried to intimidate the Minister by unrolling a map of the world and showing him the extent of the territories belonging to King Philip. According to James Murdoch in *A History of Japan During the Century of Early European Intercourse* (pregnant term), the Minister inquired "how it was that so many countries had been brought to acknowledge the sway of a single man. . . . 'Our kings,' said the outspoken seaman, 'begin by sending into the countries they wish to conquer *religieux* who induce the people to embrace our religion, and when they have made considerable progress, troops are sent who combine with the new Christians, and then our kings have not much trouble in accomplishing the rest.' "

This speech was carefully reported to Hideyoshi, and noth-ing, we are told, was equal to the impression it made upon his mind. "What!" he cried in fury, "my states are filled with traitors and their numbers increase every day. I have pro-scribed the foreign doctors; but out of compassion for the age and infirmity of some among them I have allowed them to remain in Japan; I shut my eyes to the presence of several others, because I fancied them to be quiet and incapable of forming any bad design, and they are serpents I have been cherishing in my bosom. The traitors are entirely employed in making me enemies among my own subjects, and perhaps even in my own family; but they will learn what it is to play with me!" He then swore that he would not leave a single missionary alive; but shortly after, taking a more moderate tone, he went on: "I am not anxious for myself; so long as the breath of life remains, I defy all the powers of the earth to attack me; but I am perhaps to leave the empire to a child, and how can he maintain himself against so many foes, do-mestic and foreign, if I do not provide for everything incessantly?"

Whereupon Hideyoshi arrested a number of the Franciscans' Japanese converts, ordered lists of converts living in the capital to be compiled, and had twenty-six Christians including six Franciscans put to death (by crucifixion; nothing personal, it was just the commonest means of execution in Japan at the time). From then on the Church kept making brave efforts but it was finished in Japan, several decades later it was suppressed altogether, and Philip had lost another of his great gambles of faith.

Hideyoshi was right to worry about the son of his old age, Hideyori (formerly Hiroi), whom he doted on and did his best to set up as his successor by securing pledges of loyalty from all his barons; but the child was only five when Hideyoshi died. The pledges quickly evaporated in the heat of battles that, beginning almost immediately, ended seventeen years later with the deaths of Hideyori and his mother at Osaka Castle and the foundation of the Tokugawa Shogunate that gave Japan two hundred and fifty years of domestic peace and total isolation from the outside world (till Commodore Perry and Madama Butterfly).

Hideyoshi was born in 1536 (three years after William, nine after Philip) and died in 1598 (fourteen years after William, the same year as Philip). Though having wiped out the house of Toyotomi his successors tried to make a clean sweep by wiping out the very memory of Hideyoshi, he matches William as father of his country and outstanding figure in its history ("It is usually agreed," says for instance George Sansom with quiet confidence in *A History of Japan 1334-1615*, and who am I to disagree? "that Hideyoshi is the greatest man in the history of Japan"). He was a peasant by birth and upbringing; through an extraordinary combination of qualities—patience and decisiveness, good humor and quick-wittedness, intelligence and practicality, military genius and a distaste for wasting lives on his own side or the enemy's, calculation and magnanimity, the will to win and the will to conciliate after winning, fearlessness and a refusal to be personally offended, plain-speaking and loyalty (for many years he was a kind of unflappable Kent to Nobunaga's wayward Lear)—he survived and mastered every condition of anarchy, savagery, caprice, duplicity, treachery to achieve sovereign power and institute responsible gov-

ernment and domestic order. The stories about him have the ring
of truth as well as the ring of legend. Imagine, for instance, what
the Duke of Alba would do hearing of a town that has supplied
Philip's enemy with provisions, as the townspeople of Sakai have
supplied Nobunaga's enemy. Hideyoshi, by this time Nobunaga's
general-in-chief, arrives on the scene and disperses the enemy;
Nobunaga, arriving later, is resolved to massacre the inhabitants
of Sakai for their treachery (the account comes from Walter
Dening's *The Life of Toyotomi Hideyoshi*):

> "Please entrust this business to me," said Hideyoshi, when
> Nobunaga spoke to him on the subject. "I have thought of
> a mode of dealing with these offenders that will most certainly
> answer. In such a matter as that which has occurred it is
> impossible to say who are guilty and who innocent. To kill
> all the inhabitants of the town would be a very crude way
> of dealing out justice. Besides it would be somewhat undig-
> nified for a noted warrior like yourself to march a number
> of troops against a defenceless set of townsmen and butcher
> them like so many cattle. As you well know, up to the present
> time the barons in power in Kyoto have treated both the
> Shogun and the Emperor with great disrespect. It is to your
> interest to strike out in a different line. In order to show our
> respect for those in authority, the first thing I am anxious
> to undertake is the repair of the Emperor's palaces. A large
> sum of money will be required for this purpose. A considerable
> portion of this I propose to obtain from the Sakai townsmen."

Hideyoshi carries out an elaborate plan in accordance with which,
first, the townspeople are threatened with fire and sword, then
sternly informed that for swallowing so slanderous a rumor about
the benign Nobunaga they must send envoys to the capital to beg
his forgiveness, there to be met by Nobunaga in an apparent
immitigable rage decreeing death for the town, then at last terrified
into petitioning a Buddhist monk to intercede with Hideyoshi,
who

> replied, "As you ask it, I will pardon the offence. But, as
> you know, in the seventeenth section of the laws of Shotoku

Taishi, these words occur, 'Where the deciding on the gravity of a man's offence is a matter of difficulty, his life should be spared and his fault atoned for by causing him to pay a fine. This is called a head-fine.' Now the only condition on which the sentence of the Sakai townsmen will be commuted is that they pay a fine of twenty thousand *ryo*."

The townsmen hailed this announcement with delight and the money was soon collected. Hideyoshi applied this amount to the repair of the palaces. Shortly after, he induced Kennyo [the interceding monk] to collect further large sums, and so by degrees the Emperor's palace and the Shogun's residence were rendered worthy of the exalted rank of their occupants.

This effort of Hideyoshi's was extremely well-timed and did much to make Nobunaga's cause popular in the country. The barons in power in Kyoto had for a very long time pursued a selfish and disloyal policy. It was something new and something that appealed to a deep-rooted feeling in the hearts of the people to see a large outlay of this kind. It went far to prove that the professions of disinterestedness on the part of Nobunaga and Hideyoshi were more than mere idle words.

Nobunaga's death sets off the inevitable maneuvering for succession, and Hideyoshi has the special disadvantage that the others hate him not only as a rival but most of all as the unpedigreed upstart whom they remember from the days when he was mascot and water-boy to their own exalted positions next to the great warlord himself. They all meet to discuss the partition of Nobunaga's territory:

Hideyoshi's enemies had previously determined to make this an occasion for provoking him to anger and, if possible, for killing him. They commenced by forcing him to drink a large amount of *sake*. This was followed by all kinds of unreasonable proposals. Hideyoshi bore all patiently, complying even with the request that he should hand over to Katsuie his castle of Nagahama. . . . This concession was so unlooked-for and, in Katsuie's eyes, so important that for the time being his anger was appeased . . .

—and Hideyoshi has escaped for the moment; but Katsuie calls
them together again for a farewell banquet, and

> made this an occasion for insulting Hideyoshi in a more
> egregious manner than he had hitherto done. After they had
> all been drinking freely, turning to Hideyoshi, Katsuie said:
> "Ah! you will remember that some twenty years ago you
> shampooed me. I have not yet forgotten with what skill you
> accomplished it. I wonder whether you still remember the
> art. I have been drinking a good deal today, and my limbs
> are languid: I should like to be shampooed by you again."
> Then, turning to Sakuma Morimasa, he said: "What think
> you, Morimasa? is not Chikuzen-no-Kami too great a man
> to do a thing of this kind?"
>
> Whereupon Morimasa, addressing Hideyoshi, said: "Since
> it is the request of Katsuie, you had better comply."
>
> The generals present were astonished at this proceeding
> and trembled for the consequences. "An outrageous piece of
> rudeness on Katsuie's part!" said they.
>
> Without changing countenance, Hideyoshi replied: "Not
> having practised shampooing for a long time, I am not sure
> that I can do it to your satisfaction. Moreover, today I too
> have been drinking, and hence my hands are somewhat out
> of gear, but as the request comes from one so great, I will
> try my best." Thus saying, he commenced the shampooing.
>
> The various lords looked on with amazement. And Katsuie,
> observing the notice which the barons were taking of the
> affair, felt sorry that he had acted so rudely. In order to
> prevent his feelings of shame from revealing themselves, how-
> ever, he pretended to be asleep. . . .

Morimasa, Katsuie's accomplice, is so exasperated by Hideyoshi's
imperturbability that he reproaches him for it: "I would rather
have my body cut into little bits than submit to such ignominy."

> Smiling, Hideyoshi replied: "Is it not recorded that the
> wife of the Emperor Shomu washed the body of a beggar?
> Compared with that, what I have done is a mere trifle. I am
> not only ready to do this, but to go much further, and all

for the sake of saving the house of Oda from ruin. Are we not surrounded by enemies? There is Mori in the west, who though he has made peace with us is not to be trusted; Hojo in the east; Uesugi in the north; and Chosokabe in the south. All these are rejoicing over the death of Nobunaga, and are waiting for an opportunity to recover their lost territory. What is it that restrains them if not the presence of such men as Shibata [Katsuie], Niwa, Ikeda, and my unworthy self? If we commence to quarrel among ourselves, our late master's cause will be irretrievably ruined. That is my reason for putting up with affronts."

The assembled barons were much struck by these remarks and Morimasa knew not what to say in reply. So Hideyoshi took his departure unscathed.

After he had left the castle, Katsuie called Morimasa close to him and said: "It will never do to let Hideyoshi escape. With the sharpness of a monkey [from childhood he was called Monkey-Face, and when in high spirits even as the elderly Regent he would dance around and carry on like a monkey], he has outwitted us so far, but do you attack and slay him on the road to his castle."

This plot fails too as all plots fail against Hideyoshi, who eventually defeats in battle those he can't win over with parleying, but does nothing for revenge and everything for reconciliation and good order.

"He was fond of placing himself unreservedly into the hands of his foes," says Dening. While consolidating his power, he saw the need to fight or come to terms with a warlord named Kagekatsu, and paid an unannounced visit to him with only a few attendants. When Kagekatsu learned that Hideyoshi had arrived unprotected in his territory, he

called a council to discuss what it was best to do under the circumstances. The majority of the councillors advised the assassination of Hideyoshi, arguing that this was by far the simplest way of ridding themselves of a dangerous enemy. But the highly renowned Naoe Kanetsugu condemned this advice as unworthy of a man holding the position of Kagekatsu. "Hideyoshi's coming among us unguarded," said Kanetsugu, "is a proof of his profound respect for our master. With lesser personages Hideyoshi would not so expose himself to danger. Knowing that our lord is a man of noble disposition, he trusts himself among us. Were we to take advantage of this and slay him, the story of our baseness and treachery would be handed down to distant posterity to our eternal shame. No: let our master meet magnanimity with magnanimity; let him have an audience with Hideyoshi and let them see whether they cannot come to an understanding. If they cannot agree, then we will fight, but not till Hideyoshi has been sent back to his own country." . . .

Kagekatsu entirely approved of the course recommended by Naoe Kanetsugu and, with about sixteen followers, immediately set out for Otsurumi. The two generals met. Hideyoshi's manner was genial and free from all restraint: no one would have supposed that he was in an enemy's country with a mere handful of men. Kagekatsu was fairly astonished at this phenomenon, and began to perceive that Hideyoshi was a greater man than himself, and hence concluded that it would be unwise to go to war with him. He held a private interview with his visitor, and the two came to terms. So pleased was Kagekatsu with the result of the negotiations that he accompanied Hideyoshi some twelve miles on his way back to the capital.

Hideyoshi is fearless, but he worries a lot. He worries about the fragility of pacts and truces (which he prefers to battles) and about possible retribution against a warrior who has renounced another allegiance and come over to Hideyoshi (whose letters are quoted here from *101 Letters of Hideyoshi*, translated and edited by Adriana Boscaro): "I am worried whether or not this was done with the agreement [of Ieyasu], and I am sending you these two persons . . . to find out the details of the matter. . . . I can hardly express how satisfied I am with the fact that you moved without any trouble. . . . This postscript is in my own hand and may include words difficult to read" (he is always apologizing for the illegibility of his handwriting, because well-educated people pride themselves on the elegance of their calligraphy and he knows he's not a well-educated man). He worries about his wife: "I think it would be better if you were less constipated, so why don't you take an enema? . . . I repeat: I would like you to take an enema to get the bowels moving. So I shall wait for a better report concerning your health and telling me how long it takes the enema to have its effect." About his mother: "you ought not to worry about me, for I am feeling better all the time and have been eating my meals regularly. Go somewhere and amuse yourself—and, please, become young once more. I beg you to do this." About his concubines and his two sons (of whom the first-born died in infancy): "please make Hiroi drink enough milk and take great care of him," he writes to Yodo, his favorite concubine and the mother of Hiroi/Hideyori. "You must not worry about anything. I end here. I am sending you five birds caught while hawking and three bamboo baskets of mandarin oranges." Especially about his son and heir-apparent: "I am very glad that you sent me a letter"— Hideyori is four years old!—"in particular, the wonderful nail-cutter made me very happy. . . . I repeat: because I love you deeply, I shall soon be back to kiss your lips. I often think that while I am absent [the child] has been kissed on the lips by other people [instead of by me only]."

His anxiety about Hideyori became a monomania, he seemed to concentrate his energies on trying to keep him alive (because, Tsurumatsu having died, only Hideyori was left to carry on after Hideyoshi) and guarantee him the succession; he lost his geniality and good judgment and flew into ungovernable rages, his last few years were darkened by grandiose and unrealizable schemes (e.g. the invasion and conquest of Korea and China, which took prodigious expenditures of men and money and came to nothing), he lost the passionate curiosity about public matters he had had all his life.

On his deathbed he wrote his last poem (all educated Japanese wrote poems; educated or not, Hideyoshi wrote poems and was so fascinated by the Noh plays that he studied them intensely and often acted in them):

I am as
The dew which falls,
The dew which disappears.
Even Osaka Castle
Is only a dream.

Seventeen years later in Osaka Castle Hideyori committed suicide
and his mother was killed by a retainer so that they shouldn't fall
into the hands of the Tokugawa forces entering the besieged castle.
The Tokugawas, who had their own legend to build, saw to it
for a quarter of a millennium that Hideyoshi's name might as well
have been writ in water. Since his rehabilitation as a national hero
by the Emperor Meiji a century ago, there have been many novels
and plays about him, but none so far as I know has been translated
into English. The only piece of fiction I know of available in
English that uses Hideyoshi as a character is Junichiro Tanizaki's
novella "A Blind Man's Tale," in his collection *Seven Japanese Tales*
(translated by Howard Hibbett), published by Knopf in 1963.

The
Publicity
Hound

These days there's a magazine called *People*, founded on the Andy Warhol axiom that in an age of publicity everybody has as much right to be famous as everybody else. Fame, which was once the last infirmity of noble mind, is now the first fruit of publicity (Warhol himself was the first fruit of publicity); but everybody's waiting in the wings to come on next and who in the world cares? except a world-famous noble mind who doesn't mind making use of publicity for the purpose of taking swipes at the culture that invented it—Solzhenitsyn, media hero, master of publicity, more than a match for mod America. Flashbulbs pop, reporters scribble away, the bearded prophet rocks the two superpowers back on their plastic launching-pads as he asks the question, Can politics stand up to publicity? and across the street in three black auto-mobiles the KGB hunches by the dozen like disgruntled extras rushed by Central Casting to the set of a movie that was canceled just before they roared in with screeching tires. What a one-man act! not only would it play in Peoria, it would be a smash in Las Vegas. He makes the sign of the cross (Russian Orthodox style, striking a Slavophile blow for religion), denounces on videotape the fat smug pagan West mired in materialism, insists that Russia must find its own moral and political way (so long as it isn't communism or liberal democracy): it's a line we've already heard, he sounds quite like Dostoevsky, though even expressing the same moral and political views as Dostoevsky he won't be forgiven by those Western intellectuals—"liberals and democratic socialists" all—for whom Dostoevsky is the great exception, the supreme moral and political writer, the patriarchal breaker of liberal and democratic illusions (Beat me, Daddy), the conscience of the modern world; but suppose Dostoevsky were alive and living in Vermont? In *The New Republic* of May 3, 1980 Irving Howe chides Solzhenitsyn for "such sweeping jeremiads" as "your recent grand pronouncements about the decay of Western will, its lack of moral fiber in resisting communism, etc.," and notes that "your attacks on 'Western intellectuals' for . . . not protesting the outrages of the slave labor camps" are unfair to "other liberals and democratic socialists," among whom he numbers himself—"*we,* the others, have not been silent about the scandals of the camps, the outrage of the dictatorship." Howe calls his complaint "An Open Letter" and expects an answer, he reminds Solzhenitsyn that in *The Oak and the Calf* (Solzhenitsyn's memoir of his last dozen years in the Soviet Union) "you write with anger about the fact that your letters to the Soviet rulers went unanswered." (Howe is sitting in a warm bath of self-approbation fondling his platitudes, Solzhenitsyn was a survivor of the camps out among the flying dead cats in the motherland worrying about rearrest and imprisonment or execution or exile while writing those letters to Kosygin or Brezhnev or Suslov or—boss of the KGB—Andropov demanding an end to the scandals of the camps and the outrage of the dictatorship, so there seems some disproportion here: Howe is Peoria, Solzhenitsyn Las Vegas.) Maybe *People* will give the two of them a page each to debate the issue.

Liberals and democratic socialists are nervous about this throwback who anathematizes decadence and makes a pitch for priests and churches—next week, the Inquisition—but they can relax because though he supports the Ten Commandments nobody supports the Bill of Rights more enthusiastically than Solzhenitsyn, sometimes indeed he supports both God and man at the same time: "that very evening Western radio stations, God bless them, broadcast the news" (of the KGB's campaign to intimidate him as soon as *Gulag Part I* was published in the West); no question that he counts his blessings religiously, but (since as he says God helps those who help themselves) he is less interested in revelation and truth than in freedom and accuracy, speaking up and spelling out, "openness, honest and complete openness" against the futility of prudence (for more than half a century "it was because of personal considerations . . . that we had used our vocal cords so sparingly and let outselves be bundled into the sack before we could raise a shout"); he never doubts that, however decadent, the West by the glare of its publicity has kept him alive (the dictatorship "goes in deadly fear" of "protests from public opinion in the West") as he decries "the crippling and cowardly secretiveness from which all our country's misfortunes come":

> We are afraid not only to say openly, in speech or in writing or even in conversation with friends, what we think and how things really were; we are afraid even to confide it privately to paper, for the headsman's ax hangs still over the neck of every one of us, and may descend at any moment. How much longer this secretiveness will last there is no knowing: many of us may be decapitated before it ends, and what we have kept to ourselves will perish with us.

If Solzhenitsyn hankers after a theocratic state (like, say, the Soviet Union, only using Jesus rather than Marx as a pretext), it's hard to imagine how he expects to get it by hammering away in the cause of freedom, freedom, freedom ("I feel that my whole life is a process of rising gradually from my knees, a gradual transition from enforced dumbness to free speech"; when he finds himself back in a prison cell because despite entreaties, warnings, threats, harassments he just won't stop exercising his mouth, the Nobel Laureate remembers all too well bleak morning in the camps—"There's nothing drearier than early morning in jail"— and is glad he raised a shout for freedom before they bundled him back into the sack); moreover sending the Soviet Writers' Union a letter that execrates censorship as, of all things! "a survival of the Middle Ages" isn't likely to brighten the prospects of another but not unrelated anachronistic institution decked out in medieval trumpery, namely Mother Church; and Jesus' "Ye shall know the truth and the truth shall make you free" seems to mean for Solzhenitsyn not so much the truth of revelation as the truth of history and of conscience, what it meant for Tolstoy:

> people want to conceal, to forget the crimes committed under Stalin, to avoid mentioning them. "Is there any point in

recalling the past?" was the question put to Lev Tolstoy by
his biographer Biryukov, and Tolstoy replied . . . : "If I had
a vile disease and I were cured and cleansed of it, I would
always be happy to talk about it. I would make no mention
of it only if I were still suffering and getting worse and I
wanted to deceive myself. We are sick—and always no more
and no less sick than before. The form of the sickness has
changed but it is still the same disease; only it is called by
a different name. . . . The disease that we are suffering from
is the disease of killing people. [Tolstoy is talking about the
war and militarism of his time.] If we recall the past and
look it straight in the face, the violence we are now committing will also be revealed."

No! We shall not succeed indefinitely in keeping silent
about Stalin's crimes, in going against the truth. The millions
of people who suffered from these crimes demand that they
be brought to light. It would be a good idea, too, to reflect
on the moral effect concealment of these crimes may have on
the younger generation. It means the *corruption* of still more
millions. The growing generation of young people are no
fools; they know full well that millions of crimes were committed and that nobody talks about them—that they are
carefully hushed up. What is there, then, to restrain any one
of us from taking a hand in other acts of injustice? These,
too, will be carefully hushed up.

(He is addressing his remarks, in person this time, to an official
meeting of the Writers' Union, and here are a few of the rejoinders
from the other members: "Your time is up—ten minutes"; "I will
honestly and frankly say that all of his recent writing—true, we
have no knowledge of it, we haven't read it, we haven't been
invited to discuss it—is at cross-purposes with what the rest of
us are writing"; "We must all toe the line, go forward together,
in orderly ranks—all acting as one—not under some kind of lash
but following the dictates of our own minds"; "I wouldn't make
any allowances for him—I'd expel him from the Union. In his
play not only everything Soviet but even Suvorov is presented

negatively. I completely agree: let him repudiate *Cancer Ward*. Our republic has reclaimed virgin and long-fallow lands and is going forward from success to success." There was a vote, and he was duly expelled.)

Finally "Christian" means "human." What Solzhenitsyn finds unique in the almost tragic but blundering and bamboozled Khrushchev is a "Christian trait" that most of us would be inclined to identify more universally as goodwill, decency, as our ticket of admission to the human race:

> Khrushchev had told Tvardovsky that three volumes of documents on Stalin's crimes had now been collected, but that they were not being published for the present. (Khrushchev never carried anything through to completion, and the deposition of Stalin was no exception. He had only to go a little further, and no one would ever again have unclenched his teeth to bay about the murderer's "great services.") "History will pronounce judgment on what we have tried to do." (Khrushchev always became solemn and subdued when he spoke of our common mortality, and of man's limited span. This note could be heard in his public speeches too. It was a Christian trait in him, of which he was unconscious. No Communist leader before or after him, to east or west of him, has ever spoken like that. Nikita was a tsar who completely failed to understand his true nature and his historical mission, who was forever cutting the ground from under the feet of those social groups which would and could have supported him. . . .)

Still, *something* was done, though so much remains to be done. Hope too is a universal obligation for which Solzhenitsyn prefers a Christian term: it looks like supernatural intervention that somebody like Khrushchev, however flawed, could rise up out of the Stalinist cesspool—"the sudden fury, the reckless eloquence of . . . [his] attack on Stalin" at the Twenty-second Party Congress—but, besides, that a knightly hero *sans peur et sans reproche* could come forward out of the petted and privileged cadres is nothing less than a miracle:

When Lenin conceived and initiated, and Stalin developed and made safe, their inspired scheme for a totalitarian state, they thought of everything, did everything to ensure that the system would stand firm to all eternity, changing only when the leader waved his wand; to ensure that the voice of freedom would never ring out, or any movement against the current ever set in. They foresaw all eventualities but one—a *miracle,* an irrational phenomenon, the causes of which could not be divined, detected and cut short beforehand.

Just such a miracle occurred when Andrei Dmitrievich Sakharov emerged in the Soviet state, among the swarms of corrupt, venal, unprincipled scientists, and what is more, in one of their most important, most secret and most lavishly favored nests—in the neighborhood of the hydrogen bomb. (If he had appeared in some obscure back room, they would have snuffed him out smartly.)

Creator of the twentieth century's most terrible weapon, Hero of Socialist Labor three times over (just like the general secretaries of Communist Parties whom he sat beside at meetings), enjoying the entrée to that narrow circle in which, whatever a man's requirements, the word "impossible" does not exist—Sakharov, like Prince Nekhlyudov in Tolstoy's *Resurrection*, woke up one morning feeling—or, more probably, he had always felt, all his life—that the abundance that threatened to overwhelm him was dust and ashes, that his soul yearned for truth. . . .

Solzhenitsyn thinks that Sakharov ought to have picked his spots more deliberately (though the government when they banished him to a city off limits to foreigners must have decided he was doing quite enough): he pays loving tribute to Sakharov's "large and generous nature, . . . his pleas for acquittal, reprieve, reduction of sentence, parole . . . [which were] the result of his constant, his incorrigible urge to champion the persecuted," but he concludes it was Sakharov's very virtues of kindness and fearlessness which impelled him to scatter his energies at every request and in every direction, which may therefore have undercut his effectiveness, made him into a sort of scarecrow figure, the skeleton at the feast, the marcher with the sign announcing doom (within minutes of Solzhenitsyn's arrest Sakharov—who else?—was picketing the Public Prosecutor's Office), and which eventually produced in him the one strong feeling that Solzhenitsyn seems incapable of—a "general hopelessness . . . [regarding] our country's future: we would never succeed in any of our endeavors, and they made sense only insofar as they satisfied a moral need. (I had no very substantial arguments against this; it was just that against all reason I had never in my life experienced this hopelessness, but on the contrary had always had a sort of stupid faith in victory.)"

Solzhenitsyn's blessedly stupid hopefulness is a matter of temperament all right: "I believed that there would be better times and even that I was destined to see them, believed that an age of complete freedom of the press would someday dawn" (and everybody would get to say everything and the Earthly Paradise would begin); even when he is arrested at last and sitting in a cell, he has "no doubt" that he will be taken to "see the government" and that there in the lowermost circle of hell on earth he will be able to "budge" them. But his hopefulness is also, from decades of frustration, reluctant to recognize the good reasons for hope: though he can hardly credit it something has happened, he keeps glancing at it though less to draw inferences from it than to brush it aside with impatience and puzzlement as if it will turn out to be an illusion or a mere lull: the fact is that despite jarring setbacks and heartbreaking missed chances, despite the country's failure to "take advantage of those first few months after the Twenty-second Congress, months of unrepeatable freedom," things have changed since the death of the Ogre. (Ogres are like mules, half horse's ass, half donkey's bray, quite sterile.) In the good old days torture and a bullet solved all problems: people disappeared and nobody thought to ask where on earth good old So-and-so might possibly be these days ("How much land does a man need?" asked Tolstoy in his parable about death, and Stalin gave the correct answer—"Six feet under"—millions of times over). Decades later, the crude and blighted bureaucrats who have inherited the Ogre's realm would dearly love to carry on in the Ogre's posthumous shadow, but they don't have his cannibal appetite for swallowing people toenails and all, the same words and tactics no

longer bear the same lethal charge—"although *Pravda* had chosen
this very time to walk all over me, Tvardovsky and I *did not so
much as mention it* in our conversation. Even to him, abuse from
Pravda no longer meant a thing. Ah me, how times had changed!"
Terror for the sake of appetite as by ogres is infinitely more
terrifying than terror for the sake of tenure as by functionaries
trying to hang on to their sinecures: "But now, with *Gulag* in
their claws, as they carried it from desk to desk (and hid it in
safes, I daresay, to keep it from their own colleagues), passing it
directly from the experts to the top bosses, right up to Andropov
himself, the blood must have turned to ice in their veins: such
a publication might be fatal to the system. (To hell with the
system: their soft jobs were in danger!)" And they are so sensitive!
"Even gangsters want to be loved," as another exiled dissident,
Vladimir Bukovsky, remarked compassionately. Their feelings are
hurt, and the culprit will have to pay.

So why don't they come and take him? "What was the point
of all this barking? . . . For my own part, I saw the very existence
of the newspaper campaign as a victory for me; in their eagerness
to deafen the world, *they* had forfeited the chance to do what they
would once have done—quietly take my throat in their teeth, and
sling me in the jug." He remembers learning earlier that " 'Your
case has been passed to the Public Prosecutor.' My 'case,' that
time, meant my confiscated archive, together with *The Feast of
the Victors* and *The First Circle*, and 'passed to the Public Prosecutor'
appeared to mean that there would be a trial. (Why they decided
against it then is an enigma. They would have done well to try
me.)" Or: "To this day I cannot quite understand why they didn't
take me at the dacha in Peredelkino, why they slept on the job
through Saturday and Sunday. . . . But why didn't they take me
on Monday or Tuesday, instead of letting me trumpet the news
to the whole world? Perhaps they had taken fright because I put
up such a noisy resistance." The strain of trying to figure out their
inaction grows so great that when at last they do the obvious and
come and take him he momentarily turns as hectic and panicky
as if these twenty years have been only a dream of deliverance and
he is back where he has always been, between the Ogre's jaws:

I said no goodbyes—I was in too much of a hurry! (how soon would I be back?)—except to my wife, right by the door: with all those Geebees around us, it was like being in a crowded trolley bus. We kissed each other goodbye, unhurriedly, and with the realization returning that it might be forever. Ought I, then, to go back in? Complete our arrangements [for the safekeeping and distribution of those of his manuscripts that haven't yet been published]? Hang back, drag my heels for all I was worth? No; I was galvanized by shock. (All because of my first false step, all because I had so stupidly let them in—and now I would be on hot bricks until I had cleared the apartment and taken them off with me. In my state of shock I was in some confusion as to who was taking whom.)

—Of course they wouldn't have let him go back in, nor in the time it would have taken them to break down the door could he have done much effective disposing of incriminating papers. The entire passage from which these excerpts are cited pulses and shudders with his (groundless) self-reproach and *embarrassment*. He listened to them barking and barking and forgot they had teeth.—

I made the sign of the cross slowly over my wife. And she blessed me. The Geebees were flummoxed.

"Look after the children."

Then, without a backward glance, down the stairs, not noticing the steps. Just as you would expect: a car had mounted the pavement to hug the main doorway (so that I would have less than one step to take over open ground—the foreign correspondents had only just left), and of course they had its door open and ready, as they always do. No point in resisting. I was well away now. I took the middle seat in the rear. One of them jumped in on each side of me, they slammed the doors, the driver and his navigator were in place already—and we moved off.

Just like in the movies. Terror has no imagination. Now at last he is regretful, now it doesn't seem so unthinkable that he ought to have got out of the country while he might have: "Not once in three years [three years earlier they had signaled that he might choose self-exile] had I regretted it: I had given them hell! The things I had said to them! Nothing like it had ever been uttered under that regime. And now I had published *Gulag* from the very best vantage point—from *here!* I had done my duty. What was there to regret? But still, it's easy enough to accept inevitable death, hard to accept death when you might have chosen to live."

As it happens they give him not death (the twenty years have passed, it wasn't a dream, the Ogre is safely stashed in the Kremlin wall) but their last twist of the thumbscrew, twenty-four hours of being arrested, taken away, frisked, stripped, physically examined, locked up that concludes with a KGB-escorted plane ride to—where in the world? they won't tell him—and then, as they shout "Put his hat and coat on him! Get him out!" and motion him (incredulous and hesitating: "I can't help looking around in bewilderment. They are not coming! The forces of darkness stay put in the plane, all of them") through the doorway and down the ramp to the airport in Frankfurt—there and then as they let him go and shout him out like an animal being shooed out of a cage they give him up willy-nilly to freedom and the full glare of Western publicity: smiling faces, photographers, movie cameras, and "A woman comes up and presents me with flowers."

Before they decide enough is enough and bundle him out of the country, he has lived lifetimes of rage and hope during these years, the calf will keep butting the oak "until the calf breaks its neck" or "the oak cracks and comes crashing down," he's a stupid optimist, he always brashly supposes that there's a community out there, that next time will be the charm because people won't indefinitely stand for what is officially and unremittingly passed off as the life of the spirit (Bukovsky recalls that already in his boyhood "I hated the humanities—history, literature, even geography—because they were so saturated with ideology that there was nothing left"): "pig swill," as for instance when "an illiterate idiot" who identifies himself as "lathe operator Zakharov," contributing to a "*diskussia*, a debate Soviet style," reviles the literary magazine *Novy Mir* (*New World*) in a letter to a newspaper: "We want everybody to march in step"; "we want a Communist answer;

any other answer the working class will not accept." Tvardovsky, editor of *Novy Mir*, demands information about the lathe operator and a photocopy of his letter; the newspaper comes up with the information—Zakharov is *real!*—and prints a photocopy of the letter ten days after first printing the letter, the two "versions" except for their identical party-line sentiments differing in every sentence: "Observe," says Solzhenitsyn, "the confident (and justified) impudence of Soviet newsmen; no Soviet reader would want to compare two issues with ten days between them, so they had not bothered to touch up the single short page they now reproduced, and make it match the original article!" Surely sooner or later our common humanity will be moved to laugh or cry at such heartless cynicism and impudence, such insults.

A generation after Stalin's death freedom still beckons, the purifying tide of "openness, honest and complete openness" is inevitable, look! there's the light at the end of the tunnel, prosperity is just around the corner, the stone-faced clique of pen-pushers and paper-shufflers and pint-size despots can with a little luck be made to listen to reason. Solzhenitsyn uses every opportunity exactly as if it's the right one. Addressing the Writers' Union he observes that "The censorship . . . is not provided for in the constitution and is therefore illegal—a fact that is never publicly mentioned." He doesn't point out the interesting irony that the Constitution which fails to provide for censorship is Stalin's very own (written to his order by Bukharin shortly before he had Bukharin liquidated) or that anybody in Stalin's time who objected to censorship vanished instantly in a puff of smoke, or that anybody nowadays who objects to it is bundled off to jail or a mental hospital or internal exile or Frankfurt; but it's true that the Soviet government can "legally," on the authority of their Constitution, stop the censorship anytime they please. Yes indeed. Here's Solzhenitsyn's "dream" of the Soviet government: "Some photographer should put together an album called *Dictatorship of the Proletariat*. There would be no captions, no text, just faces: two or three hundred ugly mugs, self-important, overfed, lethargic, bloody-minded people getting into cars, mounting public platforms, towering over their desks—with no captions, just the words 'Dictatorship of the Proletariat'!" Why, except out of inertia, out of fear of losing their jobs, out of fear of anything new, out of the historical impotence they impute to the rest of the world, out of the logic of their ugly, self-important, overfed, lethargic, bloody-minded natures do they keep their fat hands closed round the throat of the present while blaming Stalin for the awful past? as Solzhenitsyn must be thinking when he reads a "new-era" anti-Stalin poem by his friend Tvardovsky and in comic despair is ready to absolve the Ogre himself—"Well, yes, here was Stalin again (as though he, poor lamb, mattered anymore!)"—if only to bring to everybody's attention the suffocating present. Stalin (only a man after all) showed what one man can do, Solzhenitsyn is showing what one man can do, and now if ever it's time for everybody else to get into the act.

During the 'fifties and 'sixties Tvardovsky, a man of goodwill (another "unconscious" Christian), the regime's token humanist and respectful explainer, was editor of *Novy Mir*, the one Soviet magazine that maintained any moral and literary standards: with an okay from Khrushchev he published *One Day in the Life of Ivan Denisovich*; he regarded himself as a "Marxist-Leninist" and the horrors of Stalinism as an unlucky political accident; he was flattered to be "consulted" by "the men up top" on artistic matters and while in the halls of power was painstakingly fed bits of gossip he could carry back like an insider to his gratifyingly impressed artistic associates; he was a poet and critic by nature and talent and a flunky by conviction, a good man and a party hack, a loyal friend except when ideological pressures persuaded him otherwise (not black or white but tattle-tale gray), and he drowned his chronic uneasiness in drunken binges; he would take occasional unexpected brave stands on principle against ideology, but they never continued and cohered; at literary conclaves abroad he defended his country and his beliefs by telling high-sounding lies about his government and his friends; he tried for years to cajole and bully Solzhenitsyn into toning down his writing to an approximation of innocuousness that would allow it to pass the censorship, but after *Ivan Denisovich* nothing passed, the few sweet months of freedom were no longer even a permissible memory; he was forced to resign from *Novy Mir* and lost the will to work or live; after he is laid low by cancer and a paralytic stroke Solzhenitsyn visits him, tells him the latest news—since there's no news in *Truth* (*Pravda*) and no truth in *News* (*Izvestia*)—and reads him his latest unanswered letter of protest to one of the men up top, this time Suslov, the party ideologist, relic of the Stalin gang (on the occasion of Solzhenitsyn's attendance at a Kremlin meeting soon after the publication of *Ivan Denisovich*, Suslov "came up, took me firmly by the hand and shook it vigorously as he told me how very much he had enjoyed *Ivan Denisovich*, shook it as though from now on I would never have a closer friend"):

> [Tvardovsky] took it all in eagerly and sympathetically, and with movements of the head and inhibited gestures showed his far from inhibited feelings. He nodded vigorously, iron- ically, when I recalled that he had introduced me to Suslov. At times it even looked as though he were laughing, laughing heartily, but only with his eyes and his busily nodding head, not out loud. . . . You would start thinking that he under- stood everything—and a minute later that he understood only intermittently, when he concentrated. . . .
>
> When A.T. was particularly anxious to finish saying some- thing and could not manage it, I helped him out by taking his left hand—which was warm, and free and alive. He squeezed my hand in reply, and in this way we understood each other well enough. . . . [ellipsis in text] Understood that all was forgiven between us. That all the bad things, the hurts, the troubles, might never have been.

Three months later Solzhenitsyn visits him for the last time, and even then affection for a dying friend can't altogether overcome the indispensable distrust of the underground man for the courtier:

> to my surprise I found A.T. considerably better. He was sitting in the same hall, in the same armchair, still with his face toward the path by which people from the outside world came and went, while he himself could not struggle as far as the gate. But he had the use of his left leg, and of his left hand (which kept reaching for and lighting cigarettes), and his facial movements were almost as expressive as of old, but best of all, his speech was easier, so that he could say

quite lucidly that my book [*August 1914*] (he'd read it! he'd
understood it!) was "marvelous" and reinforce it by movements of his head and eyes, and by moaning. . . .

Alas, even at this last meeting I had to hide things from
him, as so often before. I could not confide that the book
would be coming out in Paris in two weeks' time.

Tvardovsky was the best that the system could claim for its
own, and at his funeral it can do no better than (as if in relief
at the passing of the last citizen of pride and taste) flaunt its
ugliness and provoke a characteristic protest from Solzhenitsyn:

> Long stretches of the adjoining streets were cordoned off—
> they had been lavish with policemen—and at the cemetery
> there were troops too (for a poet's funeral!), and hideously
> barking megaphones directed buses and lorries. The entrance
> hall of the Central Writers' Club was also cordoned off, but
> even so they dared not bar my way. (They regretted this
> afterward.) Against the incongruous crimson silk on which
> the dead man's head rested (his look of good-natured, childlike
> resignation, his best expression, had returned soon after his
> death) and in which the whole coffin was swathed, against
> the truculent robot faces of the Writers' Club secretaries,
> against the grating insincerity of the speakers, I had no way
> of defending him except to make the sign of the cross after
> each round of speeches, once at the Writers' Club and once
> at the cemetery. But that, I think, was plenty for the powers
> of darkness.

Every eye in sight—policeman's, soldier's, robot-faced function-
ary's, kept writer's—must have been peripherally on this flagrant
publicity hound; but Christian symbols have been used for worse
purposes.

The Romance
of Leon
Trotsky

Solzhenitsyn's colleagues at the Writers' Union, those who weren't simply KGB agents, were of course practitioners of socialist realism because it's the sole permissible Soviet artistic genre, and no doubt he would have been pleased to rub their noses in the following definition of it: "The realism consists in imitating provincial daguerreotypes of the third quarter of the last century; the 'socialist' style—in using tricks of salon photography to represent events that have never taken place. One cannot without revulsion and horror read the poems and novels or view the paintings and sculptures in which officials armed with pen, brush, or chisel, and supervised by officials armed with revolvers, glorify the 'great leaders of genius.'" No doubt Solzhenitsyn would have been equally pleased to endorse the observation that "the present ruling stratum . . . considers itself called upon not only to control spiritual creation politically, but also to prescribe its roads of development. The method of command-without-appeal extends in like measure to the concentration camps, to scientific agriculture, and to music. The central organ of the party prints anonymous directive editorials having the character of military orders, in architecture, literature, dramatic arts, the ballet, to say nothing of philosophy, natural science, and history." Certainly Solzhenitsyn would have agreed that by the time of the purges Stalin "could buy consciences like sacks of potatoes," and that "*L'état c'est moi* is almost a liberal formula by comparison with the actualities of Stalin's totalitarian regime. Louis XIV identified himself with both the state and the Church—but . . . Stalin can justly say, unlike *le Roi Soleil, la société c'est moi.*" Solzhenitsyn might even have given his blessing to this rather sacrilegious gloss on Stalin's excommunication of all his revolutionary comrades: "Of Christ's twelve Apostles Judas alone proved to be traitor. But if he had acquired power, he would have represented the other eleven Apostles as traitors, and also all the lesser Apostles whom Luke numbers as seventy." The author of every one of the foregoing quotations is Leon Trotsky, assassinated over forty years ago by a Stalin hit-man; and Solzhenitsyn ought to be delighted to have such early and incontestable corroboration of his own independently arrived-at feelings and convictions, but in fact he never mentions Trotsky except to link him with the other mischief-makers, he can't bring himself to cite anything at all which would oblige him to acknowledge Trotsky as in power and in exile Stalin's principled, untiring, and fearless opponent, as the preëminent writer of that place and time, as the pariah who outlived everything except his irrepressible talents.

In *The Gulag Archipelago*, for instance, brushing aside all the "enigmatic" and "inexplicable" talk about the confessions by the defendants in the Moscow frameup trials of the 'thirties, Solzhenitsyn notes that these party leaders "had, in their revolutionary pasts, known short, easy imprisonment, short periods in exile, and had never even had a whiff of hard labor. . . . Until they were arrested and imprisoned in the Lubyanka, they hadn't the slightest idea what a real prison was nor what the jaws of unjust interrogation were like." Perfectly true; and he goes on to maintain that if Trotsky had been among the defendants he too would have cracked:

> There is no basis for assuming that if Trotsky had fallen into those jaws, he would have conducted himself with any less self-abasement, or that his resistance would have proved stronger than theirs. He had had no occasion to prove it. He, too, had known only easy imprisonment, no serious interrogations, and a mere two years of exile in Ust-Kut. The terror Trotsky inspired as Chairman of the Revolutionary Military Council [i.e. founder and commander of the Red Army during two continuously embattled years of civil war] was something he acquired very cheaply, and does not at all demonstrate any true strength of character or courage. Those who have condemned many others to be shot often wilt at

the prospect of their own death. The two kinds of toughness are not connected.

But, as Solzhenitsyn himself concedes, a number of the accused very likely *did* hold out: "For some reason, they did not, after all, put on public trial Rudzutak, Postyshev, Yenukidze, Chubar, Kosior . . . even though their names would have embellished the trials. They put on trial the most compliant. A selection was made after all." Moreover Solzhenitsyn's reference to Trotsky's leadership of the Red Army is disingenuous. The "terror" inspired by a leader in a desperate civil war—Lincoln, for example, who like Trotsky lent his authority to the shooting of soldiers for desertion or dereliction of duty—differs significantly from the Stalin "peacetime" terror of eliminating "just for the hell of it" (as Solzhenitsyn says) a quarter of the country's population. (Bukovsky: "It was a tremendous shock to learn that your countrymen have been involved in killing sixty million people. . . . A totalitarian state has to try to put you within a bloody circle—everyone has to be stained with blood." Maybe Solzhenitsyn's nerves told him that only if *all* the actors of the October Revolution—Lenin and Trotsky and the rest as well as Stalin—were pushed far back into the shadows deep inside the bloody circle could he himself stay completely out.) The fact is that irrespective of the political issues Trotsky, with no previous military training or experience whatever, proved to be one of the great military leaders of history, within months after the utter disintegration of the Tsarist army putting together an army that protected the revolutionary enclave centering on Moscow and ultimately defeated the White and foreign-interventionist forces that often hugely outnumbered his own. His headquarters was a military train that traveled to every front bringing supplies, collecting information, inspiriting the troops: he often showed up in the thick of battle with bullets flying; during the siege of Petrograd, over the objections of Lenin who thought it should be abandoned, he insisted on defending it (according to an eyewitness, "Trotsky's orders, clear and precise, sparing nobody and exacting from everybody the utmost exertion and accurate, rapid execution of combat orders" immediately rallied the defenders), on one critical occasion he galloped in on horseback among troops who had been panicked by the appearance of British tanks on the other side, exhorted and persuaded them to turn and face the enemy, and led them to victory: it sounds like *Boys' Life* but it's in the record and Solzhenitsyn must have read the accounts of it with an intransigent mind and an aching heart.

Indeed no historical figure gives a more seamless impression of being immune to the risk of self-abasement even under torture than Trotsky: his superb confidence in his abilities and beliefs is important, he has nothing of the opportunist or hanger-on, he's one of those human beings who seem physically and morally incapable of fear, but he isn't a fanatic, neither his serenity nor his indignation is incompatible with geniality and a sense of humor: Solzhenitsyn ought to have considered the example of the Christian martyrs, many of whom though they hadn't been hardened by preliminary ordeals put up quite cheerfully with their last rites. (Solzhenitsyn despite his experience of long, hard imprisonment so lost his presence of mind when the secret police came calling that he opened the door to them and a moment later was furiously reproaching himself; Trotsky, though lacking such experience, kept the door locked—Solzhenitsyn would have known the story!—and made them break it down, refused to go along with them, they were compelled to carry him away bodily: the arresting officer in charge who had been a subordinate of his on the military train burst out, "Shoot me, Comrade Trotsky! Shoot me!" but Trotsky persuaded him to pull himself together.) After Lenin's incapacitation and death, at the regime's violent meetings—inkwells and books as well as threats and insults were hurled at speakers who dared to defend themselves against Stalin's calumnies—when Stalin had already stacked the government with thugs and stooges and his hangman personality had already terrorized the other old Bolsheviks (Kamenev and Zinoviev; Bukharin, who babbled in panic and prophecy, "He's the new Genghis Khan!"), Trotsky while the others trembled in their seats and waited for the sky to fall treated him with outrage and loathing (shouting at him over the din of his stooges, "Gravedigger of the Revolution!"; Stalin stood up in agitation and rushed out of the room, slamming the door behind him) or with ostentatious contempt (reading novels during sessions where Stalin had rigged the proceedings past hope and could do his dirty work in peace: "the peace of the tomb!" as Schiller's Posa operatically and accurately exclaims to the tyrant King Philip). Nor was it as if he didn't know whom he was dealing with: in his diary he recalled Kamenev's having told him about spending a day of " 'heart-to-heart' conversation" with Dzerzhinsky (founder of the Soviet secret police) and Stalin. "After the wine, on the balcony, the talk touched upon a sentimental subject—personal tastes and predilections, something of that sort. Stalin said, 'The greatest delight is to mark one's enemy, prepare everything, avenge oneself thoroughly, and then go to sleep.' " The enemy of such an enemy knew he was marked for death but notwithstanding never deflected or renounced an hour of his activities or recreations—he loved to go hunting and fishing in wild and remote areas—to limit the risk; till his last day he never stopped anatomizing with unsparing attentiveness the nature and conduct of the gravedigger of the Revolution; and he turned on and mauled like a wounded lion the assassin who had just driven an Alpine ice-axe into the back of his skull.

Solzhenitsyn needs to demonstrate the hatefulness and *baseness* of the despotic regime *ab initio* and *ad nauseam* from Lenin through Stalin (hence his comic-book image of Lenin, canting pettybourgeois "hero" of *Lenin in Zurich*, reduced to a piddling stream of consciousness: "To feel alarm in the face of threats means that you are prepared, not that you are panicky"), but no sequence of human associations is so uncomplicated, ogres are exceptions, things keep changing (dialectically?) all the time, remember what Solzhenitsyn finds to say about Khrushchev. In *August 1914* Solzhenitsyn intends to show that if not for their "wooden-headed" generals the Imperial Russian Armies might well have defeated the Germans and thus precluded the Revolution; in the same book he scornfully dismisses the populist determinism that Tolstoy insists on in *War and Peace*; but everywhere else he's unwilling to suppose for a moment that in the Soviet Union the obvious favoring conditions for tyranny and the undeniable beginnings of it might not necessarily have developed into the Stalin nightmare if somebody other than Stalin—say, Trotsky—had succeeded Lenin. People matter; individuals matter: though, coincidentally, Trotsky out of his Marxist determinism as well as Solzhenitsyn out of his painful hatred of the Revolution can hardly allow for the possibility that things might have been different if the people in charge had been different.

Trotsky like Solzhenitsyn is at his best piling up, sorting out for precise definition, and with every proper rhetorical emphasis imprinting on the conscience of the world the irrefutable historical evidence of irresponsibility, stupidity, malice, villainy. Further, Trotsky used such evidence as a basis for warnings and predictions that if they had been taken seriously might have headed off the Second World War. For instance, already in exile, he foresaw the Hitler horror down to its grisly details long before Hitler took power, urged an immediate coalition between the Soviet Union and Western Europe to prevent his accession, argued that unless Hitler was blocked the German working class would be destroyed and there would be a world war within a decade; but the line laid down by Stalin and followed heel-and-toe by the German Communists was that Hitler would do their job for them by overthrowing the German democratic republic whereupon they would push him aside and pick up the pieces. Nor were the British any smarter: Trotsky in a 1933 article remarked how happily British diplomats paying their respects to the new German Chancellor had applauded his "moderation" and "peaceful intentions"—Hitler talked this way every other week in 1933—because after all they "had expected to meet a madman brandishing an axe; instead they met a man hiding his revolver in a pocket—what a relief!" (A few years later Bernard Shaw, who took pride in being a reasonable Fabian-type socialist unlike those excitable Russians, couldn't quite bring himself to believe in accordance with the testimony at the Moscow trials that Trotsky had conspired with the German General Staff, the Mikado of Japan, and seventeen Soviet engineers to disrupt Soviet railway service and poison reservoirs, but he rebuked Trotsky for as it were responding in kind—that is, denouncing Stalin as a bloody tyrant and an unprecedented forger of history: "Trotsky spoils it all by making exactly the same sort of attack on Stalin. Now I have spent nearly three hours in Stalin's presence and observed him with keen curiosity, and I find it just as hard to believe that he is a vulgar gangster as that Trotsky is an assassin." Regrettable that Shaw didn't pop off the train for a couple of hours in Berlin and discover what a lovely chap Hitler was too. When as a political refugee Trotsky was refused a visa by the British Labour government, he commented that "This 'one act' comedy on the theme of democracy and its principles might have been written by Bernard Shaw, if the Fabian fluid which runs in his veins had been strengthened by as much as five per cent of Jonathan Swift's blood"; though it must be added that Shaw was one of the celebrities who sent letters protesting the government's decision.)

But Trotsky like Solzhenitsyn has a need to impose his abstract historical grid on the convolutions and accidents of individual human lives. When you're listening to Solzhenitsyn, Bolsheviks and (their second- and third-generation clones) Communists are fools or scoundrels or weaklings or, if not, then merely well-intentioned homunculi with one fatal flaw (they are wrong): a thesis that undermines his fiction because there he's making such an effort to be abstractly *fair!* and it shows in his judicious representation of Types A through B of these boring no-goods (what Harold Rosenberg, in another connection, called "the herd of independent minds"), whereas it hardly bothers his memoirs and histories in which either affection complicates things satisfactorily (as with Tvardovsky) or he can personally lord it over everybody else and snarl and scream to his heart's content. Or, when you're listening to Trotsky (even in his most genial books, *My Life* and the only readable Marxist history as well as the only history of a revolution written by one of its leaders, *The History of the Russian Revolution*), kings and constitutional democrats and Mensheviks are fools or scoundrels or weaklings or, if not, then merely well-intentioned homunculi with one fatal flaw (they are wrong)—as the slightest lively patch of characterization will prove at once: "Both [Tsar] Nicholas and Louis XVI give the impression of people overburdened by their job, but at the same time unwilling to give up even a part of those rights which they are unable to use"; "[Lieber] was a Menshevik . . . with a long revolutionary past, very sincere, very temperamental, very eloquent, very limited, and passionately desirous of showing himself an inflexible patriot and iron statesman . . . beside himself with hatred of Bolsheviks"; "A well-read rather than educated man, with considerable but unintegrated learning, Chernov [a member of Kerensky's constitutional democratic government that was overthrown by the Bolsheviks] always had at his disposal a boundless assortment of appropriate quotations, which for a long time caught the imagination of Russian youth without teaching them much"; and this double portrait of two friends from left and right of the Marxist spectrum who split on the rock of ideology because the left was right and so the right got left:

> Lenin was "hard" and Martov "soft." And they both knew it. Lenin would glance at Martov, whom he highly esteemed, with a critical and somewhat suspicious look; and Martov, feeling this glance, would look down and his thin shoulders would twitch nervously. When they met and talked afterwards, at least in my presence, one missed the friendly inflection and the jests. Lenin would look beyond Martov as he talked, while Martov's eyes would grow glassy under his drooping and never quite clean pince-nez. And when Lenin spoke to me of Martov, there was a peculiar intonation in his voice: "Who said that? Julius?"—and the name Julius was pronounced in a special way, with a slight emphasis, as if to give warning: "A good man, no question about it, even a remarkable one, but much too soft."

Those thin shoulders and especially that never quite clean pince-nez tell us all (and more) about the well-intentioned small soul that makes the mistake of being mistaken; but, in an article he wrote when the Bolsheviks had already had four years to stake their claim to "proletarian democracy," Martov shrugged his lean shoulders with electric intensity and wiped his pince-nez sparkling spotless with Jiffy Lens Lube as he spoke for himself shortly before he quit the country for good:

> The Soviet State has not established in any instance electiveness and recall of public officials. . . . It has not suppressed the professional police. . . . It has not done away with social hierarchy in production. It has not lessened the total subjection of the local community to the power of the State. On the contrary, the Soviet State shows a tendency in the opposite direction. It shows a tendency toward intensified centralism of the State, a tendency toward the utmost possible

strengthening of the principles of hierarchy and compulsion. It shows a tendency toward the development of a more special apparatus of repression then before. . . .

. . . [The Bolsheviks] continue to repudiate democratic parliamentarism. But they no longer repudiate, at the same time, those instruments of State power *to which parliamentarism is a counterweight within bourgeois society*: bureaucracy, police, a permanent army with commanding cadres that aren't accountable to the soldiers, etc.

Three years later Lenin was dead; weepy Bukharin the coward, time-server, and cynic whom Lenin in his Testament called "the favorite of the party" was making sour jokes about Soviet "democracy" ("There are many political parties in the Soviet Union: one in power, the others in jail"); Trotsky was being howled down at meetings of the Central Committee; Stalin had taken over, and Martov's well-warranted apprehensions were rapidly turning into full-fledged realities (but Solzhenitsyn, who doesn't like Mensheviks either, doesn't cite poor Martov either).

The trouble with a comprehensive ideology like Marxism (though Trotsky denies it's an ideology except for "vulgar Marxists," he contends it's properly only a tool) is that once it stops looking quite right down to the tiniest detail it doesn't look right even in the tiniest detail and all the answers reverse themselves into questions. For instance, in Trotsky's *History*, Lenin demands the "immediate transfer of land to the peasants" without governmental deliberations (Kerensky's government is still in power) or the passing of laws: " 'The important thing for us [says Lenin] is revolutionary initiative: the laws should be the result of it. If you wait until the law is written, and do not yourself develop revolutionary energy, you will get neither law nor land.' Are not these simple words [comments Trotsky] the voice of all revolutions?" They certainly are, as they are also the voice of every other headlong and self-justifying mass action, the consequences of which, as Martov is pointing out and prophesying, as Trotsky himself pointed out and prophesied a dozen years earlier in his controversies with Lenin, somehow veer off from the immediate and longed-for advantage: as it happened, Lenin had the revolutionary initiative, law was low on his agenda, and when the Bolsheviks came to power the peasants got neither law nor land. (Solzhenitsyn, having awaited in a tizzy of impatience the upheaval in the Soviet state that was bound to result from the publication of his subversive books, nevertheless after it fails to happen concedes wryly that history is safer with "gradualists, in whose hands the fabric of events does not tear.") Trotsky is a less convincing writer when he expounds as a Marxist the ideology of mass action than when he concentrates narratively on the mass action itself in its colors and eddyings of the moment—e.g. a Petrograd workers' demonstration which a detachment of Cossacks seems ready to break up (though even here the Marxist moral gets more and more pat till at the end he makes it explicit):

> Cutting their way with the breasts of their horses, the officers first charged through the crowd. Behind them, filling the whole width of the Prospect, galloped the Cossacks. Decisive moment! But the horsemen, cautiously, in a long ribbon, rode through the corridor just made by the officers. "Some of them smiled," Kayurov recalls, "and one of them gave the workers a good wink." This wink was not without meaning. The workers were emboldened with a friendly, not hostile, kind of assurance, and slightly infected the Cossacks with it. The one who winked found imitators. In spite of renewed efforts from the officers, the Cossacks, without openly breaking discipline, failed to force the crowd to disperse, but flowed through it in streams. This was repeated three or four times and brought the two sides ever closer together. Individual Cossacks began to reply to the workers' questions and even to enter into momentary conversations with them. Of discipline there remained but a thin transparent shell that threatened to break through any second. The officers hastened to separate their patrol from the workers, and, abandoning the idea of dispersing them, lined the Cossacks out across the street as a barrier to prevent the demonstrators from getting to the center. But even this did not help: standing stock-still in perfect discipline, the Cossacks did not hinder the workers from "diving" under their horses. The revolution

does not choose its paths: it made its first steps toward victory under the belly of a Cossack's horse.

And Trotsky is entirely convincing and magnetic only when his subject isn't political at all, as when laying out for every eye to see Stalin's all-purpose non-denominational crassness and savagery, or leaving politics and ideology altogether to present these images of his childhood in *My Life*:

> I am with my mother in Bobrinetz, visiting the Z. family, where there is a little girl of two or three. I am the bridegroom, the little girl is the bride. The children are playing on the painted floor of the parlor; the little girl fades away; the little boy is standing dazed and petrified beside a chest of drawers. His mother and the hostess come in. His mother looks at the boy, then at the puddle beside him, and then at the boy again, shakes her head reproachfully and says: "Aren't you ashamed of yourself?" The boy looks at his mother, at himself, and at the puddle, as if it all had nothing whatever to do with him.
>
> "Never mind," the hostess says, "the children have played too long."
>
> The little boy feels neither shame nor repentance. How old was he then? About two years, possibly three. . . .
>
> I remember another early scene that took place in our main kitchen. Neither my father nor my mother is at home. The cook and the maid and their guests are there. My older brother, Alexander, who is at home for the holidays, is also buzzing about, standing on a wooden shovel, as if on a pair of stilts, and dancing on it across the earthen floor. I beg my brother to let me have the shovel, and try to climb up on it, but I fall down and cry. My brother picks me up, kisses me, and carries me out of the kitchen in his arms.
>
> I must have been about four years old when someone put me on the back of a big gray mare as gentle as a sheep, with neither bridle nor saddle, only a rope halter. I spread my legs wide apart and held on to the mane with both hands. The mare quietly took me to a pear-tree and walked under a

branch, which caught me across the middle. Not realizing
what the matter was, I slid over the mare's rump, and hit
the grass. I was not hurt, only puzzled.

(Mauriac in his *Memoirs* rated Trotsky's evocations of childhood
with Tolstoy's and Gorky's. Mauriac was also the Nobel Laureate
who pushed Solzhenitsyn's candidacy for the Nobel Prize: "But
then Mauriac," writes Solzhenitsyn in *his* memoirs, "God rest his
soul, started his dogged campaign to obtain a Nobel Prize for me,
and spoiled the game for *our masters* once again: if they exiled me
now it would look like a riposte to Mauriac, and a stupid one."
Yet Solzhenitsyn turns a blind eye to Trotsky's memoirs as well
as to Mauriac's admiration of them.)

Isaac Deutscher's three-volume biography of Trotsky is one of
the perennial biographies, sympathetic and scrupulous throughout
its encyclopedic length, continuously illuminating on history and
politics, crammed with information all of which is interesting and
some of which (having been drawn from Trotsky's closed archives
by permission of his widow) isn't publicly available anywhere else;
but on occasion it's distractingly sectarian and political because
Deutscher when he steps forward and speaks his mind is even more
of a deterministic and optimistic Marxist than Trotsky, believes
that the Revolution would have occurred without Lenin or Trotsky,
believes that Stalin in spite of himself was a servant of history,
a homicidal barbarian involuntarily doing the essential dirty work
of the Revolution, viz. the industrialization of the economy and
the collectivization of agriculture which Trotsky had advocated
earlier and Stalin had long objected to, which (as Deutscher believes) in a country as backward as Russia had to be done by
compulsion and terror, and barring which the Soviet state would
have foundered and vanished (of course he believes, as Solzhenitsyn
thunderously doesn't, that such an eventuality would have been
bad not only for Russia but for the world). So for Deutscher the
ultimate and paradoxical greatness of Trotsky is that in his very
failure and obloquy, in exile, through the vileness of his mortal
enemy, and after his death he triumphed as the conscious and
voluntary servant of history.

On the other hand, Irving Howe's *Leon Trotsky*, "a political essay with a narrative foundation" which "borrows liberally" if not radically from Deutscher "in telling the story of Trotsky's life," takes the position that compulsion is bad and terrorism even worse (though we are left in the dark about motherhood), and that Trotsky's greatness lies in his lonely and comfortless opposition to both. Here is Howe's image of Trotsky in exile, as caustic, trenchant, and acutely urgent as a can of Drano, "shaking off his personal griefs in order to return to the discipline of work":

> Caustic and proud, . . . Trotsky continued to write his trenchant analyses of the totalitarian regime in Russia, exposing before a disbelieving world (rather, a world that did not want to believe) the terrorism which Stalin was directing against helpless millions. Time blurs memories; the shame of those years is covered by apologia [Howe seems to think this is plural, but anyhow the word has a fine polysyllabic resonance]. It becomes acutely urgent to remember that a good portion of the Western liberal and radical intelligentsia was celebrating the wisdom and humanity of the Stalin dictatorship—some of these people did not acknowledge the truth about the Moscow Trials until Nikita Khrushchev finally revealed it in 1956, and then only because it was he who revealed it. All through the 1930s Trotsky stood almost alone in pointing to the facts—for they were facts—about the Stalin regime.

(Time—for it *was* time—blurs memories and alters perspectives. In Howe's Trotsky book, published in 1978, Trotsky "stood almost alone in pointing to the facts about the Stalin regime"; but just two years later Howe in his "Open Letter" to Solzhenitsyn was demanding to know why this Vanya-come-lately didn't say thanks to those Western anti-Stalinist "liberals and democratic socialists"—"*we* have not been silent"—who presumably have been carrying on the work all these years since Trotsky led the way and were now available to Solzhenitsyn if only he looked around, but whom Howe hadn't mentioned two years earlier, perhaps because he rather fancied his image of Trotsky alone on the heights pointing down to the depths, possibly out of temporary modesty because "*we*" had been among them. When after fifteen years of Stalin's shenanigans the editors of *Partisan Review* found the frameup trials too much to swallow and decided Trotsky was a good fellow after all, they invited him to contribute with Western anti-Stalinists to a symposium impartially titled "What is alive and what is dead in Marxism?"—they were also preparing to invite the Pope to contribute to a symposium titled "What is alive and what is dead in Christianity?"—but Trotsky declined with the polite comment, "It is my general impression that the editors of *Partisan Review* are capable, educated, and intelligent, but have nothing to say." Maybe Solzhenitsyn has a similar if less polite impression of Western anti-Stalinists he happens to have heard about, maybe he considers them just not worth mentioning. At any rate Solzhenitsyn's job, because if he had looked around he would have noticed Howe, doesn't seem to Howe as lonely as Trotsky's; and Solzhenitsyn compounds his malefactions by ignoring not only Trotsky but Howe.)

The Marxist historian and the soulful journalist disagree on just where Trotsky's historical niche is, but they agree that he deserves one (to point a moral and adorn a tale), whereas the raging survivor of Gulag denies that Trotsky deserves anything more than a hole to bury him in (as Khrushchev had the embalmed and deified Stalin dragged from his slab next to Lenin in the Great Mausoleum and buried out of sight in a hole in the Kremlin wall). But if the rule is that historical niches or holes in the wall are prepared for their occupants long in advance by history, then the deterministic Marxist Trotsky is an exception: unlike Lenin and Stalin, who give the impression of having been completely accounted for and used up by history, Trotsky is a kind of luxury, an extravagance, not only because he lost the chance to do as much as he might have done but because whatever he had had the chance to do would not have been enough, he was all excess energy and surplus value, he went out of his way to attract the lightning, took pains to stand out and off from others even beyond the natural conspicuousness and exuberance of his talents: according to Lunacharsky, first Soviet Commissar of Education, who met him in Geneva in 1905,

Trotsky was then unusually elegant, in distinction from all
of us, and very beautiful [a few years later Stalin, already
though not yet openly an enemy, spoke privately of Trotsky's
"beautiful uselessness"]. That elegance of his, and especially
a kind of careless, high-and-mighty manner of talking with
no-matter-whom, struck me very unpleasantly. I looked with
great disapproval on that dandy, who swung his leg over his
knee, and dashed off with a pencil an outline of the extem-
poraneous speech he was going to make at the meeting. But
Trotsky spoke very well. . . .

A tremendous imperiousness and a kind of inability or
unwillingness to be at all caressing and attentive to people,
an absence of that charm which always surrounded Lenin [and
which Solzhenitsyn refused to dramatize or acknowledge in
his fictional image of "Lenin" in Zurich], condemned Trotsky
to a certain loneliness. . . .

For work in political groups Trotsky seemed little fitted,
but in the ocean of historic events, where such personal features lose their importance, only his favorable side came to
the front. . . .

In public argument he characteristically went too far, overleaped
the proprieties for the sake of panache, ground his opponents into
the dust. Martov (the skeleton at the feast), just after the October
Revolution, which he called a *coup d'état*, threatened to lead his
group out of the Congress of Soviets unless the Bolsheviks de-
mocratized the government by including the smaller left parties.
Trotsky came to the platform, stood face to face with Martov, and
answered him: "You are miserable, isolated individuals. You are
bankrupt. You have played out your role. Go where you belong:
to the dustheap of history!" (And Trotsky's role here was mega-
phone to the accursed dialectic.) He had no doubt that history
was in course of making the necessary discriminations, he was
unafraid of calling down on himself historical retribution or personal revenge, he never saw any reason to curry favor or hedge
his bets. In his early controversies with Lenin he argued with such
(as it might have seemed to Lenin) supererogatory and insulting
vehemence that their relations, even when for years they were firm

political allies and virtually shared state power, never became relaxed and intimate; and one late effect might have been the comparative coolness of the tone of Lenin's Testament toward Trotsky, which encouraged Stalin and his accomplices not only to brazen out the Testament's recommendation that Stalin be removed from his post but eventually to deny the Testament's very existence. Nor did Trotsky do any better with petty bureaucrats, who feared and hated him because he never cultivated them (as Stalin did from the outset: colleagues, drinking-companions, fall-guys, suspects arrested and tortured, counterrevolutionary wreckers exposed, criminals shot as they developed from one use to the next). Molotov, whom Lenin called "the best filing-clerk in the Soviet Union" and who must have had some sort of agility because he was almost the only jumped-up clerk who survived his lord and master Stalin, was secretary of the Central Committee when Trotsky strode in one day to make a complaint about the incompetence of Molotov's office: " 'Comrade Trotsky,' Molotov stammered out, 'Comrade Trotsky, not everyone can be a genius.' " At first it was impossible not to grant his abilities and achievements. He was twenty-six when he led the 1905 Revolution as President of the Petrograd Soviet. In October 1917, while Lenin was in hiding from Kerensky's police, Trotsky organized and led the uprising that brought the Bolsheviks to power: "You see, the great revolution is come," remarked the Bolshevik Uritsky, "and no matter how intelligent Lenin is, he begins to dim a little beside the genius of Trotsky"; "All the work of practical organization of the insurrection," wrote Stalin reviewing the event as editor of *Pravda*, "was conducted under the immediate leadership of the President of the Petrograd Soviet, Comrade Trotsky. It is possible to declare with certainty that the swift passing of the garrison to the side of the Soviet, and the bold execution of the work of the Military Revolutionary Committee, the party owes principally and first of all to Comrade Trotsky." Lenin himself proposed that as leader of the insurrection which brought the government to power Trotsky should head the Soviet government, but deferring to Lenin's seniority Trotsky refused. With typical superabundance, as it were incidentally, Trotsky may have been the greatest or in any case the most persuasive orator ever, speaking several times a day for months on end capturing and holding immense miscellaneous audiences with hour after hour of impromptu political disquisition:

> I consider Trotsky [writes Lunacharsky] probably the greatest orator of our times. I have heard in my day all the great parliamentary and popular orators of Socialism, and very many of the famous orators of the bourgeois world, and I should have difficulty in naming any of them, except Jaurès, whom I might place beside Trotsky.
>
> Effective presence, beautiful broad gesture, mighty rhythm of speech, loud, absolutely tireless voice, wonderful compactness, literariness of phrase, wealth of imagery, scorching irony, flowing pathos, and an absolutely extraordinary logic, really steel-like in its clarity—those are the qualities of Trotsky's speech. He can speak epigrammatically, shoot a few remarkably well-aimed arrows, and he can pronounce such majestic political discourses as I have heard elsewhere only from Jaurès. I have seen Trotsky talk for two and a half to three hours to an absolutely silent audience, standing on their feet, and listening as though bewitched to an enormous political treatise.

He was a leader without followers, a leader by excellence and accomplishment only, and as soon as Lenin died the others bared their teeth at him because he was vulnerable and superior. Zinoviev, a vain and spiteful man who resented Trotsky's precedence and regarded himself as the senior partner in the triumvirate with Kamenev and Stalin against Trotsky, very soon proposed that Trotsky be expelled from the party, but Stalin (who, as Bukharin remarked with rueful admiration, had a genius for gradation and timing—i.e. for avenging and murdering degree by degree, all in good time) vetoed the idea: "Today they chop off one head, tomorrow another, the day after tomorrow still another—who, in the end, will be left with us in the party?" (Actually Zinoviev hadn't said a word about chopping off heads, and it's futile but fascinating to wonder how metaphorical or sly Stalin was being at this moment. Probably he was just taking advantage of a momentary opportunity to appear generous and forgiving—made him seem wise and presidential, with malice toward none—because he knew the time wasn't ripe yet, but images of sanctioned bloody murder must have occurred to him as regularly as hunger or thirst.) Bukharin too, toady and "theoretician" to Stalin, snapped and fulminated obediently at the Trotskyists as if he himself were the wild beast. In the end, all in good time, nobody was left but Stalin.

If one believes in chance, luck, accident, character, personality, and will, a great deal of the trouble came from Lenin's continuous—until just before the end of his life—esteem for Stalin. Trotsky himself, working in his last years on his biography of Stalin, tried to puzzle it out, as Trotsky's widow recollects: "Stalin's origins were obscure, the part he played in 1917 difficult to establish, and the reasons for the warmth Lenin had shown him before he came to know him better—much too late in the day—were hard to discover." At times it appears that Lenin felt toward Stalin something of the hero-worship a timid and well-behaved schoolboy might feel toward cardsharps and burglars, *real* men: "During the civil war," Trotsky recalls, "when certain sections of the army, usually the cavalry branches, became unruly and went in for violence and roistering, Lenin was likely to say, 'Hadn't we better send Stalin there? He knows how to talk with people of that kind.' " (Lenin was addressing this wistful remark to the founder and leader of the Red Army, who, as Lenin proudly exclaimed to Gorky, had "conjured up an army out of nothing!" and whose unexampled gift for winning "people of that kind" over—any number of workers, peasants, or soldiers from a single interlocutor to immense gatherings—was as famous and uncontested as his intrepidity plunging directly into battle in the vanguard of his troops as soon as he arrived at any of the active fronts.) One of Trotsky's early disagreements with Lenin had to do with the question of supporting raids on Russian state banks to finance the party: Trotsky disapproved, Lenin didn't wish to discuss it but supported it, and the chief of the bank-robbers was Stalin (a *practical* man).

The first general secretary of the party was Yakov Sverdlov, by all accounts an intelligent and reliable man who was inconsiderate enough to die young, only two years after the Revolution, and

who had seemed so irreplaceable that at his death the Central
Committee left the post vacant for years. Slowly but surely, however, Stalin moved in on the appointment *faute de mieux* and once
he had it set about packing the offices, bureaus, departments,
commissariats with flunkeys whose unquestioning devotion to him
was guaranteed by their unfitness for the jobs he had bestowed
on them as well as by their grudges against his colleagues (e.g.
Trotsky, who was notorious for believing that the obligation of
a job-holder was to do his job). Stalin had already so immovably
entrenched himself before Lenin's death that at length even Lenin
grew uneasy, at first vaguely and impersonally: in Deutscher's
account "he said that often he had the uncanny sensation which
a driver has when he suddenly feels that his vehicle is not moving
in the direction in which he steers it. Powerful forces diverted the
Soviet state from its proper road: the semi-barbarous peasant in-
dividualism of Russia, pressure from capitalist surroundings, and
above all, the deep-seated native traditions of uncivilized absolutist
government." (And beyond everything Stalin, who had discon-
nected the steering mechanism from below and set the wheels on
the iron tracks straight to his version of pig heaven.) Trotsky
didn't help either. He alone had distrusted and despised Stalin
from the beginning; for years he had tried to warn or caution
Lenin and was put off; when Lenin started worrying about the
succession after he had suffered his first stroke, he several times
pleaded with Trotsky to become Vice-Premier, but Trotsky, perhaps in something of a pet, irritated him by declining each time,
on the ground that he had more important things to do in the
government (he was still Commissar of War): it was Stalin who
placed Trotsky's name in nomination, Stalin who complained of
Trotsky's irresponsibility to the party in spurning it! During the
last few months of his active political life Lenin let the Stalin
blindfold fall from his eyes, he saw Stalin as a liar, a manipulator,
and a terrifying all-round menace, he began desperately urging
Trotsky to form a bloc with him dedicated to bringing Stalin
down. But Lenin too managed to undercut himself (as if all luck
were bad, or as if the bloody farce of history were determined that
Stalin succeed): in the body of his Testament addressed to the
party, he called Trotsky and Stalin "the two ablest members of

the Central Committee" and he expressed reservations about both which made him seem unresolved between them; it was only in his grim postscript written weeks later, after more light had been cast on Stalin's treacheries, that he demanded Stalin's dismissal as general secretary. It was Lenin's *infatuation* with Stalin ("He would often fall in love with people, in the full sense of the word," Trotsky recalled. "And on such occasions I would tease him: 'I know, I know, you are having a new romance.' Lenin realized this characteristic of his, and would laugh by way of reply, a little embarrassed but a little angry, too") that kept Stalin in a position to move in as soon as Lenin was dead and gone. It was at least in part Trotsky's disappointment, perhaps his pique, over Lenin's failure to see Stalin for what he so repellently was that prevented Trotsky from, say, accepting the vice-premiership in time to head off Stalin's cabal with Kamenev and Zinoviev. As Lunacharsky noted while Trotsky still had the second strongest voice in the government, Trotsky was incompetent as a politician (the only activity he ever undertook that he was incompetent at). Lenin's last, frantic advice to Trotsky was to avoid being taken in by one of Stalin's "rotten compromises," and sure enough soon after Lenin's death Trotsky allowed himself to be persuaded not to press for Stalin's dismissal though Stalin blandly offered his resignation and there is no doubt that the Central Committee would have accepted it if Trotsky had argued that Lenin's Testament must be carried out. A couple of years after Lenin's death, the "iron curtain" of Stalin's tyranny had come down with a bang (the term was an invention by Bukharin, who as Stalin's quaking Cerberus was admonishing certain fainthearts to make their way back inside "before the iron curtain came down"), and "If Ilyich were alive today," Lenin's widow remarked bitterly, "he would be in one of Stalin's jails." Degree by degree, step by step, taking advantage of every slip and kindness by his opponents and every assistance by fate (such as Sverdlov's and Lenin's premature deaths), Stalin not only took charge of the corporation but, just to be on the safe side, sooner or later got round to murdering all the administrative holdovers. Trotsky was pushed out early, beyond easy range, so he lasted somewhat longer.

Toward the end of his life he was particularly anxious to organize a genuine Marxist party, a band of true believers (like the one to which he had pledged himself so many years ago, all of whose members except himself and Stalin were by now dead), but the— as he had no doubt—grotesquely misleading instance of Stalinist Russia and the terrible threat of Hitler kept the world's attention elsewhere, and the "Fourth International" never held the allegiance of more than a very small group who had already split into factions before his death. (He had never been a clever politician.) Publicly he was dauntless, fighting the good fight: "Trotsky was, perhaps, the only man in the whole world able to grasp the real depths to which the Russian Revolution had sunk," wrote his widow. "He worked on, because it was imperative that truthfulness, steadfastness, intelligibility, and Marxist integrity be seen to oppose Stalin's degradation of the socialist conscience; and because it was essential to rid revolutionary knowledge and thought of the monstrous nightmare that had descended upon them. Trotsky planned new books; he wrote articles for the New York *Times* almost daily for a time, worked on analyses and essays in the *Opposition Bulletin*, and brought out *Stalin's Crimes*, a work of 376 pages [it would be interesting to know how closely this book prefigured the "three volumes on Stalin's crimes" that Khrushchev told Tvardovsky he had put together but that he never quite got up the nerve to publish]. . . ." In private, though, his spirit sometimes came near to failing. Even before he had been banished the Stalinist pollution was already beginning to seem irreversible: "Leon Davidovich, overworked and tense, continued to feel weak and feverish. . . . In the mornings, at breakfast, we [she and their two sons] would watch Leon Davidovich open the papers. He would glance at them and then throw them all over the table with disgust. They contained nothing but stupid lies, distortions of even the plainest fact or speech, hateful threats, and telegrams from all over the world, vying with each other to repeat the same infamies with boundless servility. What had they done to the Revolution, the Party, Marxism, and the International! It was impossible to remain silent." Finally, as Stalin and Hitler came to dominate the period like a matched pair of bad smells and eventually made their short-lived peace with each other (which would very soon end, as Trotsky immediately foresaw but didn't live to see, with a Nazi invasion of the Soviet Union), the inflexible Marxist in Trotsky yielded just a little to pessimism and charity and the awful prospect of an age-long hell-black night for mankind. The good society had finally come to seem farther away than he had ever before been willing to imagine.

Anti-Semitism, for example, had always seemed to him a social aberration that would be cleared up in a proletarian democracy by assimilation (though as a Jew in the land of pogroms he had experienced anti-Semitism at first hand, knew how virulent it could be, had early suggested that because he was Jewish he should stay out of a Bolshevik government to forestall anti-Semitic attacks against it, but was overruled by Lenin; he liked to tell a story from the revolutionary-train days about overhearing a Cossack soldier shouting indignantly at another Cossack, "Trotsky is *not* a Jew! He's one of *us!*"). But Trotsky the humanist and Jew was soon aware of "the anti-Semitic undertones of the Moscow trials" (though the American-Jewish press of the 'thirties, accustomed to considering the Soviet Union "our only consolation as far as anti-Semitism is concerned," disagreed, calling "unforgivable" Trotsky's "groundless charges against Stalin"; Trotsky didn't live to see the full flowering of Stalinist anti-Semitism in the "Doctors' Plot" of Stalin's last years); and by 1937, in an interview with an American-Jewish newspaper, "he admitted that recent experience with anti-Semitism in the Third Reich and even in the U.S.S.R. had caused him to give up his old hope for the 'assimilation' of the Jews with the nations among whom they lived. He had arrived at the view that even under socialism the Jewish question would require a 'territorial solution,' i.e. that the Jews would need to be settled in their own homeland." (But the inflexible Marxist had to add his two cents: "He did not believe, however, that this would be in Palestine, that Zionism would be able to solve the problem, or that it could be solved under capitalism. The longer the decaying bourgeois society survives, he argued, the more vicious and barbarous will anti-Semitism grow all over the world.")

The other issue he left ajar in spite of Marxist prescriptions was one raised by Bruno Rizzi, an Italian ex-Trotskyist, who just before the Second World War published *La Bureaucratisation du Monde*, where he presented the hypothesis of "the managerial revolution" from which James Burnham and Milovan Djilas later derived their popularized and simplified studies. Rizzi's argument, as Deutscher sums it up, was that Trotsky's defense of the Soviet Union as a workers' state with bureaucratic deformations was mistaken, that the bureaucracy did in fact for all practical purposes own the means of production and exploit the workers, that "bureaucratic collectivism"—whether under Stalin, Hitler, or Roosevelt—was a "new system of exploitation, destined to prevail the world over. As long as bureaucratic collectivism stimulated social productivity . . . it would be invulnerable. The workers could only do what they had done under early capitalism—struggle to improve their lot and wrest concessions and reforms from their new exploiters. Only after the new system had begun to decay and to retard and shackle social growth, would they be able to resume the fight for socialism successfully. This was a remote prospect, yet it was not unreal: bureaucratic collectivism was the last form of man's domination by man, so close to classless society that bureaucracy, the last exploiting class, refused to acknowledge itself as a possessing class."

Trotsky in his last major theoretical essay, "The U.S.S.R. in War," treated Rizzi's argument with respect even while countering it detail by detail, but toward the end of his refutation he made a (for him) unique doomsday prediction: If the Second World War "were not to lead to proletarian revolution in the West, then the place of decaying capitalism would indeed be taken not by socialism, but by a new bureaucratic and totalitarian system of exploitation. And if the working classes of the West were to seize power, but then prove incapable of holding it and surrender it to a privileged bureaucracy, as the Russian workers had done, then it would indeed be necessary to acknowledge that the hopes which Marxism placed in the proletariat had been false. In that case the rise of Stalinism in Russia would also appear in a new light":

> We would be compelled to acknowledge that [Stalinism]
> . . . was rooted not in the backwardness of the country and
> not in the imperialist environment, but in the congenital
> incapacity of the proletariat to become a ruling class. Then

it would be necessary to establish in retrospect that . . . the present U.S.S.R. was the precursor of a new and universal system of exploitation. . . . However onerous this . . . perspective may be, if the world proletariat should actually prove incapable of accomplishing its mission . . . nothing else would remain but to recognize openly that the socialist program, based on the internal contradictions of capitalist society, had petered out as a Utopia.

If all this turns out to be the case, what is the obligation for men of good will? "It is self-evident," concludes Trotsky with the last defiant breath of nineteenth-century humanism, "that a new minimum program will be required—to defend the interests of the slaves of the totalitarian bureaucratic system."

So Trotsky was a very busy man, but all his years from the age of twenty-three he had time for a happy marriage with a brave and loving woman. Here is his widow's account of their first meeting:

It was during my adolescence that I became acquainted with "revolutionary ideas," ideas that, in Tsarist Russia, were often no more extreme than liberal ideas are in the West. . . . When my secondary studies were over, I wanted, like so many others, to breathe the air of a free country, and so I went to Geneva to study science, . . . but I was more interested in the problems of society. . . .

In 1902, I was living in Paris. I used to take my meals in a flat in the rue Lalande, where we pooled our meager resources to save money. Julius Martov [the same!] used to come there; at the age of twenty-nine, he was already known as a founder of one of the earliest Russian social democratic groups and as a veteran of Turukhansk, the notorious Siberian place of exile. It was he who one day at table announced the arrival of a young fugitive from Siberia. . . . Leon Davidovich came to the rue Lalande on the same day he arrived in Paris. He was twenty-three and had just spent three years' exile in Eastern Siberia. His keen mind, his vitality, and his capacity for hard work already set him apart as a forceful and mature figure. He was not greatly impressed by Paris at the time.

He used to joke that Odessa was worth a lot more. Although he had come to Paris with the main object of making contact with the Russian émigré socialist movement, it just happened that one day the two of us were standing together looking at Baudelaire's tomb in the Montparnasse Cemetery . . . and from that time on, our lives were inseparable. I had an allowance of about twenty roubles a month, say fifty francs, from my family, and Leon Davidovich earned about as much from his writing. We could only just make ends meet, but then we had Paris, the comradeship of the refugees, the constant thought of Russia and the great ideas to which we were devoting our lives. . . .

In the private diary he kept while he was in exile back in France a generation later, he permits himself to write about her (they are in their middle fifties): "Today on our walk we went up a hill. N. got tired and unexpectedly sat down, all pale, on the dry leaves (the earth is still a bit damp). Even now she still walks beautifully, without fatigue, and her gait is quite youthful, like her whole figure. But for the last few months her heart has been acting up now and then. She works too much—with passion, as in everything she undertakes, and today it showed during the steep ascent up the hill. N. sat down all of a sudden—she obviously just *could not* go any further—and smiled apologetically." And he remembers her youth:

What a pang of pity I felt for youth, *her* youth. . . . One night we ran home from the Paris Opera to the rue Gassendi, 46, *au pas gymnastique*, holding hands. It was in 1903. Our combined age was 46. . . . N. was probably the more indefatigable one. Once, while a whole crowd of us were walking somewhere in the outskirts of Paris, we came to a bridge. A steep cement pier sloped down from a great height. Two small boys had climbed on to the pier over the parapet of the bridge and were looking down on the passersby. Suddenly N. started climbing toward them up the steep smooth slope of the pier. I was petrified. I didn't think it was possible to climb up there. But she kept walking up with her graceful stride, on high heels, smiling to the boys. They waited for

her with interest. We all stopped anxiously. N. went all the
way up without looking at us, talked to the children, and
came down the same way, without having made, as far as
one could see, a single superfluous effort or taken a single
uncertain step. . . . It was spring, and the sun was shining
as brightly as it did today when N. suddenly sat down in
the grass. . . .

They had two sons. One, not political and studying engineering
at the university, decided against accompanying his parents into
exile. For a few years they corresponded regularly, but on family
matters only (of course the letters were read by the censorship),
and then the parents heard no more. The father died without
definite news of the son: years later, it came out that he had been
arrested and imprisoned, had refused to make any "confession,"
and was done away with in Gulag. The other son went with his
parents and served as secretary and assistant to his father till he
died "under mysterious circumstances" in a Paris hospital, probably
poisoned, while Trotsky was still alive to share the grief with
Natalya. (Trotsky also had two daughters by an earlier marriage.
One died very young of a prolonged illness while Trotsky, because
Stalin hadn't yet dared to do worse than banish him to a far corner
of Siberia, might still have confronted the authorities with a request
to visit her before she died; so the bureaucratic solution was to
hold back the letters to Trotsky about her illness till she was safely
dead. The other, having left Russia, as she thought, temporarily,
for psychoanalytic treatment in Germany, deprived of her child
during her treatment, unexpectedly forbidden—Stalin didn't miss
a trick—to return to Russia to rejoin her husband, having tried
to be helpful to her father—but "I know, I know," she cried,
"that children are not wanted, that they come only as punishment
for sins committed"; and she loathed herself for being "mostly
stuck in psychoanalytic swinishness"—ended in Berlin three weeks
before Hitler took power: "The *Horst Wessel Lied* in her ears, her
own country closed to her and herself torn from her family, driven
from Germany, and too sick to look for another refuge, Zina locked
and barricaded herself in her room and opened the gas taps." She
was thirty.)

All these family tragedies fell on them like buildings within a few years, all their children were dead and all died far away:

> Concerning the blows that have fallen to our lot, I reminded Natasha the other day of the life of the archpriest Avvakum [a seventeenth-century "Old Believer" who would not bow to the doctrinal and ceremonial changes that resulted in the modern Russian Orthodox Church]. They were stumbling on together in Siberia, the rebellious priest and his faithful spouse. Their feet sank into the snow, and the poor exhausted woman kept falling into the snowdrifts. Avvakum relates: "And I came up, and she, poor soul, began to reproach me, saying: 'How long, archpriest, is this suffering to be?' And I said, 'Markovna, unto our very death.' And she, with a sigh, answered: 'So be it, Petrovich, let us be getting on our way.' "

She was in the next room when the assassin struck. "There was a terrible piercing cry.... Leon Davidovich appeared, leaning against the door-frame. His face was covered with blood, his blue eyes glittered without his spectacles, and his arms hung limply by his sides ... 'What has happened,' I cried, 'what has happened?' I put my arms round him in utter confusion. He answered calmly, 'Jacson,' he said, as if he had wished to tell me: 'Now it is done.' I helped him, as he slumped down on the mat on the dining-room floor. 'Natasha,' he said, 'I love you ...' He spoke with an effort and indistinctly, as if in a dream, while I mopped the blood from his face and put ice on the wound in his head." In the ambulance his left side was already paralyzed, "his right arm kept making circles in the air." At the hospital: "A nurse started to cut his gray hair. Leon Davidovich smiled at me and whispered, 'You see, here's the barber.' We had spoken that day of sending for one." A little later "The nurses began to cut his clothes. Suddenly he said to me distinctly but very sadly and gravely, 'I don't want them to undress me ... I want you to do it ...' [all ellipses in the text] These were his last words to me. I undressed him, and pressed my lips to his. He returned the kiss, once, twice, and again. Then he lost consciousness." He died August 21, 1940. He was sixty years old.

Big Mama
and Her
Fatherless Boy

Coriolanus isn't a politician either but he too is in politics willy-nilly. He is Shakespeare's only durable tragic hero because the rest of them always turn out to be Shakespeare himself in greasepaint and fancy getup (a player's heart wrapt in a tiger's hide) carrying on like a bad actor, craving indulgence and looking for trouble, stepping on everybody else's lines, the dyspeptic and irresponsible young ham let loose to play the role of himself or some other bawling benighted Shakescene as redolent of pathos as the orphan who having murdered his parents throws himself on the mercy of the court: dyspeptic and irresponsible old man, remorseful assassin, would-be cuckold, worn-out world-weary lover; ever ready with speeches of self-absolution (more wind from the Shakespearean bowels of compassion); right royal or at least viceregal, and why not? if they haven't a better claim on anybody's attention. Coriolanus, though, is as pure as an idea in the mind of Plato, everything a man's supposed to do Coriolanus does at once without the shadow of a doubt, he's all martial virtue (and therefore as far as he knows all civic virtue), he's as free of flaws as the marble that will some day impersonate him in the gallery of fame. He isn't a poor excuse for bad actions like Lear or Macbeth, he's a case like Oedipus, an unadaptable large mammal (a tiger's heart wrapt in a player's hide), and Shakespeare is impartial and curious about Coriolanus as he isn't for a moment about the various sentimental projections of himself.

When Coriolanus in the heat of battle exhorts the fleeing Romans to stand and fight, he doesn't deliver the usual Shakespearean peptalk ("Once more unto the breach, good friends") because this isn't the usual idealized tin-soldier battle:

> *All the contagion of the south light on you,*
> *You shames of Rome! you herd of—Boils and plagues*
> *Plaster you o'er, that you may be abhorred*
> *Farther than seen, and one infect another*
> *Against the wind a mile! You souls of geese,*
> *That bear the shapes of men, how have you run*
> *From slaves that apes would beat! Pluto and hell!*
> *All hurt behind! backs red, and faces pale*
> *With flight and agued fear! Mend and charge home,*
> *Or, by the fires of heaven, I'll leave the foe*
> *And make my wars on you! Look to 't. Come on!*
> *If you'll stand fast, we'll beat them to their wives,*
> *As they us to our trenches. Follow me!*

It's no surprise then that he's too much to take, like Trotsky he's a leader without followers, his closing few words of encouragement are an afterthought that doesn't do a thing for the troops, and when he storms the gates of Corioles it's all by himself:

> *So, now the gates are ope. Now prove good seconds.*
> *'Tis for the followers fortune widens them,*
> *Not for the fliers. Mark me, and do the like.*
>
> Enter the gates.

FIRST SOLDIER: *Foolhardiness, not I.*
SECOND SOLDIER: *Nor I.*
FIRST SOLDIER: *See, they have shut him in.*

Alarum continues.

ALL: *To th' pot, I warrant him.*

Whereupon one of the Roman generals comes on to pronounce his premature eulogy of Marcius (not yet "Coriolanus," the name of honor he'll be dubbed with when his exploits here are celebrated back in Rome):

LARTIUS: *What is become of Marcius?*
ALL: *Slain, sir, doubtless.*

FIRST SOLDIER: *Following the fliers at the very heels,*
    With them he enters, who upon the sudden
    Clapped to their gates; he is himself alone,
    To answer all the city.
LARTIUS: *O noble fellow!*
    Who sensibly outdares his senseless sword,
    And, when it bows, stand'st up. Thou art left, Marcius.
    A carbuncle entire, as big as thou art,
    Were not so rich a jewel. Thou wast a soldier
    Even to Cato's wish, not fierce and terrible
    Only in strokes; but with thy grim looks and
    The thunder-like percussion of thy sounds,
    Thou mad'st thine enemies shake, as if the world
    Were feverous and did tremble.

Marcius, however, rematerializes in the nick of time, "bleeding, assaulted by the Enemy," and this Roman sight is such a tonic to the rank and file that "all enter the City" and pack it up for Rome, especially the loot that Marcius shouts his disgust to see them lugging out afterward:

> *See here these movers that do prize their hours*
> *At a cracked drachma! Cushions, leaden spoons,*
> *Irons of a doit, doublets that hangmen would*
> *Bury with those that wore them, these base slaves*
> *Ere yet the fight be done, pack up. Down with them!*

When later he reports on the battle, he recollects "The common file,—a plague! tribunes for them!—" and thus sums up with a curse the patrician's evidence against party politics and representative government. The rest of the play keeps trying to tell him to his astonishment and against his will that there are other ways of reacting to such evidence if not other kinds of evidence in the world.

Though in the history plays and the Roman plays Shakespeare is dealing continuously with politics and government, his attitude except in *Coriolanus* tends to be negative, defensive, anxious, even demoralized: things are in the saddle; if there were deeds to be done, there isn't anybody to do them (the only English exception is that mean-spirited layabout and cold pretender Prince Hal who turns into Shakespeare's and England's favorite king, the efficient and sanctimonious jingo Henry V); usurpers are a fact of history but they're just on a power trip so they don't change things, if they aren't out-and-out villains they're sooner or later stricken with feelings of guilt for having bumped off God's anointed and as a penance they promise to restore Jerusalem (in those days, from the Arabs) to Christ before they die but they don't live long enough (nobody lives long enough to change one damn thing); the awful truth is that government probably can't be good but it ought to be sluggish, preferably based on some such external guarantee of legitimacy as the holy oil that's sprinkled over hereditary kings (so that *Richard II* remains in the memory as a single interminable maudlin meditation by the deposed king on his divine right to do as much middling mischief as his malice and incompetence can dream up).

The world of difference is Coriolanus's Rome, where politics having just been born has a future, will and energy count, individuals have a say, power is up for grabs so factions pull and haul against each other for their share or all of it, divine right is still off in the wings because, Jesus being as yet no more than a gleam in God's eye, there's no church to announce it. But the pre-Christian license that Shakespeare issues to *Coriolanus* isn't in effect anywhere else: the other Roman plays, and *Troilus and Cressida*, are as mortified as the English history cycle is by a superstitious hopelessness about history and politics. The worst is *Troilus and Cressida*, which is Shakespeare's top entry for ugliest play in the world. Coriolanus railing at the common file knows what he believes and what a man can do or at least endeavor if he believes rightly; but Thersites railing at Ajax, Achilles, Agamemnon, Menelaus, Ulysses, Troilus, Cressida takes every cheap shot at "lechery, lechery, still wars and lechery!" with Shakespeare's full approval because love and war depend on belief which incites to action, and he hasn't a doubt that belief is delusion and action is folly. Though *Coriolanus* isn't a pretty play it isn't ugly either, its rhetoric is as gritty and functional as sandpaper, it can almost match *Troilus and Cressida* for insults and invective, but it hasn't written anything off.

It's Shakespeare's only play without pathos, it doesn't solicit
sympathy or pity or charity for any of its characters, and it has
a unique sort of comedy—the comedy of embarrassment, as if
proud parents ask their six-year-old to recite a poem for after-
dinner guests and the child proceeds to deliver despite every polite
cough and ahem! a word-perfect and eloquent reading of *Paradise
Lost.* The patricians are all proud of Coriolanus as of a very bright
and right-thinking child, but in company—in the presence of
outsiders, e.g. the plebeians and their representatives the tribunes—he's liable to embarrass them by the superabundance of his
virtues, by the force and guilelessness with which he expresses the
convictions they have taught him by lesson and example and now
are delighted to praise him for feeling and exemplifying though
they rather wish he would keep a little quieter about some of the
family secrets; as when Menenius, the old patrician who is in place
of a father to him, tries to ease him past the suspicious tribunes
into the ceremony at which, having been designated consul by the
Senate, he must formally seek approval from the people:

MENENIUS: *The Senate, Coriolanus, are well pleased*
  To make thee consul.
CORIOLANUS: *I do owe them still*
  My life and services.
MENENIUS: *It then remains*
  That you do speak to the people.
CORIOLANUS: *I do beseech you,*
  Let me o'erleap that custom; for I cannot
  Put on the gown, stand naked, and entreat them
  For my wounds' sake to give their suffrage. Please you
  That I may pass this doing.
SICINIUS: *Sir, the people*
  Must have their voices; neither will they bate
  One jot of ceremony.
MENENIUS: *Put them not to 't.*
  Pray you, go fit you to the custom and
  Take to you, as your predecessors have,
  Your honor with your form.

CORIOLANUS: *It is a part*
  That I shall blush in acting, and might well
  Be taken from the people.
BRUTUS: [to Sicinius] *Mark you that?*

Later, when they're alone, Menenius chides him for his reluctance to conform, i.e. to bow and scrape in speech for the sake of taking charge in fact: "O sir, you are not right. Have you not known / The worthiest men have done 't?" and he retorts in exasperation,

                    What must I say?
"I pray sir"—Plague upon 't! I cannot bring
My tongue to such a pace. "Look, sir, my wounds!
I got them in my country's service, when
Some certain of your brethren roared and ran
From th' noise of our own drums."

—because he isn't ambitious and could live without the consulship, he's used to his own sort of freedom, he hates to brag, he isn't snobbish or spiteful or a beastly drill-sergeant type, he mainly despises the plebeians for bearing the name of soldier and shirking the job of it, and he is even amused by the comedy of a situation that Menenius doesn't want him to think about at all, that he just wants him to pass through quickly as through a short dark tunnel (and, Coriolanus might add, on his hands and knees):

MENENIUS: *You'll mar all.*
  I'll leave you. Pray you, speak to 'em, I pray you,
  In wholesome manner.   Exit.
CORIOLANUS: *Bid them wash their faces*
  And keep their teeth clean.

(Maybe it's all in the way they were brought up.) The best that Coriolanus can manage in a pinch is another dose of unseasonable wit—word-play and ironic courtesy:

THIRD CITIZEN: *Tell us what hath brought*
  you to 't.
CORIOLANUS: *Mine own desert.*
SECOND CITIZEN: *Your own desert?*

CORIOLANUS: *Ay, not mine own desire.*

THIRD CITIZEN: *How not your own desire?*

CORIOLANUS: *No, sir, 'twas never my desire yet to trouble the poor with begging.*

THIRD CITIZEN: *You must think if we give you anything, we hope to gain by you.*

CORIOLANUS: *Well then, I pray, your price o' th' consulship?*

FIRST CITIZEN: *The price is to ask it kindly.*

CORIOLANUS: *Kindly, sir, I pray, let me ha 't. I have wounds to show you, which shall be yours in private. Your good voice, sir. What say you?*

SECOND CITIZEN: *You shall ha 't, worthy sir.*

CORIOLANUS: *A match, sir. There's in all two worthy voices begged. I have your alms. Adieu.*

THIRD CITIZEN: *But this is something odd.*

SECOND CITIZEN: *An 'twere to give again—but 'tis no matter.*

But the tribunes, who have just assumed their new and untried office and don't relish contesting with so intractable a consul what they may be able to pick up of state power, will guarantee, by goading Coriolanus into a rage, that there will be a chance for the citizens to give again or rather to take back what they have given.

He's a paragon though. To say he isn't covetous—his friends say so with pride and his enemies with apprehension—is to say the least of it: he's a sheer monument of unattemptability: not only does he loathe the plundering soldiers, he also declines his legitimate lion's share of the spoils of a battle won by him almost single-handed and in consequence rouses his troops to a predictable outburst of enthusiasm (because the less he takes the more is left for them), which characteristically provokes him to denounce them for overrating the deeds of a man who has simply done his duty:

MARCIUS: *I thank you, general,*
 But cannot make my heart consent to take
 A bribe to pay my sword. I do refuse it,
 And stand upon my common part with those
 That have beheld the doing.
                              A long flourish. They all cry, "Marcius!

> Marcius!" and cast up their caps and lances.
>   Cominius and Lartius stand bare.
> MARCIUS: *May these same instruments which you profane*
> *Never sound more! When drums and trumpets shall*
> *I' th' field prove flatterers, let courts and cities be*
> *Made all of false-faced soothing! When steel grows*
> *Soft as the parasite's silk, let him be made*
> *A coverture for th' wars. No more, I say! . . .*

(For somebody who keeps saying "No more!" he does go on and keeps on going quite a while even after this; in fact he never runs out of words—how else can he let us know how little they matter?—but then Shakespeare, who's never one to crib or confine himself merely out of deference to characters who trumpet the virtues of deeds over words, can even come up with a plausible justification for Coriolanus: "What his breast forges," says Menenius, "that his tongue must vent; / And being angry, does forget that ever / He heard the name of death." Hotspur is another nononsense warrior who dismisses rhetoric in the course of delivering a bushel and a peck of it.)

For Romans war is the honorable and necessary vocation: true, those who recall that you can get killed at it aren't mad about it, but not Coriolanus, last of the Romans, who was born to it and raised for it but most of all supremely thrives on it; his vocation coinciding with his pleasure as well as his patriotic duty, he's a lucky man who doesn't crave indulgence or recognition or reward but simply welcomes opportunity, the riskier the better; worse luck, however, that war is also the strong right arm of politics because unlike, for example, Julius Caesar later on, Coriolanus isn't a would-be politician temporarily disguised as a conquering hero, yet his friends and family are too proud of him to let him pass, their child-prodigy, their already anachronistic and superannuated boy-wonder:

> *The deeds of Coriolanus*
> *Should not be uttered feebly. It is held*
> *That valor is the chiefest virtue, and*
> *Most dignifies the haver. If it be,*
> *The man I speak of cannot in the world*

> *Be singly counterpoised. At sixteen years,*
> *When Tarquin made a head for Rome, he fought*
> *Beyond the mark of others. Our then dictator,*
> *Whom with all praise I point at, saw him fight,*
> *When with his Amazonian chin he drove*
> *The bristled lips before him; he bestrid*
> *An o'erpressed Roman and i' th' consul's view*
> *Slew three opposers; Tarquin's self he met,*
> *And struck him on his knee. In that day's feats,*
> *When he might act a woman in the scene,*
> *He proved best man i' th' field, and for his meed*
> *Was brow-bound with the oak. . . .*

When the Third Citizen says pertly and ingenuously to Coriolanus, "You must think if we give you anything, we hope to gain by you," he's introducing him to the new Rome, the Rome of interests, factions, parties, just after the Senate has been panicked (as Coriolanus thinks) into yielding up some of its authority to the plebeians—

> *Five tribunes to defend their vulgar wisdoms,*
> *Of their own choice. One's Junius Brutus,*
> *Sicinius Velutus, and I know not—'Sdeath!*
> *The rabble should have first unroofed the city*
> *Ere so prevailed with me; it will in time*
> *Win upon power, and throw forth greater themes*
> *For insurrection's arguing.*

Brutus and Sicinius are the first Roman politicians and maybe Coriolanus begins to understand he hasn't a chance against such, he doesn't have the temperament ("His nature," says Menenius, "is too noble for the world," in which the nobles are after all greatly outnumbered by the common people and therefore ought to be content to seem a bit less noble than they are), he lacks the mere animal instinct for survival to be devious with them lest they decide that for their effectiveness as politicians if not for their very lives they have no choice but to challenge and outface him.

Shakespeare's greatest scene ever is the opening scene of Act III of *Coriolanus* (more grown-up than his usual evil against good or

good mistaking good for evil), in which the tribunes, having done
their preliminary dirty work with the populace, move in on Coriolanus directly. Lucky for them, their cause is better than they
are and emboldens (almost ennobles) them to take on and wait
out the man who is the opposing cause incarnate, its champion
and fatal burden:

> BRUTUS: *The people cry you mocked them; and of late,*
> *When corn was given them gratis, you repined;*
> *Scandaled the suppliants for the people, called them*
> *Time-pleasers, flatterers, foes to nobleness.*
> CORIOLANUS: *Why, this was known before.*
> BRUTUS: *Not to them all.*
> CORIOLANUS: *Have you informed them sithence?*
> BRUTUS: *How! I inform them!*
> CORIOLANUS: *You are like to do such business.*
> BRUTUS: *Not unlike,*
>   *Each way, to better yours.* [to do better than you would as
>   consul]
> CORIOLANUS: *Why then should I be consul? By yond clouds,*
>   *Let me deserve so ill as you, and make me*
>   *Your fellow tribune.*
> SICINIUS: *You show too much of that*
>   *For which the people stir. If you will pass*
>   *To where you are bound, you must inquire your way,* [ask for
>   directions]
>   *Which you are out of, with a gentler spirit,*
>   *Nor yoke with him for tribune.*

"Let's be calm," Menenius puts in desperately, but the game's
already over, the tribunes know their man and how to let him
go on, and Coriolanus, never bound to prudence and no longer
bound to any destination, goes (bounding) on like an uncaught
ball out of all bounds:

> CORIOLANUS: *Tell me of corn!*
>   *This was my speech, and I will speak 't again—*
> MENENIUS: *Not now, not now.*
> FIRST SENATOR: *Not in this heat, sir, now.*

CORIOLANUS: *Now, as I live, I will. My nobler friends,*
  I crave their pardons.
  For the mutable, rank-scented meiny, let them [multitude]
  Regard me as I do not flatter, and
  Therein behold themselves. I say again,
  In soothing them we nourish 'gainst our Senate
  The cockle of rebellion, insolence, sedition,
  Which we ourselves have ploughed for, sowed, and scattered
  By mingling them with us, the honored number,
  Who lack not virtue, no, nor power, but that
  Which they have given to beggars.
MENENIUS: *Well, no more.*
FIRST SENATOR: *No more words, we beseech you.*
CORIOLANUS: *How? no more?*
  As for my country I have shed my blood,
  Not fearing outward force, so shall my lungs
  Coin words till their decay against those measles
  Which we disdain should tetter us, yet sought
  The very way to catch them.
BRUTUS: *You speak o' th' people*
  As if you were a god to punish, not
  A man of their infirmity.

—in response to which Coriolanus, if he weren't off and out, ought to be willing to contemplate the possibility of another side to the question of who bosses whom and, however grudgingly, cry "Touché!" in acknowledgment of their common mortality ("Comrade Trotsky, not everyone can be a genius"); but brooding over his vision of absolute order he doesn't even hear what Brutus is saying—

SICINIUS: *'Twere well*
  We let the people know 't.
MENENIUS: *What, what? His choler?*
CORIOLANUS: *Choler!*
  Were I as patient as the midnight sleep,
  By Jove, 'twould be my mind!

SICINIUS: *It is a mind*
   That shall remain a poison where it is,
   Not poison any further.
CORIOLANUS: *Shall remain!*
   Hear you this Triton of the minnows? Mark you
   His absolute "shall"?

—and now the "shall" is on the other foot, with which Coriolanus
still wildly imagines he'll be kicking the pesky tribunes and all
their constituents sky high over the moon. But it's Coriolanus
himself who soars from one passionate oration to the next up and
up into regions of self-evident truth-telling so rare ("In a rebellion,
/ When what's not meet, but what must be, was law, / Then were
they chosen. In a better hour, / Let what is meet be said it must
be meet, / And throw their power i' th' dust") and so scandalous
that at last in the racket and confusion of a preview of civil war
in the streets of Rome the tribunes consider themselves within
their rights to call the cops to do their duty (if they can), viz.
seize Coriolanus and carry him off as a traitor to be hurled from
the Tarpeian Rock ("Hence, rotten thing!" exclaims Coriolanus
with a shudder of violated fastidiousness when Sicinius sets his
authoritative hand on our hero's shoulder, "or I shall shake thy
bones / Out of thy garments"), and of course Coriolanus doesn't
doubt that he's within his rights to draw his sword and stand
ready to die fighting against the gathered rabble and their officers:

BRUTUS: *Lay hands upon him,*
   And bear him to the Rock.   Coriolanus draws his sword.
CORIOLANUS: *No, I'll die here.*
   There's some among you have beheld me fighting:
   Come, try upon yourselves what you have seen me.

He may not be a god to punish, but for his assembled enemies
the resemblance is close enough to send all of them one last time
flying.
   There's a major aspect of the play that's a little dilly of a
Freudian bedtime story: Big Mama and her fatherless boy, who
has to chop up the rest of the world and be cut and scarred in

the act to satisfy her bloodlust ("O, he is wounded; I thank the gods for 't") because he can't satisfy it in any other way: the early scenes with Volumnia and Coriolanus's timid wife ("My gracious silence, hail!" her loving husband greets her) and his butterfly-tormenting little son are in a style of grotesque farce that could be out of the Grimms' folktales. But, halfway through the play, the old battleaxe turns into Mother Machree: she didn't after all raise her boy to be the most decorated corpse in the Arlington National Cemetery, she wants him to be—of all things!—consul, and even if necessary tell *lies* to the plebeians:

> *I muse my mother*
> *Does not approve me further, who was wont*
> *To call them woollen vassals, things created*
> *To buy and sell with groats, to show bare heads*
> *In congregations, to yawn, be still and wonder,*
> *When one but of my ordinance stood up*
> *To speak of peace or war.*

"I would dissemble with my nature," says Volumnia, "where / My fortunes and my friends at stake required / I should do so in honor"; and she doesn't blink at advising him to ask the people's pardon "bonnet in thy hand" and "thy knee bussing the stones." He's a good son (he would erupt instantly if anybody else even hinted at the desirability of such behavior), he tries, but one baited word from the tribunes hooks him instantly, and so they banish him "as enemy to the people and his country" and their greatest soldier grandly banishes them in turn with a prophecy:

> *You common cry of curs, whose breath I hate*
> *As reek o' th' rotten fens, whose loves I prize*
> *As the dead carcasses of unburied men*
> *That do corrupt my air, I banish you!*
> *And here remain with your uncertainty.*
> *Let every feeble rumor shake your hearts!*
> *Your enemies, with nodding of their plumes,*
> *Fan you into despair! Have the power still*
> *To banish your defenders, till at length*
> *Your ignorance—which finds not till it feels,*

Making but reservation of yourselves, [Seeking to preserve only]
Still your own foes—deliver you as most
Abated captives to some nation
That won you without blows!

Volumnia is one of the two very important persons in his life; the other is his nearest match as a soldier, Tullus Aufidius (Menenius fondly imagines himself yet another till he suffers a heartbreaking disillusionment late in the play), and in exile Coriolanus joins Aufidius to lead an army against Rome. They have always fascinated each other: Aufidius's "hate to Marcius" is such that "Where I find him, were it / At home, upon my brother's guard, even there, / Against the hospitable canon, would I / Wash my fierce hand in 's heart"; when Coriolanus learns that Lartius has met with Volscians under a truce, he is all girlish questions— "Saw you Aufidius? . . . Spoke he of me? . . . How? what? . . . At Antium lives he?" The nuptial vibration isn't accidental (but it's all Shakespeare's, there isn't a trace of it in his source, the North translation of Plutarch): Shakespeare has already had Coriolanus express it as affection to the old general Cominius—

O, let me clip ye
In arms as sound as when I wooed, in heart
As merry as when our nuptial day was done,
And tapers burned to bedward!

—and now, when Coriolanus ("in mean apparel, disguised and muffled") throws off his disguise and reveals himself to Aufidius as Coriolanus still, though no longer his enemy but his partner, Aufidius can scarcely contain himself (he wants to make love, not war):

Let me twine
Mine arms about thy body, whereagainst
My grained ash an hundred times hath broke,
And scarred the moon with splinters. Here I clip
The anvil of my sword, and do contest
As hotly and as nobly with thy love
As ever in ambitious strength I did
Contend against thy valor. Know thou first,

I loved the maid I married; never man
Sighed truer breath. But that I see thee here,
Thou noble thing, more dances my rapt heart
Than when I first my wedded mistress saw
Bestride my threshold.

Soon one of Aufidius's servants has noticed that "Our general
himself makes a mistress of him; sanctifies himself with 's hand,
and turns up the white o' th' eye to his discourse." Shakespeare
isn't shy about documenting for no particular dramatic reason the
intensity of male bonding (Antonio-Bassanio in *The Merchant of
Venice* is another instance), these images of humid bliss are his
most explicit but he probably has piles of evidence he could pop
right out with if only the groundlings were inclined to settle for
Romeo and Julius or Troilus and Christopher. Nonetheless Aufidius
is envious rival as well as priapic bridegroom, and, observing that
Coriolanus can't resist Big Mama's plea to choose nobly rather
than hotly (to close his maidenly eyes on his wedding night with
this rough male stranger and think of Rome), Aufidius renounces
the blushing bride and restores the roaring boy:

AUFIDIUS: *. . . at his nurse's tears*
   He whined and roared away your victory,
   That pages blushed at him and men of heart
   Looked wondering each at other.
CORIOLANUS: *Hear'st thou, Mars?*
AUFIDIUS: *Name not the god, thou boy of tears!*
CORIOLANUS: *Ha!*
AUFIDIUS: *No more.*
CORIOLANUS: *Measureless liar, thou hast made my heart*
   Too great for what contains it. Boy? O slave!
   Pardon me, lords, 'tis the first time that ever
   I was forced to scold. [!] *Your judgments, my grave lords,*
   Must give this cur the lie; and his own notion—
   Who wears my stripes impressed upon him, that
   Must bear my beating to his grave—shall join
   To thrust the lie unto him.
FIRST LORD: *Peace, both, and hear me speak.*

CORIOLANUS: *Cut me to pieces, Volsces. Men and lads,*
   Stain all your edges on me. Boy? False hound!
   If you have writ your annals true, 'tis there
   That, like an eagle in a dovecote, I
   Fluttered your Volscians in Corioles.
   Alone I did it. Boy?

—defiance enough, as Coriolanus stands alone once more among the Volscians, to give Aufidius a pretext for unleashing his minions: "Draw the Conspirators, and kill Marcius, who falls. Aufidius stands on him."

Coriolanus's incredulous choked outrage at Aufidius's "boy"— after what I've done, how can anybody say I'm anything but a man? because nobody sends a boy to do a man's work—is his last tantrum; uncertain at last whether Mama knows best, this most obedient of mama's boys commits a kind of suicide by proxy on the horns of his first dilemma. Still, boys only dream of doing what Coriolanus has actually done. He's like a great dancer or athlete, exciting to think about, paralyzing to meet, terrific to watch in action, but you wouldn't want to have to live with him; but then who would want to have to live with *you*?

Dark Angel
and
Last Hope

In Plutarch's *Lives of the Noble Grecians and Romans*, which is the source of three of Shakespeare's plays, the Life of Coriolanus directly follows the Life of Alcibiades and directly precedes a comparison between the two men, but Shakespeare didn't write a Tragedy of Alcibiades; instead (with a dull thud) he drops into *Timon of Athens* a character called Alcibiades as similar to his noble Grecian namesake as Hamlet is to Hercules: instead of Plutarch's dark angel of Athens, Shakespeare's Alcibiades is a plain, blunt, choleric soldier devoted to Lord Timon and ready to pull down the city to satisfy a soldier's rough sense of justice; if he weren't mere archetype he would be a monster half-Coriolanus and half-Kent. Then, consistency be damned! Shakespeare recollects that the historical Alcibiades was a rakish sort, and in one of the scenes fixes him up with two "mistresses" so that for the length of the scene he can serve as a horrible example—representing The Vileness of Whoremongering—to exercise the rhetorical powers of his erstwhile friend and patron turned self-styled misanthrope (but at least here in this scene Timon is wrong about himself, he's just another mouthpiece for the usual Shakespearean misogyny, which the Bard is indulging here even more gratuitously than usual because women have had nothing to do with Timon's loss of affluence and of fairweather friends but whore! whore! whore! nevertheless: "This fell whore of thine / Hath in her more destruction than thy sword, / For all her cherubin look"; "Be a whore still. . . . / Give them diseases, leaving with thee their lust"; "Be strong in whore, allure him, burn him up"; and so forth).

Now there's no question that the historical Alcibiades consorted with women of ill repute, as well as with maidens, wives, boys, and men (to stop right there), including several attempts—which he gallantly said, or Plato said he said, were unsuccessful—on the virtue of Socrates himself; but there's a question why Shakespeare ducked the opportunity to consider *in extenso* and at stage center an Athenian sixty zillion times more influential, more amusing, and more tragic than Timon. Maybe Coriolanus, unmanageable but blessedly simple, was as far as Shakespeare could let himself go toward taking will and energy seriously, in an unaccustomed region beyond the preoccupations of private citizens (masquerading as kings and princes) quite like you and me who try to keep their children in line by gifts and threats or wonder whether their wives are making out with the TV repairman or renounce executive vice-presidencies for love: pathos, suffering, good and evil by the book, repentance, forgiveness, suspense; adultery, murder, filial ingrat-itude (how sharper than a serpent's tooth), death in a welter of Wagnerian declamation as the coronary climax to middle-aged sex: domestic tragedy: soap opera: Double, double (Bubble, bubble) toil and trouble. Anyhow Shakespeare's Timon railing at Alcibiades is full of the usual Shakespearean bullshit and hot air (which boil down to the usual Shakespearean *verb. sap.*: Beware the foul fiend Hankypanky, from whose crotch and armpit come all diseases—baldness, fallen noses, and severe depression), but Plutarch's Timon keeps his eye on the target and although saying much less has something to say (I quote from Sir Thomas North's translation of Plutarch, which was the Plutarch Shakespeare read):

> as . . . [Alcibiades] came from the counsaill and assembly of the cittie, where he had made an excellent oration, to the great good liking and acceptation of all the hearers, and by meanes thereof had obteined the thing he desired, and was accompanied with a great traine that followed him to his honour: Timon, . . . meeting Alcibiades thus accompanied [whereas Shakespeare has him accompanied by the two cour-tesans that give Timon a pretext for offering the usual Shake-spearean courtesies to those abominations the women that men can't deny they do the deed of darkness with], dyd not passe by him, nor gave him waye (as he was wont to doe all

other men), but went straight to him, and tooke him by the hande, and sayed. O, thou dost well my sonne, I can thee thancke, that thou goest on, and climest up still: for if ever thou be in authoritie, woe be unto those that followe thee, for they are utterly undone. When they heard these wordes, those that stoode by fell a laughing: other reviled Timon; other againe marked well his wordes, and thought of them many a time after. . . .

Alcibiades was the talk of the town all of his life, born to rank and wealth, brilliant, fearless, shameless, hugely ambitious, courting the populace like a lover ("his curtesies, his liberallities, and noble expences to shewe the people so great pleasure and pastime as nothing could be more"), boundlessly sensual, the nonpareil of beauty ("he was wonderful fayer, being a child, a boye, and a man, and that at all times, which made him . . . beloved of every man"), the complete charmer: "his company and manner to passe the time awaye, was commonly marvelous full of mirthe and pleasure, and he had suche pleasaunt comely devises with him, that no man was of so sullen a nature, but he would make him merie, nor so churlishe, but he would make him gentle. So that both those that feared him, and also envied him: they were yet glad to see him, and it did them good to be in his companie, and use talke with him." He was also perverse, impetuous, unruly, violent, unpredictable, capable of abrupt reversals, incapable of moderation or apology: "he kept Agartharcus the painter prisoner in his house by force, untill he had painted all his walles within: and when he had done, dyd let him goe, and rewarded him very honestly for his paines"; "he gave a boxe of the eare unto Hipponicus, Callias father: who was one of the greatest men of power in the cittie, being a noble man borne, and of great possessions, which was done upon a bravery and certaine lustines, as having layed a wager with his companions he would doe it, and for no malice or quarrell that he bare the man. This light parte was straight over all the cittie, and every one that heard it, sayed it was lewdly done. But Alcibiades the next morning went to his house, and knocking at his gate was let in: so he stripping him selfe before him, delivered him his bodie to be whipped, and punished at his pleasure. Hipponicus pardoned him, and was friends with him, and gave him his daughter Hipparete afterwards in mariage." At eighteen or nineteen he served valorously in the campaign at Potidaea with Socrates, who saved his life there, and at Delion, where he returned the favor by saving Socrates' life several times over during a retreat. He was the best chariot-racer of the age, and Euripides composed a song of praise celebrating Alcibiades' victories at the Olympic games as well as his military prowess (which the Greeks valued about equally): "thou art bold in martiall dedes, and overcommest allwayes"; "at thOlympike games . . . thy head hath twise bene crownde / with olive boughes." In his childhood his tutor (and a near kinsman) was Pericles; in his youth and manhood his teacher and—when prospects of polymorphous peccadilloes weren't luring him off—his favorite companion was Socrates:

> Socrates love which he bare him, though it had many mightie and great adversaries, yet it dyd staye much Alcibiades, somtime by his gentle nature, somtime by his grave counsell and advise: so as the reason thereof tooke so deepe roote in him, and dyd so pearce his harte, that many times the teares ranne downe his cheekes. Another time also being caried awaye with the intisement of flatterers, that held up his humour with all pleasure and delightes, he stale awaye from Socrates, and made him ronne after him to fetche him againe, as if he had bene a slave that had ronne awaye from his masters house: for Alcibiades stoode in awe of no man but of Socrates only, and in deede he dyd reverence him, and dyd despise all other. And therefore Cleanthes was wont to saye, that Alcibiades was held of Socrates by the eares: but that he gave his other lovers holde, which Socrates never sought for: for to saye truely, Alcibiades was muche geven over to lust and pleasure. And peradventure it was that Thucydides ment of him, when he wrote that he was incontinent of bodie, and dissolute of life.

Plutarch, writing about Alcibiades five centuries after the mischief he made, could afford to reinvest him with some of the glamor he lavishly had in person; but Thucydides was a contem-

porary who didn't dazzle easily and who was obliged to live with
the results of the mischief, so his account of Alcibiades in the
History of the Peloponnesian War has no glamor at all but a dry,
keen edge from the outset, when he introduces him as leader of
the Athenian faction that wants to break the uncertain peace that
has interrupted the war with Sparta: "a man who was still young
in years (or would have been thought so in any other city in
Hellas), but who reached a position of importance owing to the
respect in which his family was held [Thucydides never acknowledges the fact or the effect of Alcibiades' charm]. He was genuinely
convinced that the best thing for Athens was an alliance with
Argos [Thucydides is scrupulous in giving their moral due even
to those he detests]—though it is true also that considerations of
his own dignity affected his opposition to the peace with Sparta.
He did not like the fact that the Spartans had negotiated the treaty
through Nicias and Laches, paying no attention to him because
of his youth." A deputation from Sparta arrived in Athens with
full powers to conclude agreements on all issues in dispute; but,
having resolved to discredit both the deputation and Nicias, who
was the principal Athenian advocate of peace, Alcibiades tricked
the Spartans into disclaiming their powers, then publicly denounced them for misrepresenting themselves, cut the ground out
from under Nicias, was able to push the treaty with Argos (which
was hostile to Sparta) through the assembly, and assured the resumption of the war with Sparta. It was his first sizable and a
very promising act of political skulduggery.

Alcibiades and Nicias were also linked in the catastrophic expedition to Sicily, which ended with the annihilation of the largest
Athenian army ever assembled, and which assured the eventual
downfall of Athens. Although the war with Sparta was going
strong again, it wasn't enough for Alcibiades, who considered
Sicily ripe for inclusion in the Athenian Empire and a staging area
on the way to Carthage and the Mediterranean coasts of Africa and
Europe as far as the Pillars of Hercules, himself of course the
conquering hero. Once more Nicias objected, but all he got for
his pains was joint command with Alcibiades of the expedition.
Just before they embarked, there was a matter of last-minute
sacrilege that Alcibiades was accused of: profaning the Eleusinian

mysteries in an orgiastic mock-ritual, himself of course the mock-priest, part of which consisted in defacing sacred images throughout the city (he and his cronies apparently held a kind of going-away party). Alcibiades protested his innocence and demanded a trial, but the assembly decided that the ships oughtn't to be delayed and insisted that he leave with them though the charge would be hanging over his head. Scarcely landed in Sicily he was recalled by the assembly, who had determined not only that he was guilty of sacrilege but that it was associated with a plot to overthrow the democracy and establish a dictatorship. Alcibiades, who had more interesting things to do than die so young, instead of returning to Athens fled to Sparta: somebody asked him, "Why, how now Alcibiades, darest thou not trust the justice of thy countrie? Yes very well (quoth he) and it were in another matter: but my life standing upon it, I would not trust mine own mother, fearing least negligently she should put in the black beane, where she should cast in the white. For by the first, condemnation of death was signified: and by the other, pardone of life. But afterwards, hearing that the Athenians for malice had condemned him to death: well, quoth he, they shall knowe I am yet alive." Indeed they did know, very soon too, because it was Alcibiades' urgent advice to the reluctant Spartans that persuaded them to send to Sicily the fleet that seconded the Syracusans and guaranteed the defeat of the Athenians there.

Well, now he had gone and done it, surely there was no way for him from now on except down down down; but he was in the vigor of his impatient manhood, and he had a suppleness and a sense of humor that (no wonder Shakespeare didn't make a tragic hero out of him) didn't take to breast-beating or villainy for the sake of villainy. In Sparta he could plunge into a new life with the enthusiasm of an athlete:

> if he were welcome, and well esteemed in Sparta, for the service he dyd to the common wealth: muche more he wanne the love and good willes of private men, for that he lived after the Laconian manner. So as they sawe his skinne scraped to the fleshe [i.e. clean-shaven], and sawe him washe him selfe in cold water, and howe he dyd eate browne bread, and

suppe of their blacke brothe: would have doubted (or to saye
better, never have beleeved) that suche a man had ever kept
cooke in his house, nor that he ever had seene so muche as
a perfuming panne, or had touched clothe of tissue made at
Miletum. For among other qualities and properties he had
(whereof he was full) this as they saye was one, whereby he
most robbed mens hartes: that he could frame altogether with
their manners and facions of life, transforming him selfe more
easely to all manner of shapes, then the Camelion.

He could also refresh himself with more familiar activities, as when
he "entertained Queene Timaea, King Agis wife of Sparta, so well
in his absence, he being abroad in the warres: that he got her
with childe, and she her selfe denied it not. . . . And Alcibiades
jeasting out the matter, sayed he had done it for no hurte, nor
for any lust of fleshe to satisfie his desire: but only to leave of his
race, to reigne amongest the Lacedaemonians." Because Timaea
(whose pet name for the child was Alcibiades) and Alcibiades seem
to have told everybody, and because King Agis remembered that
he hadn't slept with his wife for ten months before the child was
born ("For lying with his wife one night when there was a terrible
earthquake, he ranne out of his chamber for feare the house would
fall on his head: so that it was tenne moneths after ere he laye
againe with her"), the King disavowed the child and Alcibiades
failed to become the Banquo of Sparta, no king himself but father
of kings.

Alcibiades continued to goad and rally the Spartans, who were
an unleavened and torpid bunch and, even after the Athenian
debacle in Sicily, liable to be discouraged and intimidated by
minor setbacks. (Thucydides' Spartans aren't the Classic Comics
Spartans, consummate soldiers ready and eager for war on the
double against the highly civilized but relatively effete Athenians.
In fact it took a lot of flukes, bad breaks, Alcibiades' defection,
acts of God—e.g. two devastating visitations of the plague—to
bring Athens down, because it's obvious that they had not only
better leadership and an incomparably better navy but, as it turned
out, even a better army than Sparta.) Alcibiades also kept busy
traveling from city to city of those allied with Athens arguing that

they should join Sparta if they knew what was good for them, and he fought on the Spartan side in the thick of the battle at which the Athenians tried but failed to regain one of these cities. Meanwhile, however, the Spartans had grown disenchanted with him, and a letter was sent to the Spartan field commander with orders to put him to death: "He was a personal enemy of [King] Agis," says Thucydides laconically, having never mentioned the personal cause, "and was generally considered unreliable." (Especially with lonely wives.) The Spartans had made an alliance with the Persian governor of Sardis (across the Aegean in Asia Minor), Tisaphernes, to whom Alcibiades, tipped off in the nick of time (by whom? someone he had charmed, no doubt), fled for refuge, and "with whom he wanne incontinently suche credit, that he was the first and chiefest persone he had about him":

> For this barbarous man being no simple persone, but rather malicious, and subtill of nature, and that loved fine and crafty men: dyd wonder how he could so easely turne from one manner of living to another, and also at his quicke witte and understanding. . . . In so muche as this Tisaphernes (that otherwise was a churlishe man, and naturally hated the Grecians) dyd geve him selfe so muche unto Alcibiades flatteries, and they pleased him so well: that he him selfe dyd studie to flatter Alcibiades againe, and make muche of him. For he called Alcibiades his fayer house of pleasure, and goodly prospect: notwithstanding he had many goodly gardens, sweete springes, grene arbours and pleasaunt meadowes, and those in all royall and magnificent manner.

To outsmart Alcibiades you had to get up very early in the morning. Thucydides, who isn't interested in Alcibiades' love life, does enjoy spelling out the details of his Argus-eyed if not always triumphant trickery. As soon as he went over to Tisaphernes he started trying to persuade him to take a more neutral stance toward the Greek antagonists, in other words to cool off toward his allies the Spartans and ease up on the Athenians, Alcibiades' reason being that he was already thinking about returning to Athens. He began to intrigue with leaders of the Athenian forces stationed at Samos, urging them to seek an alliance with the Persian king

and show their faith in Oriental despotism by overthrowing the
democracy in Athens. He persuaded everybody at Samos except
the Athenian general there, Phrynicus, who "believed, quite correctly, that oligarchy and democracy were all one to Alcibiades
and that what he was really after was to get recalled by his friends
and come back to Athens as a result of a change in the existing
constitution"; and that, in any case, the Persians were unlikely
to switch sides for no particular advantage. Phrynicus was outvoted,
and, fearful that Alcibiades once recalled would punish him for
his opposition, sent a secret message to Astyochus, the Spartan
admiral, informing him that Alcibiades was plotting to bring
Tisaphernes over to the Athenian side. Astyochus immediately
took off to their headquarters and informed Alcibiades and Tisaphernes, because he was already on Tisaphernes' secret payroll.
Alcibiades wrote the authorities at Samos accusing Phrynicus of
treason (against Athens! which Alcibiades had long since forsaken
for its mortal enemy) and demanding that he be put to death.
Phrynicus, understandably upset, wrote to Astyochus chiding him
for spilling the beans but, because he held no grudge, went ahead
to provide information that would allow the Spartans to capture
Samos and wipe out the Athenian forces (of which he was the
commanding general); and this letter also

> was passed on by Astyochus to Alcibiades. Phrynicus, how-
> ever, was told in time that Astyochus was betraying his
> confidence and that a letter on the subject could be expected
> any moment from Alcibiades. He therefore got in first with
> the news and informed the army that, Samos being unfortified
> as it was and the whole fleet not being at anchor in the
> harbour, the enemy was going to make an attack on the
> camp; he said that he was quite sure of this and that they
> ought to fortify Samos as quickly as possible and generally
> be on the alert. As he was in command himself, he had the
> power to see that all this was done. The Athenians set to
> work at the fortifications and so, as a result of all this, Samos,
> which would have been fortified in any case, was fortified all
> the sooner. Not long afterwards the letter arrived from Al-

cibiades saying that the army was betrayed by Phrynicus and that the enemy were going to attack. However, people did not think that Alcibiades' evidence could be trusted; instead it was assumed that he knew what the enemy's plans were and, out of personal ill-feeling, had tried to fasten on Phrynicus the charge of being concerned in them too. His message, therefore, so far from doing Phrynicus any harm, merely confirmed what he had said already.

Thus the episode ended unsatisfactorily for Alcibiades because Phrynicus had learned to get up and get moving at the crack of dawn, before all of Argus's eyes had opened.

And then, for the rest of his life, as if by a choice he made, Alcibiades was the last great leader and the tragic hero of Athens, a fitting subject—if they had been willing to consider a contemporary—for the great tragic poets of whom Sophocles and Euripides were still alive and writing till two years before his death. Now, the Athenian democracy having been overthrown, "The Four Hundred" with street squads of Hitler-youth-type bullyboys ruled Athens; Alcibiades, who had done his bit to bring about this latest mischief, was invited to Samos and, having arrived, was elected general there, to face almost at once an unexpected crisis: the Athenian army in Samos overwhelmingly favored a restoration of the democracy at home, furiously rejected pleas by delegates from The Four Hundred, and were ready to sail against Athens; and here is the skeptical Thucydides' handsome tribute to Alcibiades for what he did in the crisis:

> It was at this point, it seems, that Alcibiades did his first great act of service to his country, and a very important act it was. For when the Athenians at Samos were all eager to sail against their own countrymen—which would certainly have meant the immediate occupation of Ionia and the Hellespont by the enemy—it was Alcibiades who stopped them.
>
> There was not another man in existence who could have controlled the mob at that time. Alcibiades stopped them from sailing against Athens, and used his tongue to such

effect that he diverted them from the anger which they felt
against the delegates on personal grounds. It was he who
gave the reply to the delegates when they were sent away. . . .

His reply was a demand for restoration of the democracy. The Four
Hundred thereupon tried to shore up their regime by making an
effort to negotiate a quick peace with Sparta, and, when it failed,
they virtually instructed the Spartan fleet to move in and take
over; but the Spartan admiral was too suspicious or stupid to enter
the defenseless harbor, the city was spared, The Four Hundred
were deposed, the restored democracy officially recalled Alcibiades
to Athens; and, though Thucydides himself lived another dozen
years, his narrative stops short right here in the year 411 B.C.,
before every one of Alcibiades' greatest victories and saddest defeats,
seven eventful years before Athens was vanquished at last and
Alcibiades, in exile again, assassinated.

And it was three full years before Alcibiades accepted the city's
pardon and returned to Athens (as we learn, together with the rest
of the story, from Plutarch), because he spent these three years
sweeping the seas clear of the Spartan fleet and recapturing all the
Greek cities of Asia Minor that had defected from Athens: he
intended to return home not as a prodigal son but as a conquering
hero. First he sought out and destroyed a Spartan fleet in the
Hellespont; and—he was Alcibiades still—he was so proud of his
victory that, all dressed up and bearing gifts, he paid a visit to
Tisaphernes to brag about it; but he "found not that entertainment
he hoped for": Tisaphernes, who was afraid to fall into disgrace
with his king because the Spartans were already accusing him of
ignoring his treaty obligations to them, had Alcibiades arrested
and imprisoned; but within a month Alcibiades escaped on horseback and took a characteristic revenge by telling everybody that
it was Tisaphernes himself who had set up the escape. He resumed
his command and continued his campaign in Asia Minor as if
there were no way for Athens to lose, his exploit at Selybrea
strikingly resembling the exploit of Marcius soon-to-be-Coriolanus
trapped inside the gates of Corioles:

upon the sodaine he did take the cittie of Selybrea: bicause
he valliantly put him selfe in hazard before the time appointed

him. For certain of his friends within, with whom he had
secret practise, had geven him a token, that when time served,
they would shewe a burning torche in the ayer at midnight:
but they were compelled to shew this fyer in the ayer before
they were readie, for feare least one of their confederacie would
bewraye the matter, who sodainly repented him. Now this
torche burning in the ayer, was set up before Alcibiades was
readie with his companie. But he perceyving the signe set,
tooke about thirtie men with him in his companie, and ranne
with them to the walles of the cittie, having commaunded
the rest of his armie to followe him with all speede possible.
The gate was opened to him, and to his thirtie men: besides
them there followed twentie other light armed men. Howbeit
they were no soner entered the cittie, but they heard the
cittizens armed come against them: so that there was no hope
to scape, if he dyd tarie their comming [await the coming
of his army]. Nevertheles, considering that untill that present
time he was never overcome in battell, where he had taken
charge, it greved him very muche to flye: wherefore it straight
came in his head to make silence by sound of trumpet, and
after silence made, he caused one of them that were about
him to make proclamation with a lowde voyce, that the
Selybrianians should not take armes against the Athenians.
This cooled them a litle that would fayne have bene doing,
bicause they supposed that all the armie of the Athenians had
bene already in the cittie: the other on the contrarie side,
were very glad to talke of peace, without any further daunger.
And as they beganne to parle upon composition, the rest of
Alcibiades armie was come on. Now he thincking in deede
(which was true) that the Selybrianians sought nothing but
peace, and fearing least the Thracians which were many in
number (and came with good will to serve him in that jorney)
would sacke and spoyle the cittie, he made them all to goe
out againe: and so concluding peace with the chiefe of the
Selybrianians, he dyd them no more hurte, apon their humble
submission, but made them paye him a summe of money,
and so leaving a garrison of the Athenians within the cittie,
he departed thence.

He was one of the few commanders whose word could be trusted on the conditions of a surrender: when he was besieging Byzantium, certain leading citizens "promised him to deliver it into his hands, so they might be assured he would doe them no hurte," and, even though there was heavy fighting, he honored the pledge:

> Nevertheles they went not away unfought with. For those that laye in garrison within the cittie, some of them Peloponnesians, other Boeotians, and other Megarians, dyd so valliantly repulse them that came out of their gallyes, that they drave them to retire abord againe. Afterwardes hearing how the Athenians were entred the cittie on thother side, they put them selves in battell raye, and went to mete them. The battell was terrible of both partes: but Alcibiades in the ende obtained victorie, leading the right winge of his battell, and Theramenes the lefte. The victorie being gotten, he tooke 300 of his enemies prisoners, who had escaped the furie of the battell. But after the battell, there was not a Byzantine put to death, neither banished, nor his good confiscated: bicause it was capitulated by Alcibiades with his confederats, that neither he, nor his, should hurt any of the Bizantines either in persone or goodes, nor any way should rifle them.

One of the enemies he routed and humiliated was another Persian governor, Pharnabazus (who would play a double role, savior and avenger, in the last year of Alcibiades' life), first at the battle of Cyzicum: "Alcibiades leaving his fleete, followed the chase with twentie of the best gallyes he had, and drave them a lande. Thereupon he landed also, and pursued them so corageously at their heeles, that he slue a great number of them on the mayne lande, who thought by flying to have saved them selves. Moreover, Mindarus [the Spartan general], and Pharnabazus, being come out of the cittie to rescue their people, were overthrowen both. He slue Mindarus in the field, fighting valliantly: as for Pharnabazus, he cowardly fled away. So the Athenians spoyled the dead bodies (which were a great number) of a great deale of armour and riches, and tooke besides all their enemies shippes. After they tooke the cittie of Cyzicum, Pharnabazus having left it." Alcibiades' troops exulted to be under his command, they "grewe to suche a pryde and reputation of them selves, that they would not, and disdained also to serve with the other souldiers that had bene beaten many times": for instance when an Athenian army under Thrasyllus was defeated at Ephesus, "Alcibiades souldiers did very muche rebuke Thrasyllus men, and dyd exceedingly extoll their captaine and them selves, and would neither encampe with them, neither have to doe with them, nor yet keep their companie,"

> Untill suche time as Pharnabazus came with a great armie against them, aswell of footemen as horsemen, when they ranne a forraging upon the Abydenians: and then Alcibiades went to the rescue of them, and gave Pharnabazus battell, and overthrewe him once againe, and dyd together with Thrasyllus chase him even untill darke night. Then both Alcibiades and Thrasyllus souldiers dyd companie together, one rejoycing with another: and so returned all with great joye into one campe. The next morning Alcibiades set up a triumphe for the victorie he had the daye before, and then went to spoyle and destroye Pharnabazus countrie, where he was governour, and no man durst once come out to meete him.

So in 408 B.C., at the age of forty-two, in the prime of his pride and beauty, the conquering hero set sail for Athens, "desirous in the ende to see his native countrie againe (or to speake more truely, that his contry men should see him) after he had so many times overthrowen their enemies in battell":

> he hoysed saile, and directed his course towardes Athens, bringing with him all the gallyes of the Athenians richely furnished, and decked all about, with skutchines and targettes, and other armour and weapon gotten amongest the spoyles of his enemies. Moreover, he brought with him many other shippes, which he had wonne and broken in the warres, besides many ensignes and other ornaments: all which being compted together one with the other, made up the number of two hundred shippes.

Yet "he returned in great feare and doubt," he was still afraid that they didn't love him, or that at best they loved him but knew they shouldn't, as Aristophanes sourly summed up the Athenians' feeling for Alcibiades: "The people most desire, what most they hate to have"; and (though the lion feared and needed his keepers as much as they feared and needed him) "if they nedes will keepe, a lyon to their cost, / then must they nedes obeye his will, for he will rule the roste"—

> when he was arrived in the haven of Piraea, he would not set foote a lande, before he first sawe his nephewe Euryptolemus, and divers other of his friendes from the hatches of his shippe, standing apon the sandes in the haven mouthe. Who were come thither to receyve and welcome him, and tolde him that he might be bolde to lande, without feare of any thing. He was no soner landed, but all the people ranne out of every corner to see him, with so great love and affection, that they tooke no heede of the other captaines that came with him, but clustred all to him only, and cried out for joye to see him. Those that could come neere him, dyd welcome and imbrace him: but all the people wholy followed him. And some that came to him, put garlands of flowers upon his head: and those that could not come neere him, sawe him a farre of, and the olde folkes dyd pointe him out to the yonger sorte. But this common joye was mingled notwithstanding, with teares and sorrowe, when they came to thinke upon their former misfortunes and calamities, and to compare them with their present prosperitie: waying with them selves also how they had not lost Sicilia, nor their hope in all things els had failed them, if they had delivered them selves and the charge of their armie into Alcibiades hands, when they sent for him to appeare in persone before them. Considering also how he found the cittie of Athens in manner put from their seigniorie and commaundement on the sea, and on the other side how their force by lande was brought unto such extremitie, that Athens scantly could defend her suburbes, the cittie self being so devided and turmoiled with civil dissention: yet he gathered together those fewe, and small force that remained, and had now not only restored Athens to her former power and soveraintie on the sea, but had made her also a conquerer by lande.

He was chosen general, all his confiscated property and possessions were restored, and the priests who had cursed him for his
sacrilege, which now again he solemnly denied, revoked their
curses. At once he began preparing a fleet for a resumption of the
campaign, because the Spartans had a new admiral, Lysander, who
was making inroads in Asia Minor. Alcibiades, characteristically
wanting to do something really spectacular before he left again,
decided to restore the annual ceremonies of the Eleusinian mysteries
(against which his alleged sacrilege had started all the trouble for
him) to their former splendor. The Spartans under King Agis had
taken and fortified a city on the road from Athens to Eleusis, and
the initiates could no longer make the journey by land. Alcibiades
decided to reinstitute the traditional procession and accompany
it with an escort of soldiers, reasoning that either Agis "would
not sturre at all against the sacred ceremonies, and by this meanes
should much imbase and diminishe his reputation and glorie: or
if he dyd come out to the field, that he would make the battell
very gratefull to the goddes, considering it should be in defence
of their most holy feasts and worshippe, and in the sight of his
countrie, where the people would see and witnesse both, his val-
liantnes, and also his corage." The procession traveled without
incident both going and coming, without a sign from the hapless
Agis or his troops: the people were so confirmed in their enthusiasm
for Alcibiades that they urged him to become king but "the greatest
men of the cittie, fearing least in deede he ment some suche thing,
dyd hasten his departure as sone as they could." Off he went with
his fleet; but the odds had changed, Lysander was the best commander the Spartans had ever had as well as the best diplomat,
his parleys with the in any case pro-Spartan son of the Persian
king had gained him more than enough money for his military
operations, whereas Alcibiades was compelled to leave his own
fleet repeatedly to try to raise money from allied cities. On one
such occasion he gave temporary command of the fleet not to one
of his captains but to his pilot and drinking-companion Antiochus,
with express instructions to avoid battle till his return; but Antiochus, a brash sailor no doubt yearning for glory, challenged
Lysander to battle and was quickly beaten (he himself was killed
and fifteen ships were lost). In fact it wasn't a major engagement,

but, once the news got back to Athens, it was enough to scandalize the volatile Athenians into deposing Alcibiades from his command.

Again he fled, this time into the wilds of Thrace, where for two years he lived the life of a bandit chieftain on a grand scale, moving from fortress to fortress with his army of mercenaries, raiding settlements and carrying off booty, and incidentally protecting the northern borders of Greece against Thracian incursions (he may have been planning a new empire of his own, half-Thracian and half-Greek, and he wouldn't have wanted anybody else to get the same idea). During the second year of his second exile the Athenian fleet scored a great victory, its first without Alcibiades since his first exile; and the Athenian admirals tried to press their advantage by forcing a battle with Lysander, who however, being far outnumbered, refused to engage. Finally Lysander took a strategic harbor town on the Asian side of the Hellespont and established his ships there. One hundred and eighty ships—the entire Athenian navy—followed him and set up their station on the European side at Aegospotami, a very poorly chosen anchorage without a proper harbor or a town for provisioning. From the walls of one of his castles a few miles to the north, Alcibiades observed for four days the disposition of the two fleets: the discipline of the Spartans, who were drawn up ready for battle every day from sunrise to sunset yet refused to be challenged out of their harbor into an engagement; the overconfidence and disorder of the Athenians, who sailed out every day to challenge the enemy, were refused, sailed back, and dispersed from the ships as if the Spartans deserved a handicap. Then he rode alone into the Athenian camp, no doubt astonishing the troops who were seeing him for the first time since he had led them, and explained to the admirals exactly what they were doing wrong and how they could correct it, but they "stowtely commaunded him to get him awaye, as one that had nothing to doe with the matter"; and Alcibiades rode back to his castle. Twenty-four hours later he looked on as the Spartans fell upon the unprepared Athenian fleet, destroyed all but eight of the hundred and eighty ships, and took three thousand prisoners all of whom were put to death; it was all over but the shouting: soon afterward Lysander occupied Athens and won for Sparta the war that had begun twenty-seven years earlier.

Alcibiades, knowing that the Spartans would want his head, hoped to reach the court of the Persian king and start a new career there (as another illustrious Athenian exile, Themistocles, had done sixty years before), so he took refuge with Pharnabazus, who welcomed him but declined to recommend him to the king; Pharnabazus settled him in a remote village of his district and provided him, as befitted his status, with a princely income. Meanwhile Lysander had appointed as the new rulers of Athens thirty oligarchs, of whom Critias (like Alcibiades, one of Socrates' students) warned Lysander that as long as Alcibiades lived the oligarchy and Sparta's ascendancy would be imperiled by the people's expectation of his glorious return:

> the Athenians founde them selves desolate, and in miserable state to see their empire lost: but then much more, when Lysander had taken all their liberties, and dyd set thirtie governours over their cittie. Now to late, after all was lost (where they might have recovered againe, if they had been wise) they beganne together to bewaile and lament their miseries and wretched state, looking backe apon all their wilfull faultes and follies committed: emong which, they dyd reckon their second time of falling out with Alcibiades, was their greatest faulte. So they banished him only of malice and displeasure, not for any offense him selfe in persone had committed against them, saving that his lieutenaunt in his absence had shamefully lost a fewe of their shippes: and they them selves more shamefully had driven out of their cittie, the noblest souldier, and most skilfull captaine that they had. And yet they had some litle poore hope lefte, that they were not altogether cast awaye, so long as Alcibiades lived, and had his health. For before, when he was a forsaken man, and led a banished life: yet he could not live idely, and doe nothing. Wherefore now much more, sayed they to them selves: if there be any helpe at all, he will not suffer out of doubt the insolencie and pryde of the Lacedaemonians, nor yet abyde the cruelties and outrages of these thirtie tyrauntes.

Yet Lysander refused to proceed against Alcibiades, till from Sparta came a royal despatch (King Agis was back home with his wife and her son) containing the order for Alcibiades' assassination; Lysander passed it on to the Spartans' ally Pharnabazus; and Pharnabazus delegated the job to a party of soldiers led by his brother and his uncle:

> Now was Alcibiades in a certen village of Phrygia, with a concubine of his called Timandra. So he thought he dreamed one night that he had put on his concubines apparell, and how she dandling him in her armes, had dressed his head, friseling his heare, and painted his face, as he had bene a woman. Other saye, that he thought Magaeus [Pharnabazus' brother] strake of his head, and made his bodie to be burnt: and the voyce goeth, this vision was but a litle before his death. Those that were sent to kill him, durst not enter the house where he was, but set it a fire round about. Alcibiades spying the fire, got suche apparell and hanginges as he had, and threwe it on the fire, thincking to have put it out: and so casting his cloke about his left arme, tooke his naked sworde in his other hande, and ranne out of the house, him selfe not once touched with fyer, saving his clothes were a litle singed. These murderers so sone as they spied him, drewe backe, and stoode a sonder, and durst not one of them come neere him, to stande and fight with him: but a farre of, they bestowed so many arrowes and dartes of him, that they killed him there. Now when they had left him, Timandra went and tooke his bodie which she wrapped up in the best linnen she had, and buried him as honorably as she could possible, with suche things as she had, and could get together.

But nothing is simple in the life or death of Alcibiades (nothing simple enough for Shakespeare to make a big tragedy out of), and there is quite another story with which Plutarch closes: "Notwithstanding, touching the death of Alcibiades, there are some that agree to all the rest I have written, saving that they saye, it was neither Pharnabazus, nor Lysander, nor the Lacedaemonians, which caused him to be slaine: but that he keeping with him a young gentlewoman of a noble house, whom he had stolen awaye and intised to follie: her brethern to revenge this injurie, went to set fire upon the house where he was, and that they killed him as we have tolde you, thinking to leape out of the fyre." Maybe both stories are true, and Pharnabazus' assassins joined up with the young gentlewoman's exasperated brothers en route to Alcibiades' den to do in for good and all the lion of Athens, this beautiful cat with nine lives who had always landed on his feet running.

Nobody Here
But Us
Chickens

If Shakespeare's on the verge of having a good time he begins to
brood about time ("Devouring Time"); if he's on the verge of
enjoying his own or anybody else's body he begins to think about
it as the slave of time, because first it ripes and ripes and next
it rots and rots:

> Thy glass will show thee how thy beauties wear,
> Thy dial how thy precious minutes waste;
> The vacant leaves thy mind's imprint will bear,
> And of this book this learning mayst thou taste.
> The wrinkles which thy glass will truly show,
> Of mouthed graves will give thee memory;
> Thou by thy dial's shady stealth mayst know
> Time's thievish progress to eternity.

—and (Time's fool) he's at his gloomiest when he means to spread
the good word that love ("the marriage of true minds" rather than
of treacherous because deteriorating bodies) is stronger than time,
which however by the strength of the images he can't help giving
it is unaccommodating enough to beat love all hollow:

> Love's not Time's fool, though rosy lips and cheeks
> Within his bending sickle's compass come;
> Love alters not with his brief hours and weeks,
> But bears it out even to the edge of doom.

The bridegroom cometh (if you'll excuse the expression), unless
en route he gets so depressed by visions of doom and bending

sickles that he can't help dropping in at Barney's Bar and Grill to drown his sorrows.

For Jesus there's all the time in the world till there's no time at all; and the body, far from being enslaved to time, thumbs its pretty nose at Shakespeare's inventory of dependable horrors—decay, disease (e.g., fallen noses), death—and rises on the third day out of all time. Restoring the body is as simple as stopping or reversing time: healings happen twice to a paragraph and dozens per chapter if the force be with you; leprosy and blindness are easy, deaf-mutes are easy and the technique is interesting ("he took him aside from the multitude, and put his fingers into his ears, and he spit, and touched his tongue"), raising from the dead is a lead-pipe cinch; still, there are a few hard cases that take a bit of doing, like one of the epileptics the Jews imagined were possessed by devils:

> And one of the multitude . . . said, Master, I have brought unto thee my son, which hath a dumb spirit;
>
> And wheresoever he taketh him, he teareth him: and he foameth, and gnasheth with his teeth, and pineth away: and I spake to thy disciples that they should cast him out; and they could not.
>
> He answereth him, and saith, O faithless generation, how long shall I be with you? how long shall I suffer you? bring him unto me.

(Jesus, whose pipeline to the Infinite ought to fill him with Christian charity, often takes this holier-than-thou attitude toward his rather dense disciples—you don't deserve me, and I really don't know why I put up with you—like the snotty headmaster of a highly recommended boys' school with mass calisthenics and cold showers before breakfast.)

> And they brought him unto him: and when he saw him, straightway the spirit tare him; and he fell on the ground, and wallowed foaming.
>
> And he asked his father, How long is it ago since this came unto him? And he said, Of a child.

And ofttimes it hath cast him into the fire, and into the waters, to destroy him: but if thou canst do any thing, have compassion on us, and help us.

Jesus said unto him, If thou canst believe, all things are possible to him that believeth.

And straightway the father of the child cried out, and said with tears, Lord, I believe; help thou mine unbelief.

—which, the most touching utterance in the Gospels, Jesus discreetly lets pass without a comment (though everywhere else he'll accept nothing less than total submission)—

When Jesus saw that the people came running together, he rebuked the foul spirit, saying unto him, Thou dumb and deaf spirit, I charge thee, come out of him, and enter no more into him.

And the spirit cried, and rent him sore, and came out of him: and he was as one dead; insomuch that many said, He is dead.

But Jesus took him by the hand, and lifted him up; and he arose.

And when he was come into the house, his disciples asked him privately, Why could not we cast him out?

And he said unto them, This kind can come forth by nothing, but by prayer and fasting.

Keep following me around and watch closely! you clods, and after a few thousand years you'll master the whole bag of tricks.

Then there's lust (or sexual desire), which according to Shakespeare is the body's outrageously repetitive dirty trick on the mind, a snare and a delusion, and which he wouldn't have anything to do with if he could keep it out of his mind (by prayer and fasting? but Shakespeare has no religion, and no belief in anything except the dominion of hell on earth—he's in thrall to the personage Jesus calls "the prince of this world"):

The expense of spirit in a waste of shame
Is lust in action; and till action, lust
Is perjured, murd'rous, bloody, full of blame,
Savage, extreme, rude, cruel, not to trust;

> *Enjoy'd no sooner but despised straight;*
> *Past reason hunted; and no sooner had,*
> *Past reason hated, as a swallow'd bait,*
> *On purpose laid to make the taker mad:*
> *Mad in pursuit, and in possession so;*
> *Had, having, and in quest to have, extreme;*
> *A bliss in proof, and proved, a very woe;*
> *Before, a joy proposed; behind, a dream.*
> > *All this the world well knows; yet none knows well*
> > *To shun the heaven that leads men to this hell.*

Jesus would give an indignant snort at that—"O adulterous and sinful generation!" ("O, what fools these mortals be!") because he won't have any truck with the body except for curing it of tetters, cankers, imposthumes, and every other ill short of dismemberment and decapitation—

> if thy hand or thy foot offend thee, cut them off, and cast them from thee: it is better for thee to enter into life halt or maimed, rather than having two hands or two feet to be cast into everlasting fire.
>
> And if thine eye offend thee, pluck it out, and cast it from thee: it is better for thee to enter into life with one eye, rather than having two eyes to be cast into hell fire.

—because the body is either at best an emblem of grace or (cf. Shakespeare's "Lascivious grace, in whom all ill well shows") at worst an emblem of grace so who needs it? and Jesus won't concede that mind can't (maybe even shouldn't) always master the body and its bent for pleasure: the rich man in the parable decides to use some of his accumulated wealth to "eat, drink, and be merry"; "But God said unto him, Thou fool, this night thy soul shall be required of thee: then whose shall those things be, which thou hast provided?" and the rich man might have answered impishly, "Consider the lilies of the field" or "Sufficient unto this night is the evil thereof" (because rich men have been known to quote Scripture—"ye have the poor always with you"—to their own purposes). The body can be very hell (as when Hamlet denounces his mother for, he likes to think, enjoying sex with her present husband: "Oh, shame! Where is thy blush? Rebellious Hell, / If thou canst mutine in a matron's bones . . ."), and Jesus just won't have it:

> Ye have heard that it was said by them of old time, Thou shalt not commit adultery:
> But I say unto you, That whosoever looketh on a woman to lust after her hath committed adultery with her already in his heart.

The impression of intention that the reader may find in the Jacobean grammar here—looketh *in order* to lust (as though joining the gang on the corner to whistle at the passing girls)—is incorrect: if it were correct, Jesus would be prohibiting a conscious decision to do something (which he thinks wicked) that one can decide not to do (by wearing a blindfold, staying off the streets, taking frequent cold showers); but the Revised Standard Version reads: "looks at a woman lustfully," and so he's saying "Down, boy, even in your dreams" or still zanier, "If you're up you're out." In fact elsewhere he does indirectly acknowledge the unmanageableness of sexual appetite, when he asserts that marriage is a mistake which (like the divinely anointed Henry VIII) most are driven to make but that they oughtn't to be allowed to make it more than once:

> What . . . God hath joined together, let not man put asunder.
> They say unto him, Why did Moses then command to give a writing of divorcement, and to put her away?
> He saith unto them, Moses because of the hardness of your hearts suffered you to put away your wives: but from the beginning it was not so.
> And I say unto you, Whosoever shall put away his wife, except it be for fornication [hers of course], and shall marry another, committeth adultery: and whoso marrieth her which is put away doth commit adultery.
> His disciples say unto him, If the case of the man be so with his wife, it is not good to marry.
> But he said unto them, All men cannot receive this saying, save they to whom it is given.
> For there are some eunuchs, which were so born from their

mother's womb: and there are some eunuchs, which were made eunuchs of men: and there be eunuchs, which have made themselves eunuchs for the kingdom of heaven's sake. He that is able to receive it, let him receive it.

Sex is the enemy (he may even be advocating chop-chop; at any rate, some Christians including entire sects have thought so and acted accordingly), because in the parable God is the universal Bridegroom and won't stand for any competition. Virgins, wise or foolish, will have their reward in heaven. Religion enacts the comedy of unrequited love without the risk of requital.

Hence it isn't surprising that, like other saving-it-all-for-God preachers, Jesus whose "kingdom is not of this world" had great success with women, who make a choice among the men in this world but may well resolve in their deepest imagination to settle for a rain check. Because his relations with women are proxy courtships (he's sitting in for God), they tend to be one-act comedies within the universal comedy of unrequited love, of which the most hilarious is the meeting at the well between Jesus, who's thirsty, and the woman of Samaria, who has had five husbands and runs up against Jesus' disapproval of more than one marriage even if the husbands keep dying (Chaucer's Wife of Bath, splendidly self-justifying theologian, who has also had five consecutive husbands, professes that in this exchange she can't quite figure out what Jesus *means*):

> Jesus saith unto her, Go, call thy husband, and come hither.
> The woman answered and said, I have no husband. Jesus said unto her, Thou hast well said, I have no husband:
> For thou hast had five husbands; and he whom thou now hast is not thy husband: in that saidst thou truly.
> The woman saith unto him, Sir, I perceive that thou art a prophet.

"I perceive, Sir," said Dr. Johnson, having discovered that the man he was conversing with had unacceptable political opinions, "that you are a vile Whig"; but the bigamous woman is guileless and respectful, she and Jesus get along famously, and after a few moments Jesus feels cosy enough to confide to her that, guess what! he himself and nobody else is the one-and-only Messiah: "And upon this came his disciples, and marvelled that he talked with the woman: yet no man said, What seekest thou? or, Why talkest thou with her?" He was just being expansive, as men are likely to be with a sympathetic woman; but woe unto the troops if they dare to question the general about his latest maneuver.

Indeed his heart is warmed by women's favors and attention, the little luxuries that he doesn't *need* but laps up anyhow ("Oh, reason not the need," cries Lear in a moment of sanity: "Our basest beggars / Are in the poorest thing superfluous. / Allow not nature more than nature needs, / Man's life's as cheap as beast's"):

> Now it came to pass, as they went, that he entered into a certain village: and a certain woman named Martha received him into her house.
>
> And she had a sister called Mary, which also sat at Jesus' feet, and heard his word.
>
> But Martha was cumbered about much serving, and came to him, and said, Lord, dost thou not care that my sister hath left me to serve alone? bid her therefore that she help me.
>
> And Jesus answered and said unto her, Martha, Martha, thou art careful and troubled about many things:
>
> But one thing is needful: and Mary hath chosen that good part, which shall not be taken away from her.

They also serve that only sit and gape. For a man who denies his mother and brothers in favor of his circle of believers, Jesus gets quite a kick out of the comforts of home (and if they aren't available in most Christian homes the Church ought to start a campaign):

> Then Jesus six days before the passover came to Bethany, where Lazarus was which had been dead, whom he raised from the dead.
>
> There they made him a supper; and Martha served: but Lazarus was one of them that sat at the table with him.
>
> Then took Mary a pound of ointment of spikenard, very costly, and anointed the feet of Jesus, and wiped his feet with

her hair: and the house was filled with the odour of the ointment.

Then saith one of his disciples, Judas Iscariot, Simon's son, which should betray him,

Why was not this ointment sold for three hundred pence, and given to the poor?

This he said, not that he cared for the poor; but because he was a thief, and had the bag, and bare what was put therein.

Then said Jesus, Let her alone: against the day of my burying hath she kept this.

For the poor always ye have with you, but me ye have not always.

There's also the woman who bears up under his shocking insult and outsmarts him into healing her daughter:

And, behold, a woman of Canaan came out of the same coasts, and cried unto him, saying, Have mercy on me, O Lord, thou Son of David; my daughter is grievously vexed with a devil.

But he answered her not a word. And his disciples came and besought him, saying, Send her away; for she crieth after us.

But he answered and said, I am not sent but unto the lost sheep of the house of Israel.

Then came she and worshipped him, saying, Lord, help me.

But he answered and said, It is not meet to take the children's bread, and to cast it to dogs.

And she said, Truth, Lord: yet the dogs eat of the crumbs which fall from their masters' table.

Then Jesus answered and said unto her, O woman, great is thy faith: be it unto thee even as thou wilt. And her daughter was made whole from that very hour.

And the feminist he outsmarts with a withering one-liner:

And it came to pass, as he spake these things, a certain woman of the company lifted up her voice, and said unto him, Blessed is the womb that bare thee, and the paps which thou hast sucked.

But he said, Yea rather, blessed are they that hear the word of God, and keep it.

(But even Jesus is speechless when without explanation from out of nowhere the first streaker on record flashes across the scene in Mark 14:51-52 and disappears without explanation forever into the back of beyond: "And there followed him a certain young man, having a linen cloth cast about his naked body; and the young men laid hold on him: / And he left the linen cloth, and fled from them naked": as if by an eyewitness who, having noticed what randomly happened, doesn't suppress it in deference to what ought to have happened: even God has accidents.)

Maybe Jesus takes his opportunities to relax with a woman (who at least can diversify her homage by such inspirations of seductive originality as smearing the master's feet with halvah and wiping them with her long and snaky yellow hair) because his disciples are such a dreary crew that, if he weren't Who He is, one would applaud his testiness with them: they're dumb as dirt, usually misunderstand him, are often afraid to question him when they have no idea what he's talking about, are as thunderstruck by the ten thousandth run-of-the-mill raising from the dead as by the first ("they marvelled"), squabble so often over precedence (who's on first?) that Jesus has to quiet them periodically by producing one of his routine upside-down inside-out wisdom-sausages (The first shall be last and the last shall be first); they keep asking anxiously whether, having turned their dreariness over to him lock, stock, and barrel, they'll get a proper quid for their quo (the moral aphorisms that sound so impressive out of context—whosoever will save his life shall lose it; whosoever hath, to him shall be given—prove in context to be weary reassurances for petty minds which, having given up nothing but their minds in this world, will verily receive the whole enchilada in the next); they aren't even good soldiers but run away in a crisis (Blessed are the poor in spirit), deny him thrice (but weep bitterly), and so on.

And not only the disciples. Jesus quite explicitly directs his appeal at the insulted and the injured, who yearn for miracles and cosmetic restoration because nothing less will help; he sounds much more like a TV preacher than like an English vicar or an Italian priest, because, though theology has tactfully obscured the issue, he himself insists that those who don't have it in this world will get it in the next and those who have it here will get it in the neck: envy is one of the prime sources of energy he draws on, and these losers are encouraged to believe that it's as easy for a rich man to enter heaven as for a camel to thread a needle with his hump—

> And he lifted up his eyes on his disciples, and said, Blessed be ye poor: for yours is the kingdom of God.
> Blessed are ye that hunger now: for ye shall be filled. Blessed are ye that weep now: for ye shall laugh.
> Blessed are ye, when men shall hate you, and when they shall separate you from their company, and shall reproach you, and cast out your name as evil, for the Son of man's sake.
> Rejoice ye in that day, and leap for joy: for, behold, your reward is great in heaven: for in the like manner did their fathers unto the prophets.

But, but, but—

> But woe unto you that are rich! for ye have received your consolation.
> Woe unto you that are full! for ye shall hunger. Woe unto you that laugh now! for ye shall mourn and weep.

If this weren't Jesus the merciful, it might sound less like Christian charity than like a demagogic heating-up of underdog self-pity and spite.

His moral connection with Shakespeare is that what anybody else calls love they call lust, and what they call love anybody else having thought about it would call pity (though their interest is less in the human condition than a clinical or morbid interest in the lame, the halt, and the blind including for Shakespeare his own precious sensibility). When in *Troilus and Criseyde* Chaucer rejoices with the lovers, he doesn't distinguish their "carnal" love from any other kind of love or merely evade the issue but binds

all together in "the holy bond of things," so that Venus and the
Prime Mover of the universe are one:

> *O blisful light, of which the bemes clere*
> *Adorneth al the thridde heven faire!*   [where
>   Venus dwells]
> *O sonnes lief, O Joves doughter deere,*   [darling
>   of the sun]
> *Plesaunce of love, O goodly debonaire,*
> *In gentil hertes ay redy to repaire!*
> *O veray cause of heele and of gladnesse,*   [health]
> *Iheryed be thy myght and thi goodnesse!*   [Praised]
>
> *In hevene and helle* [!], *in erthe and salte see*
> *Is felt thi myght, if that I wel descerne;*
> *As man, brid, best, fissh, herbe, and grene tree*
> *Thee fele in tymes with vapour eterne.*   [Feel
>   thee in season under eternal influence]
> *God loveth, and to love wol nought werne;*   [will
>   deny love nothing]
> *And in this world no lyves creature*   [living]
> *Withouten love is worth, or may endure.*

When, in his "Christian" epilogue, Chaucer mourns the passing
of love and pities the lovers, it isn't because earthly love is ugly
or sinful but because it's as transitory as he believes Christ's love
won't be, and he continues affirming to the end without recantation
the beauty, grace (his favorite and deliberately ambiguous word
for Criseyde and what she has in her keeping), and bounty of
"this world, that passeth soone as floures faire." For Jesus the
world can't pass soon enough, it's a hospital or madhouse, and
pity (what he calls love) is the form of snobbery with which he
ministers to its inmates. For Shakespeare the catch is that, though
the world is certainly a hospital or madhouse, it's all there is and
when it passes it doesn't come back: "Never, never, never, never,
never!" cries Lear with unusual emphasis, carrying Cordelia's forever dead body: no resurrection, no reward, just nothing. "To be
or not to be" is a genuine choice but a frightful one: if love is
lust and lust is hell on earth, if you've given up on sex except

as a persistent itch that you hopelessly scratch, if you've given up on history and politics except as leaky vessels manned by incompetent mariners and mad captains which may or may not capsize while you're still a passenger, if nevertheless you can't bring yourself to commit suicide because "The weariest and most loathèd worldly life / That age, ache, penury, and imprisonment / Can lay on nature is a paradise / To what we fear of death," then there isn't much left except pity, and Shakespeare's pity soon gives up any pretense to the name of love and becomes self-pity: "my pity-wanting pain" (as he cries in his own voice in Sonnet 140), which there's nobody to minister to and no laying on of hands to cure.

"My kingdom is not of this world," says Jesus with calm conviction, and there's no gainsaying the power of his promise (though it doesn't work for Shakespeare) for those who find this world as difficult and debilitating as Shakespeare does. "O Jerusalem, Jerusalem, thou that killest the prophets, and stonest them which are sent unto thee," exclaims Jesus with considerable animosity, forgetting to turn the other cheek or return love for hatred, "how often would I have gathered thy children together, even as a hen gathereth her chickens under her wings, and ye would not!" but suppose it's all a cock-and-bull story and there isn't even a mother hen and there's nobody here but us chickens? which is what Shakespeare horridly feels and fears, and it just drives him up the wall.

PART II

ART
AND
LIFE

Art is overrated though life isn't.
This section is about the life in art
and the life in artists.

Gloomy Aristotle versus Cheerful Oedipus

The experts won't let us just think how lucky we are to have our precious few Greek tragedies, they keep reminding us that what we have, however grand, is only the script so to speak, which if we could penetrate the mists of time and there in the theater of Dionysus see it realized with its songs and dances would knock us dead. Shakespeare, Mozart, and Balanchine wrapped up in the same package! An eminent classicist, H. D. F. Kitto, goes so far as to suggest that Aeschylus was "one of the finest choreographers that Europe has seen," and for evidence singles out in Aeschylus's verse some "liquid anacreontic rhythms" and a certain "slow iambic rhythm" which he hasn't a doubt were accompanied on the great stage by (respectively) liquid anacreontic and slow iambic dance steps of such irresistible charm that they would knock us dead if only they had survived and he could sit at our elbow calling attention to their finer touches. Still, he doesn't mention that Aristotle, who may be supposed to have seen them often enough to name and classify their fifty-seven varieties in a treatise since lost, was quite cool to Terpsichore, in fact to all those aspects of tragedy he lumped together as "embellishments"—staging, acting, singing, dancing—because unlike the modern professors he hasn't a doubt that the words and story do the job and everything else is marzipan. "The plot ought to be so constructed that, even without the aid of the eye, he who hears the tale told will thrill with horror and melt to pity at what takes place"; and "This is

the impression we should receive from hearing the story of the
Oedipus," because the play Aristotle most loves to be thrilled and
melted by is *Oedipus the King.* So on Aristotle's authority we're just
as lucky as we thought we were to have what we have; and surely
he can also be trusted—who if not Aristotle?—to tell us everything
else we've always wanted to know about what's left to us of Greek
tragedy, viz. the unembellished script which is all that matters
to him anyhow, and especially the script of his favorite play and
the character of his favorite hero.

In God we trust, others pay cash. Aristotle is a real fan—
whether he's at fourth row center or snug in his study his pulse
pounds and his nape hairs rise when Oedipus enters self-blinded
and bereft—but he's a critic too, and the tug-of-war between the
fan and the critic is as thrilling and pitiful as the play they tear
to shreds between them. He can't help coming back to *Oedipus,*
not only does it illustrate most of the points he's making but, as
if he were bent on showing them up in the act of making them,
it illustrates them negatively.

In a tragedy (according to the *Poetics*) "the change of fortune
presented must not be the spectacle of a virtuous man brought
from prosperity to adversity: for this moves neither pity nor fear;
it merely shocks us." Equally unsatisfactory would be an "utter
villain" as protagonist: the tragic hero must be a man "whose
misfortune is brought about not by vice or depravity, but by some
error or frailty. He must be one who is highly renowned and
prosperous—a personage like Oedipus." But if Oedipus isn't that
merely shocking case the virtuous man brought from prosperity
to adversity, it's hard to see wherein his "error or frailty" consists:
maybe too much wit and heart as he tries to foil the malign will
of the gods; and, oddly enough, Aristotle's favorite hero is the
only extant Greek tragic hero whom Aristotle's prissy stipulations
miss by a mile. At any rate tragic heroes should come to a bad
end: "The best tragedies are founded on the stories of a few
houses—on the fortunes of . . . Oedipus . . . and those others
who have done or suffered something terrible"; "the right ending"
for a tragedy is the unhappy ending characteristic of such stories,
and Euripides is "the most tragic of the poets" because he prefers
unhappy endings. But, though *Oedipus the King* has as unhappy

an ending as anybody could hope for, the story of Oedipus as Sophocles carries it forward in *Oedipus at Colonus* ends with a death but not unhappily—perhaps one of the reasons why Aristotle never brings up the later play at all. "The circumstances which strike us as terrible or pitiful" should occur "between those who are near or dear to one another. . . . The action may be done consciously and with knowledge . . . [or] it may be done in ignorance and the tie of kinship or friendship be discovered afterwards. The Oedipus of Sophocles is an example." Aristotle is of course thinking of Oedipus's killing of Laius, so he adds: "Here, indeed, the incident is outside the drama proper," and he concedes that Oedipus's present ignorance of the circumstances of Laius's death is so implausible that we accept it only because it has occurred already and long ago, it is "outside the drama proper." But Sophocles isn't worried here about plausibility (he knows as well as we do that Jocasta or a courtier would have told Oedipus about the circumstances of Laius's death), his intention is to push the "wicked" deed as far back into the past and as far away from any connection with a responsible agent as possible: the deed wasn't something willed and done, it had no actor (without volition, says Aristotle in the *Ethics*, there is no action), it simply happened like a natural disaster, hence till Oedipus recognizes its effects he needn't be aware of it: it isn't circumstances that do Oedipus in but circumstance itself, because, though rational critics are shocked and most tragic poets prefer a daisy-chain of circumstances (e.g. a thane kills his king to become king and then kills as many others as necessary to stay king), circumstance itself doesn't scruple to bring a virtuous man from prosperity to adversity. "If the irrational cannot be excluded," sighs Aristotle, "it should be outside the scope of the tragedy. Such is the irrational element in the Oedipus of Sophocles."

And such is the blind old man Oedipus at Colonus (whom Sophocles created when he was ninety and Aristotle, choosing discretion as the better part of valor, ignores altogether), outside the scope of tragedy altogether (Aristotle reports that "Sophocles said he himself made men such as they ought to be while Euripides made them such as they are"), keen, hard to handle, angrier and more impatient than ever, denouncing and repudiating the very idea of tragedy:

In me myself you could not find such evil
As would have made me sin against my own.
And tell me this: if there were prophecies
Repeated by the oracles of the gods,
That father's death should come through his own son,
How could you justly blame it upon me?
On me, who was yet unborn, yet unconceived?
If then I came into the world—as I did come—
In wretchedness, and met my father in fight,
And knocked him down, not knowing that I killed him
Nor whom I killed—again, how could you find
Guilt in that unmeditated act?

He is addressing his uncle, Jocasta's brother, the treacherous and sanctimonious Creon:

As for my mother—damn you, you have no shame,
Though you are her own brother, in forcing me
To speak of that unspeakable marriage;
But I shall speak, I'll not be silent now
After you've let your foul talk go so far!
Yes, she gave me birth—incredible fate!—
But neither of us knew the truth; and she
Bore my children also—and then her shame.
But one thing I do know: you are content
To slander her as well as me for that;
While I would not have married her willingly
Nor willingly would I ever speak of it.
No: I shall not be judged an evil man,
Neither in that marriage nor in that death
Which you forever charge me with so bitterly.—
Just answer me one thing:
If someone tried to kill you here and now,
You righteous gentleman, what would you do,
Inquire first if the stranger was your father?
Or would you not first try to defend yourself?
I think that since you like to be alive
You'd treat him as the threat required; not
Look around for assurance that you were right.

> *Well, that was the sort of danger I was in,*
> *Forced into it by the gods. My father's soul,*
> *Were it on earth, I know would bear me out.*

The gods had no business doing what they did, and I wasn't only wrong I was plain stupid to punish myself for it. What they did has nevertheless made him unclean to all who haven't shared his fate: grateful for the rescue of his daughters by King Theseus, he almost forgets himself but draws back in the nick of time before kissing the rescuer's hand ("How can a wretch like me / Desire to touch a man who has no stain / Of evil in him? No, no, I will not do it; / And neither shall you touch me"). But when at length, having outlasted his suffering and worn out the hostility of the gods, he prepares for the hour of his death, the pariah turns oracle and pollution becomes the vessel of grace (as he promised Theseus earlier: "I come to give you something, and the gift / Is my own beaten self: no feast for the eyes; / Yet in me is a more lasting grace than beauty"); and, untouchable horror having become untouchable grace, the blind old man will now take over as guide to those who guided him faithfully on his long journey from Thebes:

> *Children, follow me this way: see, now,*
> *I have become your guide, as you were mine!*
> *Come: do not touch me: let me alone discover*
> *The holy and funereal ground where I*
> *Must take this fated earth to be my shroud.*
> *This way, O come! The angel of the dead*
> *Hermes, and veiled Persephone, lead me on!*

So, dying at his appointed time and in his secret holy place, with a proper show of thunder and lightning, unresigned, benignant, exalted, Oedipus (as well as Sophocles) becomes a tutelary spirit of Athens, a god himself. Doesn't seem very tragic to me.

Old Farts,
Young Lovers,
and the
Sound of
Music

Still, comedy is another matter. Not only once but twice, in the General Prologue and the Miller's Prologue, Chaucer disclaims his indelicacies even before he sets them down—These are the Miller's words, not mine—because he knows they'll startle and shock; also because he wants them looked at with care or else he wouldn't take the trouble first and secondly to be sorry they're coming! they're coming! and then to set them down plump in their places for the popping eyeballs of posterity. They can still surprise readers as late as our own unsurprisable age, and they're no joke. Chaucer's "low" characters on the Canterbury pilgrimage aren't comic relief, they are shrewd and experienced (like his solid citizens); they have a lot to say, however preoccupied with rage or malice or fond reminiscence they sometimes are when they say it; their language when it turns blue carries them beyond decorum but not beyond the practical boundaries of Chaucer's world: the old have rights and had better not be counted out, sex and lovers have rights, women (especially beautiful young women) have rights and a few privileges too, justice is often dilatory and always possible, everybody jostles and everybody has elbow-room, everybody gets a nod from the Host and tells a story.

The Friar and the Summoner are a pair of ecclesiastical con-men working the same neighborhood. The Friar, who belongs to a mendicant order ("He was the beste beggere in his hous"), is an itinerant peddler of instant absolution—"an esy man to yeve [give] penaunce / Ther as he wiste to have a good pitaunce [Where he was sure of a good donation]"—padding from door to door paying his suave respects to well-heeled souls but not above varying the routine with an occasional friendly visit to a poor and lonely widow ("His eyen twynkled in his heed aryght / As doon the sterres in the frosty nyght"). As for the Summoner, plenary snoop and censor of the diocese and counselor to its boys and girls about all their little intimate problems, can anybody blame him for stretching his job a bit to extort money or favors from the timid, hale in on false charges the hard of heart, and restore himself at every opportunity with wine, women, and children? Well, the Friar might blame him: the amount of money (not to speak of less portable advantages) in the diocese being finite, each begrudges the other the ill-gotten gains he would rather add to his own; and the Friar taunts the Summoner by telling a graceful and witty tale about a summoner who strikes a bargain with the Devil who fairly and squarely seals it by conducting the summoner straight to hell. The Friar plumes himself on his social graces vis-à-vis the manners and appearance of the Summoner (a noisy and indelicate sort with the world's worst case of acne, which Chaucer describes at length in blazing technicolor); even so, referring to the—after all useless because both old and penniless—widow in his tale, the Friar makes the slip of calling her a "ribibe," an old fiddle (on which too many tunes have been played?): but the widow survives the Friar's gracelessness and the summoner's attempt at extortion because the tale itself can't dispense with the old fiddle that plays the tune that marches the summoner off: "The devel so fecche hym er he deye . . . but he wol hym repente! [*May the Devil fetch him before he dies . . . unless he repents!*]"; but summoners don't ever repent, anyhow not in the face of an old woman's ultimatum, and off to hell he goes in custody of the Devil, who comments that soon the summoner will "knowen of oure privetee [*private affairs*] / Moore than a maister of dyvynytee." The Friar, since for the moment his malice is directed elsewhere, doesn't mind making use of the useless widow as the necessary and energetic conscience of his tale: there's a tune in the old fiddle yet, as he might twinklingly concede if he knew what he had done.

The enraged Summoner retaliates with a story that will bring the Friar down a peg or two, indeed right down to the level of an old man's fundament. The Summoner's friar is of course (like the Friar and the Summoner) a faithless shepherd who keeps busy fleecing the faithful to the buff in a cold wind, one of those damnable begging friars who can't resist poaching on the Summoner's territory: he tries to argue and intimidate a sick old man into surrendering all he has to "my hous" until at last, exasperated past endurance, the old man says Yes, I'll deposit it all into your very own hand this minute if you promise to share and share alike with the other friars of your house; Done! cries the friar, and as instructed "gropes" down the old man's back as far as the "cleft" whereupon "he leet the frere a fart, / Ther nys no capul [*nag*], drawynge in a cart, / That myghte have lete a fart of swich a soun." The friar leaves in a dudgeon, vowing vengeance—"Thou shalt abye [*pay for*] this fart!"—and the rest of the tale engages the friar, the town's leading citizen and his wife, and their clever servant in an earnest discussion of the puzzle posed by the old man: how to divide a fart equally twelve ways. It isn't the Summoner or the fart-splitting epilogue, though, but the sick and apparently helpless old man (there's a tune in the old fiddle yet) that issues the final report on the friar's messing about. ("Don't mess over an old man," says the nameless and ominous old man to the three scoundrels in the tale told by Chaucer's Pardoner, like the Friar and the Summoner a flamboyant running sore of the spiritual bureaucracy who in spite of himself has a lot to say.)

The Wife of Bath is getting on in years, thus an old fiddle and not to be taken seriously by such as the Friar, Summoner, and Pardoner. At the end of her Prologue the Friar laughs and says, "This is a long preamble of a tale" (giving the choleric Summoner a pretext to start the fuss that culminates in their tales at each other's expense); earlier, the Pardoner interrupts her feminist disquisition on marriage with an obtrusively masculine comment (which is not only condescension toward the old fiddle but a smokescreen from the closet, since Chaucer has already observed about the Pardoner, "I trowe he were a geldyng or a mare"). The Wife is so caught up in her recollections of life and love that she can't hold back anything at all, she could never keep a secret anyway: she had a woman friend who "knew myn herte, and eek my privetee [*private affairs*] / Bet than oure parisshe preest . . . / For hadde myn housbonde pissed on a wal, / Or doon a thyng that sholde han cost his lyf, / To hire, and to another worthy wyf, / And to my nece, which that I loved weel, / I wolde han toold his conseil [*what he confided*] every deel." Furthermore it's too late for coyness if she's to have a chance at collecting another husband— maybe girls can afford the game of innocence, but time's a-wasting for a woman, who has to concentrate a man's attention on the moving target: "Have thou ynogh, what that thee recche or care [*what need have you to care*] / How myrily that othere folkes fare? / For, certeyn, olde dotard, by youre leve, / Ye shul have queynte [*cunt*] right ynogh at eve. / He is to greet a nygard [*too stingy*] that wolde werne [*forbid*] / A man to lighte a candle at his lanterne; / He shal have never the lasse light, pardee." The Wife is so transported by the vividness of her recollection here that she says the magic word she must have said during her counterattack on a jealous and miserly old husband. Elsewhere in her Prologue the terms are more ladylike and can even be foreign: "membres of generacioun," "oure thynges smale," "my instrument," "*bele chose*," "*quoniam*"; but, whatever the terms, she advertises the thing itself as enthusiastically as if it's the next grand opening though by now the old customers are long gone and there isn't a new one in sight. Never mind: the unappeasable and irrepressible old woman takes her own sweet time and tells in unequivocal language her tremendous truths, which, however, the Pardoner who rudely interrupts her and the Friar who passes his contemptuous judgment regard as senile indiscretions. "Telle forth youre tale," says the politic Host; "Al redy, sire," says the Wife imperturbably, "if I have licence of this worthy Frere" (who has boasted of being the "licenciat" of his order, i.e. the one licensed to hear confession); but she doesn't need permission or absolution, no not from God Himself (Who as she points out made at least one disastrous mistake: "Allas! allas! that evere love was synne!" exclaims the Wife for all of us), she renounces nothing of her life, warms herself with the memory of past joys in the moment of acknowledging that they are irretrievable—

> But, Lord Crist! whan that it remembreth me
> Upon my yowthe, and on my jolitee,

It tikleth me about myn herte roote.
Unto this day it doth myn herte boote   [does
    my heart good]
That I have had my world as in my tyme.
But age, allas! that al wole envenyme,
Hath me biraft my beautee and my pith.
Lat go, farewel! the devel go therwith! . . .

Chaucer's Merchant isn't (like the Wife) only now and then regretful for being past the time of youth, he's a bitter old man, the bleakest and bitterest of the pilgrims, and he tells a bitter tale about an old man, January, who is rich enough and self-deluded enough to buy himself a young bride, the beautiful May. January has his comeuppance, naturally: from a young man, Damian, who's in love with May and soon persuades her that young belongs with young. The multiple climax of the tale occurs in January's locked but still not wholly secure garden, where the King of the Underworld intervenes to expose May's infidelity but the Queen immediately saves her from its consequences: fun is fun, but such language! "Ladyes," says the Merchant nervously, no doubt bowing toward the Prioress, the Nuns, and the Wife of Bath, "I preye yow that ye be nat wrooth; / I kan nat glose [*mince words*], I am a rude [*plain*] man— / And sodeynly anon this Damyan / Gan pullen up the smok [*chemise*], and in he throng [*thrust*]. . . ." (It's been said that medieval England was a plain blunt society in which Chaucer's dirty talk didn't ruffle a feather—and that Chaucer's just kidding when he disclaims it—but nobody told the Merchant, who's so anxious about offending the ladies that he apologizes to the Wife of Bath! who has already stated her racy case so he ought to know whom he's dealing with. Violations of decorum aren't actions, they're *re*actions, they demonstrate not the absence of decorum but its continuous pressure on even strong and idiosyncratic characters, e.g. the Merchant, the Wife of Bath, Chaucer.) Still, telling his tale, the Merchant isn't any more moral than the Wife, the Friar, or the Summoner. January gets what he deserves, the old fool; but as usual Chaucer has no interest in justice of the merely distributive kind: as usual, when a woman—especially a beautiful young woman—is in question, Chaucer numbers the hairs on her head and everywhere else, he honors the source of pleasure, he is chivalrous and grateful and (if the Merchant or January had any such silly ideas) would never permit May to be punished or humiliated: fidelity and chastity aren't indispensable conditions that Chaucer attaches to the delight he takes in women. Nor is January a powerless old fool who can't even use the woman he bought, he isn't sexually impotent to say the least, in the conjugal bed he doesn't sing like a bird or look like a prince but he's fit as a fiddle (old and stringy) and ready for love on his wedding night and any night thereafter:

> *Thus laboureth he til that the day gan dawe;*
> *And thanne he taketh a soppe in fyn clarree,* [sop
>   in fine claret]
> *And upright in his bed thanne sitteth he,*
> *And after that he sang ful loude and clere,*
> *And kiste his wyf, and made wantown cheere.*
> *He was al coltish, ful of ragerye,*
> *And ful of jargon as a flekked pye.* [magpie]
> *The slakke skyn aboute his nekke shaketh,*
> *Whil that he sang, so chaunteth he and craketh.*
> *But God woot what that May thoughte in hir herte,*
> *Whan she hym saugh up sittynge in his sherte,*
> *In his nyght-cappe, and with his nekke lene;*
> *She preyseth nat his pleyyng worth a bene.*

The day of reckoning will come for January, already May wishes she were just anywhere else, but meanwhile the old man's having a wonderful time.

The Miller's Tale is an elaborate dirty joke told by the drunken Miller, involving the same triangle of an old fool (John the carpenter), his beautiful young wife (Alisoun), and her young lover (Nicholas the scholar), here augmented by an unsuccessful young suitor (Absolon the parish clerk) who comes sniffing around once too often, a dandy locked in the grip of hubris—the Miller introduces him as one afflicted with something like a tragic flaw: he's "somdeel squaymous / Of [*somewhat squeamish about*] fartyng, and of speche daungerous [*dainty*]"—who suffers a terrible humiliation that incites him to take a terrible revenge that almost brings the house down. The plot, which is as exquisite and doomful as the plot of *Oedipus*, proceeds as follows. Nicholas, having won Alisoun over but for their night of bliss needing to get the old husband out of the way, lets him in on the secret he has extracted from his astrological calculations, that next Monday a great flood like Noah's will sweep in and cover all. John can however preserve the three of them by suspending from the roof-beams three large tubs and laying in a supply of food and an axe; they will climb into the tubs the night before, and when the following morning the rains have ceased they will use the axe to cut the cords from the beams and a hole in the roof through which the three of them will float off as the Noah-like survivors and rulers of the unpopulated world. So on the appointed evening they climb the ladders into the tubs, and of course Nicholas and Alisoun soon after come down to earth and make merry in the old man's bed ("ther"—in bed together rather than sitting alone in the tubs awaiting the end of the world—"was the revel and the melodye"). It's at this juncture that Absolon, having heard that John is out of town, gets dressed in his dandy-best, chews some breath-freshening herbs, and hurries to Alisoun's window: "Awaketh, lemman myn [*my love*], and speketh to me!" Alisoun gives him fair warning, "Go fro the wyndow, Jakke fool. . . . I love another," but he persists: "Thanne kysse me" (one kiss, my queen, before I glumly go). Alisoun loses patience, and whispers to Nicholas that if he keeps quiet he'll soon have something to laugh about: "Derk was the nyght as pich, or as the cole" when "at the wyndow out she putte hir hole" (the sill is just the right height, says the Miller), and eager Absolon "kiste hir naked ers / Ful savourly," but "Abak he stirte . . . / For wel he wiste [*knew*] a womman hath no berd"; "Tehee!" giggles Alisoun; "A berd! a berd!" cries Nicholas; and Absolon, thirsting for revenge, stalks off rubbing his lips "with dust, with sond, with straw, with clooth, with chippes." He borrows a red-hot plowshare-blade from a nearby smith—"What, Absolon! . . . Why rise ye so rathe [*early*]? . . . / What eyleth you? Som gay gerl . . ."—and returns to the fatal window, where he pleads with his lady for another kiss. This time it's Nicholas who puts his backside out: "Spek, sweet bryd [*bird*]," says Absolon, "I noot nat [*know not*] where thou art," and Nicholas "anon leet

fle a fart / As greet as it had been a thonder-dent [*thunderbolt*],"
but Absolon strikes back while the iron is hot and fixes his brand
forever on Nicholas, who understandably cries out, "Help, water!
water!" which wakes up the old man who, thinking the flood has
come, cuts the cord with his axe and falls all the way to the
ground, breaking his arm but getting no sympathy when the
neighbors gather and listen to Nicholas's explanation that the old
fool had been scared out of his wits by the crazy notion that a
new flood was on the way.

Once again it's the old husband who's punished and the young
wife who comes off doubly unscathed. The Miller's attitude toward
Alisoun has a noteworthy delicacy: though she's frisky enough to
put her pretty ass out the window to be kissed, it isn't thank
goodness! she who farts into a squeamish fellow's face (no nice girl
would do *that*!), it takes male arrogance and male indelicacy to
tempt fate and the branding iron, and (therefore?) it isn't Alisoun
but Nicholas whose butt is branded. Once again, moreover, there
are touches in the old man's character and behavior that indicate
he isn't merely the local joke for others to do a job on. To begin
with, he's a kindly soul and, though he has the typical bluecollar
doubts about this flighty intellectual, he doesn't let them interfere
with his Christian concern about Nicholas, who at the moment
is pretending to have gone into a trance:

> *This man is falle, with his astromye,*
> *In som woodnesse or in some agonye . . .*   [madness]
> *"What, Nicholay! what, how! what, looke adoun!*
> *Awake, and thenk on Cristes passioun! . . .*
> *What! thenk on God, as we doon, men that swyn-*
>   *ke."*   [labor]

Besides, the old fool loves Alisoun more than life itself: when
Nicholas tells him that "in lasse than an hour / Shal al be dreynt
[*drowned*], so hidous is the shour," John instantly responds,
" 'Allas! my wyf! / And shal she drenche? allas! myn Alisoun!' /
For sorwe of this he fil almost adoun, / And seyde, 'Is ther no
remedie in this cas?' " (The remedy is to hang three kneading-
tubs from the roof-beams.) And later all he can think of is the
flood that will come surging like the sea to "drenchen Alisoun,

his hony deere. / He wepeth, weyleth, maketh sory cheere; / He siketh [*sighs*] with ful many a sory swogh [*sigh*]. . . ." Old fools aren't supposed to be capable of such feelings, which sound very much like love; but since when is love love simply because it's appropriate to the character, justified by the circumstances, savorily requited, and between young and young?

Maybe such unexpected and uncalled-for signs of life are commoner than most writers imagine, and if they aren't they ought to be.

The
Unstrung
Zero

Hamlet, concludes Tolstoy, "has no character at all": he does what he does for the sake of whatever stage effects Shakespeare is after at the moment; he says what he says in order to express whatever quips and quiddities Shakespeare wants to get off his chest at the moment; the "unsolved riddle of Hamlet" is merely the absence of the protagonist from the play that bears his name. Decipher Hamlet and he turns out to be a zero.

Is Hamlet mad (or at any rate very irritated)? has he lost his marbles? have his beads come unstrung?—rosary beads no doubt: Shakespeare specializes in R.C. images: Hamlet's father's ghost is on overnight leave from Purgatory (about which if it weren't for copyright restrictions he could tell a tale that would harrow your marrow) where he's doing time because he was careless enough to let himself be assassinated without benefit of clergy, "Un-housel'd, disappointed, unanel'd"—or is he, as he says, just pretending in order to throw Claudius off the track? but incidentally achieving a certain number of crowd-pleasing stage effects: cloud-teasing with Polonius, prurient insults to the unattempted Ophelia, jumping into an open grave to challenge forty thousand brothers. "Of the feigned madness of Hamlet," observes Dr. Johnson, "there appears no adequate cause, for he does nothing which he might not have done with the reputation of sanity. He plays the madman most, when he treats Ophelia with so much rudeness, which seems to be useless and wanton cruelty."

All right, so there he is, our representative to the world, Mr. Western Civilization, in codpiece and pantyhose up there on the boards, firing away at the rapt groundlings with his blank verses, not less of a word-slinger and spellbinder than the Bard himself and therefore not to be considered too curiously on such matters as relevance, coherence, consistency, propriety, sanity, common decency. When Hamlet happens on Claudius at prayer, he decides against doing him in here and now because it will be much juicier to catch and kill him in circumstances that will guarantee his immediate passage to Hell (not Purgatory, which if it's good enough for Hamlet's father is much too good for Uncle Claudius): "Indecent," notes Tolstoy in the margin at these lines in his copy of the play; "This speech," comments Johnson, "in which Hamlet, represented as a virtuous character, is not content with taking blood for blood but contrives damnation for the man he would punish, is too horrible to be read or to be uttered." (The ground-lings insist that their hero doesn't really mean what he says here, that Hamlet's deep Christian feelings ingeniously contrive this diabolical argument only for the moment in order to prevent his committing the murder he really shrinks from, but it suffices to recall that he does manage later to have Rosencrantz and Guil-denstern, who didn't even murder his father or sleep with his mother, "put to sudden death, / Not shriving time allowed"; and maybe Hamlet or Shakespeare is after all as nutty as a fruitcake because, unless one or the other imagines he's God Almighty, why bother?) Johnson is a Christian and can't think of a good reason why Shakespeare, who pays at least lip service to Christian notions of sin and virtue, would permit Hamlet to claim for himself the ultimate prerogative of the Christian God, as in *Measure for Measure* Johnson can't think of a good reason why Shakespeare has the stonily pious Isabella plead for Angelo's pardon with "the extraor-dinary argument" that he did all those wicked deeds, such as (so far as she and Angelo know) disposing of her brother against the deal they made, only because he fell so hard for li'l ol' me:

> Angelo's crimes were such, as must sufficiently justify pun-ishment, whether its end be to secure the innocent from wrong, or to deter guilt by example; and I believe every reader feels some indignation when he finds him spared. From what extenuation of his crime can Isabel, who yet supposes her brother dead, form any plea in his favour. *Since he was*

good 'till he looked on me, let him not die. I am afraid our Varlet Poet intended to inculcate, that women think ill of nothing that raises the credit of their beauty, and are ready, however virtuous, to pardon any act which they think incited by their own charms.

Johnson is one of the three helpful critics of Shakespeare (besides Tolstoy there's also Lawrence, who keeps dropping asides like this one in *Twilight in Italy*: "I had always felt an aversion from Hamlet: a creeping, unclean thing. . . . His nasty poking and sniffing at his mother, his setting traps for the King, his conceited perversion with Ophelia make him always intolerable. The character is repulsive in its conception, based on self-dislike and a spirit of disintegration"), but even Johnson can't bring himself to believe that (1) Shakespeare isn't Christian but only going through the motions and from time to time forgetting to keep them going, or (2) he's a cynical stage magician who will sacrifice any impression of moral coherence for the sake of a spectacular stage effect, or (3) a moral mess who tries to hold things together with any paperclip or bit of Scotch tape or splinter of the true Cross that comes his way at the moment, or (4) usually one or more of the three and sometimes all of them at once. "What coarse, immoral, mean, and senseless work *Hamlet* is," writes Tolstoy to a friend after attending a performance of the play; "everything is based on pagan vengeance, there is only one aim: to pile up as many effects as possible, it is quite without any order"; and one of the reasons for the general senselessness is that Shakespeare tricks out his source, a simple story of pagan vengeance, with Christian metaphysic and the huge purple patches of his own self-flagellating sensibility (this prince of shreds and patches). Richard Capell, writing about Wagner's *Ring*, remarks that "the simple barbarians of the old saga are endowed by Wagner with a new consciousness and a manner of expressing themselves which are by no means simple—and all the while they retain their antique savagery of action. Wotan's cunning and Siegfried's brutal prowess were all very well before these persons took to heroizing themselves, but then they became unpardonable." A simple Hamlet might go so far as to treat Ophelia "with useless and wanton cruelty" and kill

Polonius inadvertently in a fit of temper, but Shakespeare's Hamlet
doing such things and heroizing himself into the bargain is unpardonable. (Max Beerbohm's comment on soliloquies in drama
is apropos: "Talking to oneself has this obvious advantage over
any other form of oratory or gossip—one is assured of a sympathetic
audience.") Both Shakespeare and Wagner not only have their
kicks but videotape them with an accompaniment of forty thousand
violins for leisurely replays later: Macbeth, encouraged by his crazy
wife, murders Duncan and all the rest with as little provocation
and the same motive as a gangleader on his way to the top, but
he also does a lot of high-flown brooding (*The Godfather*—I didn't
read the book but I saw the movie—was an effort to classicize
movie gangsters by endowing them with Shakespearean sensibil-
ities), and it isn't till the end of the play that a passing reference
by Malcolm—to "this dead butcher and his fiendlike queen"—
defines the precious pair whom Shakespeare tries to magnify in
his blood-boltered thriller about conscience that doth make cowards
of us all though it dothn't keep us from committing dozens of
cold-blooded murders.

  G. Wilson Knight, this puny age's prime Bardolater who if he
can't explain something can always explain it away, carries on at
somniferous length (in *The Wheel of Fire*) to congratulate Tolstoy
for being so brilliant as to illuminate features of Shakespeare's art
that nobody else (save Knight) has ever even noticed; but Tolstoy
stops short of this last essential insight (Knight's): that indeed
Hamlet "has no character at all" but only because "he is more
than 'literary': he is like a real person with a real person's poten-
tiality for all things"—a pause while we little-known and long-
remaindered paperback Hamlets lay this flattering unction to our
souls—"in which he resembles Cleopatra [that boring single-noted
shrew except for her gorgeous speeches to die on]. Hamlet is
universal. In him we recognize ourselves [you bet!], not our ac-
quaintances [not a chance!]. Possessing all characters, he possesses
none." Hamlet, like me but not like you, "suffers for his pro-
fundity, for his advance, prematurely hastened by his ghost-con-
verse, beyond normality and mortality. He is on the way to superman status in the Nietzschean sense."

Tolstoy, Knight suggests, finds fault with Shakespeare because both of them indulge in "violent, exaggerated sex-satire" (Tolstoy dislikes competition?); but Knight fails to point out that Tolstoy's "sex-satire" rejects sex and marriage explicitly, unequivocally, and altogether, whereas Shakespeare's often hides behind his rabble-rousing appeals to chastity and fidelity: "That we can call these delicate creatures ours, / And not their appetites": if only women didn't rattle their chains so! "It is as though the erotic idealism of the artist's mind stimulates a repressed sex-instinct into virulent, unruly force. In the work of Shakespeare it is reflected as an almost unhealthy horror of sexual impurity, an unnecessarily savage disgust at the physical aspect of sex unless hallowed by a spiritual and faithful love." What a charitable way of putting it! because according to Knight a "horror of sexual impurity" or a "savage disgust at the physical aspect of sex" is okay, it's only the almost unhealthy or unnecessary kind that we have to take pills for. Among the symptoms that Knight doesn't specify is a hangup of Shakespeare's about laundry: Hamlet advises Gertrude to sleep on the couch in the living-room instead of wallowing with Claudius "In the rank sweat of an enseamed [you probably didn't think this means "greasy" but it also sounds like another word that Shakespeare knows as intimately as you do] bed," and almost any Shakespearean husband in that pre-enzyme age worries about "stains" on adulterous sheets (Leontes: "Sully the purity and whiteness of my sheets"; Othello: "Thy bed lust-stainèd"; the narrator of *Lucrece*: "her yet unstainèd bed"): Shakespeare, who led a sheltered life, seems to have believed that modest and lawful fucking occurs without the exudation of noisome bodily fluids, of the sort that Lear spits and holds his nose at when his thoughts are magnetically drawn into the region south of the linty navel of yond simpering dame (There's nothing like a dame! groans Lear atremble with an almost unhealthy terminal revulsion). Doubtless such fear and loathing testify to problems that a shrink would be hard put to solve (Now Adolf, do you remember exactly when it was that you started to experience these hostile feelings toward kikes?), but what they have to do with great thoughts and advances beyond normality and mortality (unless Knight's ideal is abnormality and death, and

I wouldn't put it past him) is something only a critic's mother could be interested in.

Well, Hamlet's a man who values friendship. In his first private chat with Horatio he interrupts Horatio's half-line ("O, my dear lord—") to make a speech of nineteen lines in praise of his own unexampled ability to recognize and value friendship, Horatio's in particular, then interrupts himself with the uneasy "Something too much of this," then gives Horatio his marching orders for the evening. In the graveyard scene Horatio says "It might, my lord" or "Ay, my lord" whenever Hamlet pauses to think up another eight or ten pregnant lines about death and corruption. After his scuffle with Laertes in the grave and having had a miraculous recovery from his fustian profession of boundless love for Ophelia, Hamlet is ready to tell the rather tedious story of his recent adventures to his only chum (i.e. Horatio), who says "That is most certain" or "Is't possible?" or "I beseech you" (Hamlet has brought his hands together around Horatio's throat in a fit of absent-mindedness) or "Ay, good my lord" whenever Hamlet pauses to check on whether he's paying attention. Next Hamlet says "I am very sorry, good Horatio, / That to Laertes I forgot myself . . . / But sure the bravery [*ostentatiousness*] of his grief did put me / Into a tow'ring passion" (fancy that! Laertes daring to upstage Hamlet! who however isn't sorry about Ophelia, who doesn't even rate a mention here, five minutes after her funeral and Hamlet's boundless love, but then she's dead and gone). At last, dying, Hamlet asks his fast friend (Horatio) to "Absent thee from felicity awhile . . . / To tell my story," and once Superman is good and dead Horatio breathes a sigh of relief (Goodbye and good *luck!* you unsolved riddle you—"Good night, sweet prince, / And flights of angels sing thee to thy rest!") and has his first opportunity to make a speech (to Fortinbras) since the time Hamlet was so unsettled by his encounter with the Ghost that he kept his mouth shut long enough to let Horatio have a few lines. (My favorite statement by Horatio, though, is his response to Hamlet's regicidal exclamation about Claudius: "is't not perfect conscience / To quit him with this arm?" and Horatio says cagily that there'll be bluebirds over the white cliffs of Dover—"It must be shortly known to him from England / What is the issue of the business there." Even so model a flunkey as doll-baby Horatio isn't going to put his head voluntarily into *that* noose.)

Meanwhile everybody's dead; and why do these tragic "heroes" on their angel-attended trips to oblivion have to involve and even slaughter numerous innocents? Johnson, whose feelings are as just as his reasoning, remarks about the ending of *Lear* that "I was many years ago so shocked by Cordelia's death, that I know not whether I ever endured to read again the last scenes of the play till I undertook to revise [reëxamine] them as an editor"; and about the ending of *Othello*, "I am glad that I have ended my revisal of this dreadful scene. It is not to be endured." He also remarks that the only way to endure the onstage blinding of Gloucester ("Out, vile jelly!") is to remind oneself that those are mere actors on a stage; but of course Shakespeare adores the pathos of such miseries inflicted on the helpless—Ophelia's flowery little suicide, the murder of Macduff's wife and children ("All my pretty ones? / Did you say all?") which Shakespeare is able to accomplish only by having the brave and gallant Macduff irrationally or pusillanimously run away and leave them at Macbeth's mercy. "Since all reasonable beings naturally love justice," says Johnson, "I cannot easily be persuaded that the observation of justice makes a play worse; or, that if other excellencies are equal, the audience will not always rise better pleased from the final triumph of persecuted virtue." Aeschylus and Sophocles thought so too, in fact they are careful never to persecute virtue at all, they take death seriously and allow it to come not to helpless women and children but only to characters with authority and the power of choice. The objective term for the Shakespearean preference is melodrama or journalistic sensationalism or Grand Guignol; the subjective term is what you will, so long as it's psychiatric and uncomplimentary. Good riddance, sweet prince.

None
But
Eagles

Two centuries later, along comes another fictitious lady-killer not only princely but imperial: "Charles Adams was an amiable, accomplished & bewitching young Man, of so dazzling a Beauty that none but Eagles could look him in the Face." When Mr. Johnson of Pammydiddle gives a masquerade ball for his neighbors,

> Of the Males a Mask representing the Sun, was the most universally admired. The Beams that darted from his Eyes were like those of that glorious Luminary tho' infinitely superior. So strong were they that no one dared venture within half a mile of them; he had therefore the best part of the Room to himself, its size not amounting to more than 3 quarters of a mile in length & half a one in breadth. The Gentleman at last finding the feirceness of his beams to be very inconvenient to the concourse by obliging them to croud together in one corner of the room, half shut his eyes by which means, the Company discovered him to be Charles Adams in his plain green Coat, without any mask at all.

It goes without saying that such brilliance will attract adoring females (moths to the flame), among them Mr. Johnson's daughter Alice, who persuades her father to intervene on her behalf with the superb young man, who replies in measured tones as follows:

> "Sir, I may perhaps be expected to appear pleased at & gratefull for the offer you have made me: but let me tell you that I consider it as an affront. I look upon myself to be Sir a perfect Beauty—where would you see a finer figure or a more charming face. Then, sir I imagine my Manners &

Address to be of the most polished kind; there is a certain elegance, a peculiar sweetness in them that I never saw equalled and cannot describe—. Partiality aside, I am certainly more accomplished in every Language, every Science, every Art and every thing than any other person in Europe. My temper is even, my virtues innumerable, my self unparalelled. Since such Sir is my character, what do you mean by wishing me to marry your Daughter? Let me give you a short sketch of yourself & of her. I look upon you Sir to be a very good sort of Man in the main; a drunken old Dog to be sure, but that's nothing to me. Your Daughter Sir, is neither sufficiently beautifull, sufficiently amiable, sufficiently witty, nor sufficiently rich for me—. I expect nothing more in my wife than my wife will find in me—Perfection."

Charles Adams, the actual if not nominal hero of a burlesque titled "Jack and Alice," was invented at a country parsonage in England by the Rev. George Austen's fifteen-year-old daughter Jane, who not only devoured the contemporary novels of sentiment and romance her family borrowed by the dozen from the circulating libraries but could turn them upside down and backwards without ever forgetting how indispensably they nourished the feminine sensibility.

They Took Him for a Cucumber

A year before she dreamed up Charles Adams, as early as her first glosses on sensibility Jane Austen already knew it like a book— a corrupt text that caught her eye as if she were its preordained restorer—and picked out its nonsense with beams of mere daylight that are brilliant enough to make even eagles blink. Here for instance are Laura and Sophia, her first pair of heroines (who affirm the precedence of "Love and Freindship" over everything else, though this title and the sunlike "feirceness" of Charles Adams's eyebeams and the ms. of her last novel show that at fourteen or forty our author spurned the precedence of *i* over *e*), here are these bosom buddies in the very act of grand larceny affirming the precedence of sensibility over filthy lucre:

> as Sophia was majestically removing the 5th Bank-note from the Drawer to her own purse, she was suddenly most impertinently interrupted in her employment by the entrance of Macdonald himself, in a most abrupt and precipitate Manner. Sophia (who though naturally all winning sweetness could when occasions demanded it call forth the Dignity of her sex) instantly put on a most forbidding look, and darting an angry frown on the undaunted culprit, demanded in a haughty tone of voice "Wherefore her retirement was thus insolently broken in on?" The unblushing Macdonald, without even endeavouring to exculpate himself from the crime he was charged with, meanly endeavoured to reproach Sophia with defrauding him of his money. . . . At this period of their Quarrel I entered the Library and was as you may imagine equally

offended as Sophia at the ill-grounded accusations of the malevolent and contemtible Macdonald. "Base Miscreant! (cried I) how canst thou thus undauntedly endeavour to sully the spotless reputation of such bright Excellence? Why dost thou not suspect *my* innocence as soon?" "Be satisfied Madam (replied he) I *do* suspect it, and therefore must desire that you will both leave this House in less than half an hour."

These hearts and handbags are big as all outdoors, which is where they now find themselves when they happen rather unexpectedly upon an overturned phaeton:

Two Gentlemen most elegantly attired but weltering in their blood was what first struck our Eyes—we approached—they were Edward and Augustus—. Yes dearest Marianne they were our Husbands. Sophia shreiked and fainted on the ground—I screamed and instantly ran mad—.

Both husbands having incontestably expired,

Sophia immediately sunk again into a swoon—. *My* greif was more audible. My Voice faltered, My Eyes assumed a vacant stare, my face became as pale as Death, and my senses were considerably impaired—.

"Talk not to me of Phaetons (said I, raving in a frantic, incoherent manner)—Give me a violin—. I'll play to him and soothe him in his melancholy Hours—Beware ye gentle Nymphs of Cupid's Thunderbolts, avoid the piercing shafts of Jupiter—Look at that grove of Firs—I see a Leg of Mutton—They told me Edward was not Dead; but they deceived me—they took him for a cucumber—" Thus I continued wildly exclaiming on my Edward's Death—. For two Hours did I rave thus madly and should not then have left off, as I was not in the least fatigued . . .

—because, as Lear or Edgar or Hamlet or Ophelia quickly discovers, once you get started it's fun to improvise and, though sense may fail, sensibility will quite outdo itself to vindicate the nonsense.

Honest-to-Goodness Heroines

At sixteen, turning out her high-spirited and highly personal "History of England" ("There will be very few Dates in this History"), Jane Austen already suspected that history as we have it is politics, politics, politics, for which an all too public-spirited ghostwriter like Shakespeare provides the posthumous and un-abridged campaign speeches:

> Henry the 4th ascended the throne of England much to his own satisfaction in the year 1399 [a date with a splendid terminal ring to it and therefore one of those very few that she allows in her history], after having prevailed on his cousin and predecessor Richard the 2nd, to resign it to him, and to retire for the rest of his life to Pomfret Castle, where he happened to be murdered. It is to be supposed that Henry was married since he had certainly four sons, but it is not in my power to inform the Reader who was his wife. Be this as it may, he did not live for ever, but falling ill, his son the Prince of Wales came and took away the crown; whereupon the King made a long speech, for which I must refer the Reader to Shakespear's Plays, and the Prince made a still longer. . . .

In *Northanger Abbey* she's a few years older but of the same mind about politics (reporting a conversation that "arrived at politics; and from politics, it was an easy step to silence") or history ("the men all so good for nothing, and hardly any women at all"), which however except parenthetically she now disregards because, though of course politics can kill you if it doesn't bore you to death, she now has livelier matters to deal with: women and also men.

At seventeen Catherine Morland knows nothing of politics, history, art, or other such idle matters and is "heartily ashamed of her ignorance," but it's a "misplaced shame" because "in justice to men"—even heroes—"though to the larger and more trifling part of the sex, imbecility in females is a great enhancement of their personal charms, there is a portion of them too reasonable and too well informed themselves to desire anything more in woman than ignorance." Catherine, bless her, is not only ignorant but a brave and bright-eyed darling who isn't too frightened by the hero's impromptu Gothic novel to keep pressing him for more and more:

> "[Dorothy, the housekeeper,] gives you reason to suppose that the part of the abbey you inhabit is undoubtedly haunted, and informs you that you will not have a single domestic within call. With this parting cordial she curtsies off—you listen to the sound of her receding footsteps as long as the last echo can reach you—and when . . . you attempt to fasten your door, you discover, with increased alarm, that it has no lock."

> "Oh! Mr. Tilney, how frightful! This is just like a book! But it cannot really happen to me. I am sure your housekeeper is not really Dorothy. Well, what then?"

> "Nothing further to alarm perhaps may occur the first night. After surmounting your *unconquerable* horror of the bed, you will retire to rest, and get a few hours' unquiet slumber. But on the second, or at farthest the *third* night after your arrival, you will probably have a violent storm. . . . [Stark staring wakeful with shocks and tremors] you will discover a division in the tapestry so artfully constructed as to defy the minutest inspection, and on opening it, a door will immediately appear—which door, being only secured by massy bars and a padlock, you will, after a few efforts, succeed in opening—and, with your lamp in your hand, will pass through it into a small vaulted room."

"No, indeed; I should be too much frightened to do any such thing."

"What! Not when Dorothy has given you to understand that there is a secret subterraneous communication between your apartment and the chapel of St. Anthony, scarcely two miles off? . . ."

Catherine's appetite for horrors is so insatiable that only Tilney's delight in it prevents him from improvising on and on forever:

". . . your eyes will be attracted towards a large, old-fashioned cabinet of ebony and gold, which, though narrowly examining the furniture before, you had passed unnoticed. Impelled by an irresistible presentiment, you will eagerly advance to it, unlock its folding doors, and search into every drawer—but for some time without discovering anything of importance—perhaps nothing but a considerable hoard of diamonds. At last, however, by touching a secret spring, an inner compartment will open—a roll of paper appears—you seize it—it contains many sheets of manuscript—you hasten with the precious treasure into your own chamber, but scarcely have you been able to decipher 'Oh! Thou—whosoever thou mayst be, into whose hands these memoirs of the wretched Matilda may fall'—when your lamp suddenly expires in the socket, and leaves you in total darkness."

"Oh! No, no—do not say so. Well, go on."

But Henry was too much amused by the interest he had raised to be able to carry it farther; he could no longer command solemnity either of subject or voice, and was obliged to entreat her to use her own fancy in the perusal of Matilda's woes. . . .

Catherine is direct and brimming with curiosity, she never dissembles, she cannot tell a lie: her appetite isn't only for horrors, the whole unexperienced world out there excites her and she hasn't learned not to say so: for a man of the world, even one as clever and likable as Henry Tilney, she seems too good to be true, he goes on testing her but always ends by enjoying her responses as richly as she enjoys his vivacity and attention—"listening with

sparkling eyes to everything he said; and in finding him irresistible,
becoming so herself." Who could ask for a better audience? Not
Tilney as he fabricates, embroiders, tantalizes, flatters, provokes.
When he sets about trying to talk her into fashionable agreement
on the "tiresomeness" of the resort town where she has been lucky
enough to encounter among other novelties Henry Tilney, "Oh!
Who can ever be tired of Bath?" she exclaims with astonishment,
and with corresponding astonishment he replies, "Not those who
bring such fresh feelings of every sort to it as you do." "I understand
you perfectly well," says Tilney, teasing her about her guileless
straightforwardness; "Me? Yes; I cannot speak well enough to be
unintelligible"; and "Bravo!" cries Tilney, enchanted by this all
the more apt for being modest and unintended "satire on modern
language" (Jane Austen is a no-nonsense eighteenth-century writer,
an admirer of Cowper and Johnson, and she doesn't take to the
first murky stirrings of Romanticism). Tilney keeps conducting
his interrogations and Catherine keeps coming back at him as
dauntlessly as if she's applying for a job (his wife, as it happens):

> ". . . I consider [says Tilney, Catherine's partner at a ball
> where another man has had the temerity to speak to her] a
> country-dance as an emblem of marriage. Fidelity and com-
> plaisance are the principal duties of both; and those men who
> do not choose to dance or marry themselves, have no business
> with the partners or wives of their neighbours."
> "But they are such very different things!"
> "—That you think they cannot be compared together."
> "To be sure not. People that marry can never part, but
> must go and keep house together. People that dance only
> stand opposite each other in a long room for half an hour."
> "And such is your definition of matrimony and dancing.
> Taken in that light certainly, their resemblance is not strik-
> ing . . ."

—and he gravely contemplates the "resemblance" in the light of
its imperfections:

> "In one respect, there certainly is a difference. In marriage,
> the man is supposed to provide for the support of the woman,

the woman to make the home agreeable to the man; he is
to purvey, and she is to smile. But in dancing, their duties
are exactly changed; the agreeableness, the compliance are
expected from him, while she furnishes the fan and the lavender water. *That*, I suppose, was the difference of duties
which struck you, as rendering the conditions incapable of
comparison."

"No, indeed, I never thought of that."

"Then I am quite at a loss. . . ."

But how can any man be at a loss with such an adorable girl who
has not only the good taste to adore him but the wit to tell him
so in a breathless outburst as if nothing could be more obvious?

"Oh! Mr. Tilney, I have been quite wild to speak to you,
and make my apologies. You must have thought me so rude;
but indeed it was not my own fault, was it, Mrs. Allen? Did
not they tell me that Mr. Tilney and his sister were gone
out in a phaeton together? And then what could I do? But
I had ten thousand times rather have been with you; now
had not I, Mrs. Allen?"

"My dear, you tumble my gown," was Mrs. Allen's reply.

Her assurance, however, standing sole as it did, was not
thrown away; it brought a more cordial, more natural smile
into his countenance, and he replied in a tone which retained
only a little affected reserve: "We were much obliged to you
at any rate for wishing us a pleasant walk after our passing
you in Argyle Street: you were so kind as to look back on
purpose."

"But indeed I did not wish you a pleasant walk; I never
thought of such a thing; but I begged Mr. Thorpe so earnestly
to stop; I called out to him as soon as ever I saw you; now,
Mrs. Allen, did not— Oh! You were not there; but indeed
I did; and, if Mr. Thorpe would only have stopped, I would
have jumped out and run after you."

Is there a Henry in the world who could be insensible to
such a declaration? Henry Tilney at least was not. . . .

Still, as the author sums it up eventually, it's quite unromantic
for a romance because, "though he felt and delighted in all the

excellencies of her character and truly loved her society, I must confess that his affection originated in nothing better than gratitude, or, in other words, that a persuasion of her partiality for him had been the only cause of giving her a serious thought. It is a new circumstance in romance, I acknowledge, and dreadfully derogatory of an heroine's dignity; but if it be as new in common life, the credit of a wild imagination will at least be all my own." Or, in other words, not romance but mere flat reality.

Jane Austen's honest-to-goodness heroines are honest and good without ever being lollipops or prudes or shrinking violets or— even love-struck Catherine the bonny babe-in-the-marriage-market—Desdemona-like doormats and mattress-pads to masterful (uxoricidal) husbands or, most surprisingly, at all similar to one another or (except that they're as beautiful as heroines have every right to be) otherwise reminiscent of any other heroines in the world. For instance Catherine Morland knows nothing; but in *Sense and Sensibility* Marianne Dashwood, another seventeen-year-old with sparkling eyes, knows everything and won't put up with any nonsense:

> "He is as good a sort of fellow, I believe, as ever lived," repeated Sir John. "I remember last Christmas, at a little hop at the Park, he danced from eight o'clock till four, without once sitting down."
>
> "Did he indeed?" cried Marianne, with sparkling eyes, "and with elegance, with spirit?"
>
> "Yes; and he was up again at eight to ride to covert."
>
> "That is what I like; that is what a young man ought to be. Whatever be his pursuits, his eagerness in them should know no moderation, and leave him no sense of fatigue."
>
> "Aye, aye, I see how it will be," said Sir John, "I see how it will be. You will be setting your cap at him now, and never think of poor Brandon."
>
> "That is an expression, Sir John," said Marianne warmly, "which I particularly dislike. I abhor every commonplace phrase by which wit is intended; and 'setting one's cap at a man,' or 'making a conquest,' are the most odious of all. Their tendency is gross and illiberal; and if their construction

could ever be deemed clever, time has long ago destroyed
all its ingenuity."

Sir John did not much understand this reproof; but he
laughed as heartily as if he did, and then replied—

"Aye, you will make conquests enough, I dare say, one
way or other. Poor Brandon! he is quite smitten already,
and he is very well worth setting your cap at . . ."

—because many who have ears hear not and even Beauty herself
could never beat brains into a silly man.

Clear and passionate, fearless, intolerant of cant and stupidity,
electrically attractive ("in her eyes, which were very dark, there
was a life, a spirit, an eagerness, which could hardly be seen
without delight"), mad about not just scenery but nature ("romantic," and therefore suspect to her Augustan young author),
mad about books and music (playing away at the piano for hours
oblivious of anybody else in the room, reading with unquenchable
curiosity through the libraries of well-stocked old houses where
she happens to be a guest for a week or a month), intense and
serious ("I should hardly call her a lively girl," says her sister
Elinor; "she is very earnest, very eager in all she does—sometimes
talks a great deal, and always with animation—but she is not
often really merry"), generous, affectionate, loving, head over heels
in love and making no secret of it to him or anybody else when
the right man—the young hero who danced all night without ever
taking a breather—comes along, Marianne is the grudging and
miraculous tribute that Jane Austen pays to the new age of feeling
for which she borrows the old and already outworn label of "sensibility." Mostly, afflicted by an unsympathetic author and a per-
versely manipulated plot, poor Marianne has to suffer like mad,
but nobody suffers with a steadier and more heartbreaking grace
than Marianne, as if she is totally unaware of being trapped in
a melodrama even when the man to whom she has given her heart
turns out for melodramatic reasons to be heartless and treacherous:

> Her face crimsoned over, and she exclaimed in a voice of the
> greatest emotion, "Good God! Willoughby, what is the
> meaning of this? Have you not received my letters? Will you
> not shake hands with me?"

He could not then avoid it, but her touch seemed painful to him, and he held her hand only for a moment. During all this time he was evidently struggling for composure. Elinor watched his countenance, and saw its expression becoming more tranquil. After a moment's pause, he spoke with calmness.

"I did myself the honour of calling in Berkeley Street last Tuesday, and very much regretted that I was not fortunate enough to find yourselves and Mrs. Jennings at home. My card was not lost, I hope."

"But have you not received my notes?" cried Marianne in the wildest anxiety. "Here is some mistake, I am sure—some dreadful mistake. What can be the meaning of it? Tell me, Willoughby—for heaven's sake, tell me, what is the matter?"

But the suddenly unspeakable Willoughby, for all his need to pull himself together here before he can act the consummate cad, won't tell her a thing (indeed, as for what has transmogrified him into a villain, we don't find out till much later, when he confides to Elinor the implausible story Jane Austen has imposed on him); and soon afterward she is forced to listen to Elinor, stern mouthpiece of the author, counseling prudence and "exertion": " 'I cannot, I cannot,' cried Marianne; 'leave me, leave me, if I distress you; leave me, hate me, forget me; but do not torture me so.' " There is no end to the mystery of creation: Marianne is the marvelous creature whom her creator tortures for being marvelous in a new and not yet authorized way.

In *Pride and Prejudice* Elizabeth Bennet is marvelous too, but in a familar way that doesn't threaten anybody's Augustan bias: witty, easily amused and often merry, bristling with judgments even before they have to be made, detached, strong, alert, almost the huntress Diana, armed if not quite armored against feeling, an antagonist with wounding darts for the unwary, as Darcy discovers when Miss Bingley carries her toadyism toward him a step too far by informing Elizabeth, while the two ladies share the same drawing-room with the great man, that nobody who has Darcy's "calmness of temper and presence of mind" could ever be a subject for laughter:

"Mr. Darcy is not to be laughed at!" cried Elizabeth. "That is an uncommon advantage, and uncommon I hope it will continue, for it would be a great loss to *me* to have many such acquaintance. I dearly love a laugh."

"Miss Bingley," said he, "has given me credit for more than can be. The wisest and the best of men, nay, the wisest and best of their actions, may be rendered ridiculous by a person whose first object in life is a joke."

"Certainly," replied Elizabeth—"there are such people, but I hope I am not one of *them*. I hope I never ridicule what is wise or good. Follies and nonsense, whims and inconsistencies *do* divert me, I own, and I laugh at them whenever I can.—But these, I suppose, are precisely what you are without."

"Perhaps that is not possible for any one. But it has been the study of my life to avoid those weaknesses which often expose a strong understanding to ridicule."

"Such as vanity and pride."

"Yes, vanity is a weakness indeed. But pride—where there is a real superiority of mind, pride will be always under good regulation."

Elizabeth turned away to hide a smile.

"Your examination of Mr. Darcy is over, I presume," said Miss Bingley; "and pray what is the result?"

"I am perfectly convinced by it that Mr. Darcy has no defect. He owns it himself without disguise."

"No"—said Darcy, "I have made no such pretension. I have faults enough, but they are not, I hope, of understanding. My temper I dare not vouch for. It is, I believe, too little yielding—certainly too little for the convenience of the world. I cannot forget the follies and vices of others as soon as I ought, nor their offenses against myself. My feelings are not puffed about with every attempt to move them. My temper would perhaps be called resentful. My good opinion once lost is lost for ever."

"*That* is a failing indeed!" cried Elizabeth. "Implacable resentment *is* a shade in a character. But you have chosen your fault well. I really cannot *laugh* at it. You are safe from me."

> "There is, I believe, in every disposition a tendency to
> some particular evil, a natural defect, which not even the best
> education can overcome."
>
> "And *your* defect is a propensity to hate everybody."
>
> "And yours," he replied with a smile, "is wilfully to mis-
> understand them."

Elizabeth's cutting edge here has back of it, besides her wit, certain
private justifications; and Darcy is slow and rather majestic, he
can only keep moving deliberately in against Elizabeth's fancy
footwork; but he's an impressive man (though "not to be laughed
at": a defect, not a virtue: Elizabeth is right), as close to a match
for her as she's likely to meet; and already, in spite of himself,
he's as helplessly in love with her as Marianne was with Willoughby.

Darcy's first proposal to Elizabeth must be among the most
original in fiction if not in history. "In vain have I struggled"
(he means against his feelings and on the side of his numberless
reasons for leaving her in the mud hut among savages where he
has found her): "His sense of her [social] inferiority—of its being
a degradation—of the family obstacles which judgment had always
opposed to inclination"—What a suitor! When Elizabeth, amazed
by the proposal and infuriated by his conceding how irrational he
is for having fallen into it, curtly refuses him, it's Darcy's turn
to be amazed and infuriated, though—at least he can console
himself with his good breeding as against a certain person's in-
civility—"in a voice of forced calmness": "And this is all the reply
which I am to have the honour of expecting! I might, perhaps,
wish to be informed why, with so little *endeavour* at civility, I am
thus rejected. But it is of small importance."

> "I might as well inquire," replied she, "why with so evident
> a design of offending and insulting me you chose to tell me
> that you liked me against your will, against your reason, and
> even against your character? Was not this some excuse for
> incivility, if I *was* uncivil? But I have other provocations.
> You know I have. Had not my own feelings decided against
> you, had they been indifferent, or had they even been fa-
> vourable, do you think that any consideration would tempt

me to accept the man who had been the means of ruining, perhaps forever, the happiness of a most beloved sister?"

To which, "with assumed tranquillity," he replies: "I have no wish of denying that I did everything in my power to separate my friend from your sister, or that I rejoice in my success. Towards *him* I have been kinder than towards myself." Yet within months he will propose again and be joyfully accepted: Elizabeth, our pride and joy, will have learned to love and trust him: Darcy will have come to seem, though he has undeniably said and felt and done all these unpleasant and sometimes nearly unforgivable things, not only formidable but a worthy and even likable man who deserves our paragon. Besides, with a keeper like Elizabeth how can he fail?— "She remembered that he had yet to learn to be laughed at, and it was rather too early to begin." Jane Austen, world's champion novelist, gets a kick out of setting up obstacle courses that only she can run.

In *Mansfield Park* Fanny Price is a mousy (with nipping little teeth) embarrassment, a bribe to the times, an evangelical angel with vampire wings; Emma of *Emma* is a brilliant representation of a nasty and gratuitous meddler (beloved of all including I'm afraid the author), a blooming girl of brains, beauty, and means who acts on the assumption that bullying and meanness, if one has a talent for them, aren't to be sniffed at simply because they haven't had as good a press as honesty and goodness: the fact is that neither Fanny nor Emma would last a round against indignant Marianne or ironic Elizabeth, and they would both make innocent Catherine wonder. But with Anne Elliot of *Persuasion* we're back in the best of company.

Admirable Admiral Croft, the old salt who hasn't lost his savor and loves to take really breakneck drives through the countryside with his loving wife (often upsetting the carriage round a turn and flinging the two of them out into the road), incidentally defines for all times and places the "nice girl" as he gives his opinion of the Musgrove sisters: "And very nice young ladies they both are; I hardly know one from the other." No such problem ever arises with Jane Austen's heroines; and Anne is another non-pareil, after those decisive and responsive girls of the earlier novels

a gentle and somewhat chastened woman, yet seeing Wentworth
again for the first time in eight years the first of her heroines to
whom the author attributes girlish palpitations:

> the room seemed full—full of persons and voices—but a few
> minutes ended it. Charles shewed himself at the window, all
> was ready; their visitor had bowed and was gone; the Miss
> Musgroves were gone too, suddenly resolving to walk to the
> end of the village with the sportsmen: the room was cleared,
> and Anne might finish her breakfast as she could.
> "It is over! it is over!" she repeated to herself again, and
> again, in nervous gratitude. "The worst is over!"
> Mary talked, but she could not attend. She had seen him.
> They had met. They had been once more in the same room!

Anne is a maiden aunt, like her author: what she has learned
from her singleness is that in polite society one equals zero—the
art of maiden-aunthood, of doing for family what they're too
piggish to do for themselves, "the art of knowing our own noth-
ingness," the art of living without love which in a world populated
by such as her father and sisters would seem quite natural and
indeed desirable if it weren't for the intrusion of such loving
couples as the Crofts and the Harvilles and such a dizzying presence
as Wentworth: "It was agitation, pain, pleasure, a something
between delight and misery"; "joy, senseless joy!"; "in spite of
all the various noises of the room, the almost ceaseless slam of the
door, and ceaseless buzz of persons walking through, [she] had
distinguished every word, was struck, gratified, confused, and
beginning to breathe very quick, and feel an hundred things in
a moment":

> There being nothing to be eat, [the child] . . . could only
> have some play; and as his aunt would not let him teaze his
> sick brother, he began to fasten himself upon her, as she
> knelt, in such a way that, busy as she was about Charles,
> she could not shake him off. She spoke to him—ordered,
> intreated, and insisted in vain. Once she did contrive to push
> him away, but the boy had the greater pleasure in getting
> upon her back again directly.

"Walter," said she, "get down this moment. You are extremely troublesome. I am very angry with you."

"Walter," cried Charles Hayter, "why do you not do as you are bid? Do not you hear your aunt speak? Come to me, Walter, come to cousin Charles."

But not a bit did Walter stir.

In another moment, however, she found herself in the state of being released from him; some one was taking him from her, though he had bent down her head so much, that his little sturdy hands were unfastened from around her neck, and he was resolutely borne away, before she knew that Captain Wentworth had done it.

Her sensations on the discovery made her perfectly speechless. She could not even thank him. She could only hang over little Charles, with most disordered feelings. His kindness in stepping forward to her relief—the manner—the silence in which it had passed—the little particulars of the circumstance—with the conviction soon forced on her by the noise he was studiously making with the child, that he meant to avoid hearing her thanks, and rather sought to testify that her conversation was the last of his wants, produced such a confusion of varying, but very painful agitation, as she could not recover from, till enabled by the entrance of Mary and the Miss Musgroves to make over her little patient to their cares, and leave the room. . . .

There's inevitably a happy ending because Anne is Cinderella and Penelope, fit for any marriageable prince or sailor home from sea, and feminine enough to be the lover of all men if all were like Captain Wentworth or Admiral Croft (Jane Austen had two sailor brothers, both of whom came to be admirals long after her death)—

in walking up Milsom-street, she had the good fortune to meet with the Admiral. He was standing by himself, at a printshop window, with his hands behind him, in earnest contemplation of some print, and she not only might have passed him unseen, but was obliged to touch as well as address him before she could catch his notice. When he did perceive

and acknowledge her, however, it was done with all his usual
frankness and good humour. "Ha! is it you? Thank you,
thank you. This is treating me like a friend. Here I am, you
see, staring at a picture. I can never get by this shop without
stopping. But what a thing here is, by way of a boat. Do
look at it. Did you ever see the like? What queer fellows
your fine painters must be, to think that any body would
venture their lives in such a shapeless old cockleshell as that.
And yet, here are two gentlemen stuck up in it mightily at
their ease, and looking about them at the rocks and mountains, as if they were not to be upset the next moment, which
they certainly must be. I wonder where that boat was built!"
(laughing heartily) "I would not venture over a horsepond
in it. Well," (turning away) "now, where are you bound?
Can I go any where for you, or with you? Can I be of any
use?"

"None, I thank you, unless you will give me the pleasure
of your company the little way our road lies together. I am
going home."

"That I will, with all my heart, and farther too. Yes, yes,
we will have a snug walk together; and I have something to
tell you as we go along. There, take my arm; that's right;
I do not feel comfortable if I have not a woman there. Lord!
what a boat it is!" taking a last look at the picture, as they
began to be in motion.

"Did you say that you had something to tell me, sir?"

"Yes, I have. Presently. But here comes a friend, Captain
Brigden; I shall only say, 'How d'ye do,' as we pass, however.
I shall not stop. 'How d'ye do.' Brigden stares to see anybody
with me but my wife. She, poor soul, is tied by the leg. She
has a blister on one of her heels, as large as a three shilling
piece. . . ."

The pleasure of their company, the pleasure in their pleasure: It's
a pleasure to watch Anne and the Admiral as they stroll arm in
arm up Milsom-street and to make a guess at what the Admiral
will be telling her and to think just this much about Captain
Brigden's darkest apprehensions.

And Some
Unstrung
Heroines

Except for that grim old stager Cleopatra about whom one can't help having the darkest apprehensions (she's so sick and tired of her other orifices she instructs the messenger to "ram . . . thy fruitful tidings in mine ears"), Shakespeare's middle and late heroines are chaste as snow, pure as ice, cold as comfort, null and void enough to shame the Devil; but nothing helps: "be thou as chaste as ice, as pure as snow," says Hamlet to Ophelia, "thou shalt not escape calumny." Not from him or Shakespeare, anyway: "wise men know well enough what monsters you make of them. . . . I have heard of your paintings too, well enough. God hath given you one face, and you make yourselves another. You jig, you amble, and you lisp; you nickname God's creatures and make your wantonness your ignorance." That's a lot of God to back up such routine barroom misogyny, but then it's hard to see how anybody but God can be brought in to authorize the moral line that in women virtue must be ice because vice is so obviously fire. Hamlet having insulted and rejected Ophelia and killed her father, the poor girl goes mad, uses up her last scene on earth to sing a ballad of sexual surrender ("Quoth she, 'Before you tumbled me, / You promised me to wed' "), and thus demonstrates that even the most tight-laced woman will sooner or later come unstrung and expose her secret hankering after the forbidden fire; hence a man can't trust any of 'em. "Behold yond simp'ring dame," cries mad (and therefore truthful) Lear, "whose face between her forks presages snow" (which once the wall-eyed syntax is straightened appears to mean that her ladylike expression forecasts a ninety-percent chance of not a chance between her legs); but yond dame

176

is no lady, she has the resistance of a snowball in hell, she melts and sizzles, "The fitchew [*polecat,* slang for *prostitute*] nor the soilèd horse goes to 't / With a more riotous appetite"—as if anybody but a bucolic teenager would think that prostitutes are hot numbers; but Lear thinks so and the Fool thinks so ("This is a brave night to cool a courtesan"), and Shakespeare seems to fear that whether for love or money women come to 't it's only natural they'll burn like brimstone when they do 't.

Here's the picture (the play is *Cymbeline*). Everybody but the paranoid King of Britain and his wicked Queen considers Posthumus the very flower of manhood, so when the King banishes him for no particular reason nobody is sadder than Imogen, who is Posthumus's wife, the King's daughter, and the very flower of womanhood. Next big scene, Luigi's Pizza and Pool Parlor, somewhere in Italy. Posthumus is sitting around with a few other loungers, from one of whom we learn that Posthumus has already upheld in a duel in France his opinion that Imogen (whom without provoking another duel our informer is allowed to call Posthumus's "country mistress"—i.e. sex-partner) is the best country mistress on record, "more fair, virtuous, wise, constant, qualified, and less attemptable than any the rarest of our ladies in France." Gallant Posthumus speaks up to reaffirm this opinion to the locals, Iachimo (a villain) challenges it, and their exchange develops to the point at which the two make a bet on Imogen's "attemptability": faithful Posthumus will show his good faith by furnishing Iachimo with a fulsome lying introduction to Imogen, Iachimo will attempt her, and if he succeeds he will not only pick up all the marbles but "I am no further your enemy," says good-sport Posthumus, because "she is not worth our debate"; if he fails, "you shall answer me with your sword." Iachimo makes his visit to Imogen, by a laborious ruse manages to observe her boudoir and the peculiar mole on her left breast, and carries his evidence back to trustful Posthumus, who doesn't take much convincing:

> *We are all bastards,*
> *And that most venerable man which I*
> *Did call my father was I know not where*
> *When I was stamped.*

(A recurrent theme, preoccupation, joke, conviction among Shakespeare's men: " 'Is this your son, my lord?' 'So hath his mother told me' ": Baby Bunting knows who Mama is but who except Mama knows who Papa is? and if Mama's been making the rounds it's conceivable that Mama herself doesn't know. "Thou may'st be false, and yet I know it not," laments the writer of the Sonnets, who like the presumptuous Wife in the Grimms' story "The Fisherman and His Wife" won't settle for playing God, he wants to *be* God. "Some coiner with his tools / Made me a counterfeit; yet my mother seemed / The Dian of that time"—cold, cold, cold as the moon; for Imogen too, Diana isn't the goddess of the hunt but the blue-veined lady with the "cold sheets.") The reason Posthumus trusted Imogen was that she often with a pretty little blush pleaded a splitting headache:

> *Me of my lawful pleasure she restrained*
> *And prayed me oft forbearance—did it with*
> *A pudency so rosy, the sweet view on 't*
> *Might well have warmed old Saturn—that I thought her*
> *As chaste as unsunned snow.*

(Blushful unaroused innocence—it's all mine! and in mint condition!—is a turn-on for the old Adam.) What proved her virtue was that safe between the unsullied sheets with her very own husband she could still be cold, cold, cold—virtue in women is snow and ice (and thus incompatible with flesh and blood, and thus the reliable basis for denunciations of women):

> *O, all the devils!*
> *This yellow Iachimo in an hour, was 't not?*
> *Or less? At first? Perchance he spoke not, but,*
> *Like a full-acorned boar, . . .*
> *Cried "O!" and mounted . . .*

—because Shakespeare (an odd distaste for a country boy) doesn't care for barnyard couplings, which keep fading into images of Beauty and the Beast, which keep fading into the silhouette of one beast with two backs ("an old black ram is tupping your white ewe," shouts skulking Iago at Brabantio; "you'll have your daughter cover'd with a Barbary horse"; "your daughter and the Moor are

now making the beast with two backs"—but Iago's a villain and
these depressing redundancies no doubt have a dramatic function).
When Imogen finds out that Posthumus has commanded her
murder she concludes that "Some jay [*whore*] of Italy" is responsible, and like an obedient wife prepares to die:

> *I draw the sword myself. Take it, and hit*
> *The innocent mansion of my love, my heart.*
> *Fear not, 'tis empty of all things but grief.*
> *Thy master is not there, who was indeed*
> *The riches of it.*

The irony is that Imogen hasn't felt a thing, she's as chaste as
unsunned snow and nothing would please her better than to plead
another splitting headache in response to some lawful request from
her beloved husband. But what if she winked and lolled and cried
"O!" like a full-acorned sow? These women can't win for losing:
they're damned if they do and dimmed if they don't.

Besides, they are so dumb—Hermione in *The Winter's Tale*, for
example. Polixenes, King of Bohemia, has had a visit with his
boyhood chum, Leontes, King of Sicilia, and is beginning to offer
polite excuses for his imminent departure. Hermione, Leontes'
Queen, succeeds in persuading Polixenes to stay a while longer
after Leontes has tried and failed (hmmm!). Of course when a
woman says a kind word to any other man in the presence of her
husband, there's hell to pay—five acts of fulmination, psychosis,
and misery, which according to the experts are all necessary if
there's to be a play at all. Of course Hermione is chaste as ice,
but it has to be admitted that she doesn't mince metaphors while
she sexily joshes her crazy husband with another man standing
there all ears ("Ram thou thy fruitful tidings . . ."):

HERMIONE: *He'll stay, my lord.*
LEONTES: *At my request he would not.*
   Hermione, my dearest, thou never spok'st
    To better purpose.
H: *Never?*
L: *Never but once.*
H: *What! Have I twice said well? When was't before?*

> *I prithee tell me; cram 's with praise, and make 's*
> *As fat as tame things. . . .*
> *Our praises are our wages—you may ride 's*
> *With one soft kiss a thousand furlongs, ere*
> *With spur we heat an acre.*

Very cute, if she were alone with Leontes—"cram us," "make us fat," "ride us," "one soft kiss," "heat"—but Polixenes stands there smiling nervously and Leontes has already started foaming at the mouth: "Too hot, too hot! . . . / But to be paddling palms and pinching fingers, / As now they are . . ." because Hermione is a friendly sort and though she's pure as the driven snow she's dumb as a post too, or at least Shakespeare needs to keep her so till he wraps her up in his net of elementary propositions: Women may be as icy as the chastened snowiness of pure drivel, but circumstances or sheer stupidity may make them seem as oozy as a dip in a hot tub, and often they really *are!* the nasty things, so it's hardly surprising that men go bonkers and threaten to chop them into messes trying to figure them out and hem them in.

And trying to keep up with the cock-and-bull stories of all these villains slinking around impugning a lady's honor, like Don John in *Much Ado About Nothing* (callous title which could also be the title of *Cymbeline* or *The Winter's Tale* or *Othello*: such a fuss, and what a pity that women need to lose their lives and even their reputations when they haven't done a *thing!*), who with the usual Shakespearean charade of evidence convinces Claudio that his bride-to-be not only deserves rejection and humiliation but has to have them dumped on her publicly in the very middle of the wedding ceremony, which he therefore goes through with till at the proper moment he can ceremoniously halt it for his idea of a wedding announcement to the father of the bride:

> *Give not this rotten orange to your friend;*
> *She's but the sign and semblance of her honour.—*
> *Behold how like a maid she blushes here!*
> *O, what authority and show of truth*
> *Can cunning sin cover itself withal!*
> *Comes not that blood as modest evidence*
> *To witness simple virtue? Would you not swear,*

> *All you that see her, that she were a maid,*
> *By these exterior shows? But she is none:*
> *She knows the heat of a luxurious bed;* [lustful]
> *Her blush is guiltiness, not modesty.*

(Shakespeare and the pathos of thwarted voyeurism: She's not cold and therefore true but hot and therefore false, and she doesn't even let me watch.)

True, these ladies are so unlucky they couldn't cross a city street without getting run over by a herd of stampeding buffalo. True, they are so dumb they keep pushing their bad luck and building it up in front of them as tirelessly as a dung-beetle: e.g. Desdemona begging a favor of Othello, to whom Iago has just noted that it was Cassio they saw "steal away" from Desdemona "so guilty-like, / Seeing you coming":

DESDEMONA: *I have been talking with a suitor* [!?#†*]
   here. . . .
OTHELLO: *Who is 't you mean?*

—and on and on, this all of a sudden maddeningly obtuse and persistent wife at her coyest trying it seems to wheedle a new boyfriend out of her obviously already upset husband whom she must be bent on driving to distraction: "Went he hence now?" mutters Othello; "Good love, call him back"; "Not now, sweet Desdemona"; "But shall 't be shortly? . . . Shall 't be tonight at supper? . . . Tomorrow dinner then? . . . Michael Cassio, / That came a-wooing with you; and so many a time, / When I have spoke of you dispraisingly, / Hath ta'en your part . . . "; "Prithee, no more; let him come when he will"; "Why, this is not a boon . . . "—till one begins to feel that if it weren't for the dramatic obligation of two more acts Othello would preëmpt most of Iago's inventions and strangle her on the spot.

Shakespeare cares about blockbuster scenes and the chances they give him to vent his obsessions on a grand scale, but he doesn't much care about excess or preëmption (audiences have short memories) or consistency of character. Compare the bold and knowing Desdemona of Act II Scene 1 who bandies eyelash-batting badinage with Iago—"O most lame and impotent conclusion!—Do not learn

of him, Emilia, though he be thy husband.——How say you, Cassio?
is he not a most profane [*coarse*] and liberal [*licentious*] councillor?"——to the puling child-bride of Act IV Scene 3 who asks Emilia
whether there really are wives who do, er, well, you know, *that*——

> *Dost thou in conscience think,——tell me, Emilia,——*
> *That there be women do abuse their husbands*
> *In such gross kind?*

——to the gross, gabby, and disastrous wheedling wife of Act III
Scene 3 ("Not now, sweet Desdemona") and Act III Scene 4:

> D: *Pray you, let Cassio be received again.*
> O: *Fetch me the handkerchief: my mind misgives.*
> D: *Come, come;*
>   *You'll never meet a more sufficient man.*
> O: *The handkerchief!*
> D: *I pray, talk me of Cassio.*
> O: *The handkerchief!*
> D: *A man that all his time*
>   *Hath founded his good fortunes on your love . . .*

——which sounds in isolation as if Shakespeare may have intended
Desdemona here to be running off at the mouth as much out of
panic as obtuseness, though the surprise and bewilderment she
expresses to Emilia once Othello exits suggest only the latter; but
in any case she's too dumb to live. In any case she has to be
sacrificed to the blockbuster scenes that flout consistency, common
decency, and common sense for the sake of providing us with the
self-satisfaction we take from contemplating this unmerited and
high-type misery that so strikingly reminds us of our own: Othello's
as he murders, though he would rather not, his beloved and
innocent though very dumb wife; Desdemona's as, lying beautifully
there in her stainless marriage bed strangled to death, in a metaphysical spasm of wifeliness she confounds medical science by
waking from the dead just long enough to deny that her murderer
killed her; and the blizzard of handkerchiefs that breaks out in
the audience would have sufficed to appease Othello himself. The
pity of it!

Out
Among
the Heathen II

A wet hanky and a good cry don't seem quite so popular on the other side of the planet. For instance here are some *Traditional Chinese Stories* (edited by Y.W. Ma and Joseph S.M. Lau) that take a bit of getting used to for us sentimental and slow-witted foreign devils: e.g. we barely have time to acknowledge so dependable and undemanding a mode as the picaresque—

> Around midnight that night, Sung . . . went over to Tightwad Chang's place. There was nobody else walking the streets, and the moon was covered by dark clouds. Sung took out a strange-looking, rope-like contraption and, hooking it to the eaves, clambered up to the top of the house. Having secured the contraption at the roof, he jumped into the courtyard. There were rooms on either side of the courtyard, and he saw lamplight in a room off to one side. While he listened for noises there, he heard a woman saying, "What's the matter with Third Brother? He still isn't here."

—when all of a sudden up pops a posy of album verses:

> "Ah!" said Sung to himself. "This woman must have a secret tryst with someone." He took a peep at the girl and saw:

> *Silky, silky raven locks,*
> *A glittery, glittery pale forehead,*
> *Curvy, curvy seductive brows,*
> *Pretty, pretty flirtatious eyes,*
> *A cute, cute straight nose,*
> *Bright, bright red cheeks,*

A bubbling, bubbling fragrant mouth,
A gentle, gentle smooth chest,
Round, round white breasts,
Dainty, dainty jade-like hands,
A slim, slim tiny waist, and
Shapely, shapely arched feet.

Ah! say we to ourselves, Romance! but we're wrong again, because the poor girl isn't the sort of jewel Sung has in mind, and, except for the time it takes to list her charms, she won't for a moment deflect him from his preoccupation with more negotiable treasures:

> Sung went up and covered her eyes with his two sleeves. "Third Brother, what do you think you're doing, frightening me like that?" she giggled. With a jerk, Sung secured her by the waist and, brandishing his sword, warned her, "Quiet! You make any noise and I'll kill you!"
> The woman turned into a mass of shudders. "Sir, please spare my life," she begged.
> "I'm here on business," Sung told her. "Let me ask you: How many traps are there between here and the storehouse?"

No sooner has she told him all she knows than he cries out,

> "Who's that coming over behind you?"
> Unaware of the trick, the girl turned her head. Sung dispatched her with a blow of his sword down her shoulder, and she crumpled in a splash of blood.

—and Sung the master thief goes on about his business.

In the stories we're used to, such a threat ("Quiet! You make any noise and I'll kill you!") is itself the guarantee that it won't be carried out. Moreover a catalogue of feminine charms is the guarantee that they'll last long enough to be admired and pursued. Moreover the idea of casually doing away with a pretty girl who just happens to be standing around waiting for her lover would never appeal to an Occidental storyteller—such a waste! and probably immoral. Moreover Sung is no thug or flunky, he's resourceful and stylish, the founder and inspiration of his triumphant gang of thieves; the hero: no doubt murdering the girl means one less witness, but mainly it seems intended to give the impression of a curt virtuoso gesture by the hero to clear the air, like Humphrey Bogart stubbing out a cigarette. Moreover Sung is no ascetic: later, at his ease in a tavern, he isn't averse to a little dalliance—

> Sung looked at her closely, and her face seemed somehow familiar. Taking her for a prostitute, he invited her to sit down. The woman settled herself opposite Sung and, calling for another order of wine, downed a cupful. Sung took her into his arms, gave her a pinch or two, and began to caress her. Then he started to feel her chest and exclaimed, "Hey, little girl, you haven't got any breasts!" He proceeded then to touch her privates, but felt only a dangling tool. "Dammit!" Sung blurted out. "Who the hell are you?"
>
> "I'm no prostitute," the one in disguise, with arms akimbo, said. "I'm merely Chao Cheng from the P'ing-chiang Prefecture in Soochow."
>
> "You sneaky, insolent bastard!" Sung screamed. "I'm your teacher, and you made me feel your privates! Now I know it, that captain must have been you."

—for Chao is quite a joker, and in this naughty world he has any number of opportunities because what's a bigger joke than naughtiness itself? e.g. the proprietress of a dumpling shop that Chao has just entered notices some expensive loot in his pack and muses, "Even though I sell human-flesh dumplings and my husband's a thief, we never have that much. Just wait. In a while he'll order some dumplings and I'll slip in a heavy dose." But of course Chao outsmarts her, and meanwhile has a few laughs besides:

> "My father told me not to buy dumplings on the banks of the Pien River because they are all made with human flesh there. Look at this piece. There's a fingernail, and it must be part of a human finger. And on this piece of skin are all sorts of little hairs; it's got to be flesh from the pubic area."
>
> "Seriously, sir," protested Hou Hsing's wife: "how can you say such things?"
>
> Chao Cheng ate the dumplings and heard the woman say

"Fall!" while she stood in front of the stove, watching for
Chao to topple over. But nothing happened. "Bring me another five," ordered Chao.

Soon not he but she is stretched out on the floor in a stupor;
and Chao, improving every shining hour while he waits for her
husband, "loosened his belt and began to pick fleas off his body."
Chao is an exemplary thief, just has a dirty and illegal good time,
eats human flesh piping hot from the steamer but doesn't go around
murdering innocent bystanders.

"Sung the Fourth Raises Hell with Tightwad Chang" is a great
comic story; and if, say, a score or a dozen of the other sixty stories
in this (according to the editors) representative and comprehensive
anthology of two thousand years of Chinese short fiction were
nearly so impressive, we'd be glad to conclude that art once again
has risen above mere fleapicking cultural differences. Nor is it only
that "Sung the Fourth" is vivid and inventive enough to disarm
our xenophobia, it's also that a comic story about a gang of thieves
can't spend much time reviewing its obligations to love and common decency. Anyhow the editors don't expect us to brood over
such issues or else they hope we'll refrain from asking for scholarly
assistance. One of the deficiencies of this collection is that, though
the pages are bottom-heavy with thickets of historical footnotes—
some of them mysterious: "Prince Hsiu was the father of Emperor
Hsiao-tsung (r. 1163-1189) because Kao-tsung, the first emperor
of Southern Sung, had no son of his own"—and though the editors
go through the motions of making all sorts of distinctions, usually
self-evident (these stories are about judges, those are about thieves),
it nevertheless doesn't occur to them to supply us with information
that might be far more helpful. What, if anything, is known
concerning whoever wrote the stories? Can any of the stories be
dated more closely than by attaching it to a dynasty that lasted
several centuries (on pages 535-554 we find the text of "Sung the
Fourth," which on page 598 the editors place in the Sung Dynasty,
which, we learn by flipping back to page xxvi, lasted from 960
to 1279)? For whom were they written or recited? since some (like
"Sung") are about low life, some are about emperors and princes,
many are about a middle class of shopkeepers and civil servants,

and most of them flatfootedly take for granted the—unsentimental?—attitudes and conventions that in "Sung" may seem to
be rationalized by wit, a headlong pace, and the nature of the
genre. Life, in short, is cheap. Consider, for instance, "Prince Tan
of Yen" ("pre-T'ang"; i.e. before 618 A.D. and after the Flood),
which tells of a prince whose one motive is to revenge himself for
slights he suffered while detained in another kingdom. He consults
various counselors, of whom he sends off T'ien Kuang to bring
back a champion: "Taking T'ien Kuang's hand, he advised, 'This
is an affair of state. Please be discreet about it.' 'Certainly,' T'ien
Kuang said, smiling," departs on his mission, and, having per-
formed it, says to the champion,

> "Now I've heard that a man should leave no room for doubt
> about his trustworthiness. When the prince was seeing me
> off he said, 'This is an affair of state. Please be discreet about
> it.' This means that he doesn't trust me. To be distrusted
> and still live in this world is my shame." Facing Ching K'o,
> he bit his tongue to commit suicide. Ching K'o then pro-
> ceeded to Yen.

Ching, one guesses, is a very cool customer or an unfeeling
brute, or just before T'ien bit his tongue Ching looked away and
the body was removed before he looked back, or such suicides are
as ordinary as dumplings; when the prince, however, is informed,
he "sobs" and "whimpers" because that, he says, was not what
he had meant at all. T'ien Kuang was too sensitive. Mistakes
happen. The prince thereupon makes Ching K'o quite comfortable
at court to soften him up for the job he will eventually ask him
to do:

> During the party the prince brought out a beauty skilled on
> the lute. Ching K'o remarked, "Fair are the hands of the lute
> player." The prince offered her to Ching who said, "I only
> admire her hands." The prince then had her hands cut off,
> and on a jade plate offered them to Ching K'o.
>
> The prince often ate at the same table and slept in the
> same bed as Ching K'o. Once Ching placidly told the prince,
> "I've been here in your service for three years and Your

Highness has treated me most generously. There was the gold
I threw at the frogs, the liver of the superb steeds, the beauty's
lovely hands presented to me on a jade plate. Even a common
man treated in this manner would be exceedingly happy and
willing to be employed for tasks fit for a dog or a horse. . . ."

If there is any irony here, it's invisible to an outsider; and the
editors don't say a word, they don't even say that protocol, custom,
the facts of history are more important than an American reader's
nostalgia for the wishful thinking of fiction. Maybe T'ien Kuang's
suicide can pass as an unlucky side-effect of the prince's obsession
with revenge (the prince is troubled enough to neglect protocol
and permits his tongue to wag instead of biting it); but the hand-
chopping seems calculated to strike us dumb with approbation,
as princely a gesture as killing a fine horse to serve its liver to
a valued guest who says he would like it for dinner or inviting
the guest to throw gold nuggets at frogs in a pond. At any rate
the story concludes with two more suicides—the last a sort of
cheerleader's encouragement to the warriors riding off: "Hsia Fu
[otherwise unmentioned] came before their chariot when they
passed by and slit his throat to send the two men on their way"—
and another hand-chopping, this one not hospitable but punitive:

Ching K'o took up the dagger and threw it at the king. It
cut an ear and struck a bronze pillar, striking sparks. The
king then turned back and cut off Ching's hands. Ching
leaned against a pillar and laughed. Squatting, he denounced
the king . . .

—and the editors launch one of their typical long historical footnotes, which ends with an inscrutable reference to "a moving but
unsuccessful attempt by Kao Chien-li on the life of the king of
Ch'in."

Murder, suicide, execution (of which one method is "death by
slicing"), and torture take up considerable space in these stories.
Tightwad Chang himself and his clerks, charged before the magistrate on a frameup by Sung, are "beaten until their skin split
open, their flesh curled, and blood flowed freely"; Chang is a comic
dupe and a loser all the way: loss of face isn't only a hazard of

the ruling classes, it has extreme consequences not only for T'ien the royal counselor but for Chang the pawnbroker, who, having been robbed and humiliated, "hanged himself in his storehouse." Suicide seems to recommend itself as a way out more readily than in the West: a triangle of lugubrious lovers, which ends with two suicides and one death by pining away ("The Broken Hairpin," published in 1916, the most recent story in the collection); a heart-of-gold courtesan betrayed by her lover ("Tu Shih-niang Sinks the Jewel Box in Anger": "Li, overwhelmed with remorse and shame, was about to turn to beg Shih-niang's forgiveness when, clasping the casket in her arms, she threw herself into the river"); husband and wife separated by a despotic king, against whom their only recourse is suicide ("Han P'ing and His Wife"); a widow who kills her treacherous lover and herself ("The Case of the Dead Infant"); a maiden who kills herself because the man who rescued her declines to marry her and so compromises her honor ("The Sung Founder Escorts Ching-niang One Thousand *Li*"); several defeated rebels and army commanders who kill themselves because of their disgrace or possibly for fear of the ingenious devices reserved to those who don't measure up ("Lord K'uang shouted an order to apply the ankle-squeezers"). On the evidence of many of these stories, which treat torture as an everyday matter ("When he was questioned under torture, his answers were found to coincide exactly with Mrs. Liu's statement") and which often describe it in detail, "Chinese torture" isn't a term invented by provincial Europeans. True, during the same millennia European judicial procedures included torture, and writers mentioned it ("With torment and with shameful deeth echon / This provost dooth thise Jewes for to sterve"; "Torments will ope your lips"), but they didn't mention it nearly so often, didn't seem to regard it as a feature of the moral landscape, didn't describe it in ankle-squeezing detail. Doubtless more and worse went on than anybody except the Marquis de Sade made explicit; but, as such reticence reminds us, hypocrisy isn't all bad, it bites its tongue in the Western sense, it's the tribute that vice pays to virtue, whereas honesty isn't merely the best policy, sometimes it's also the tribute that vice, having never heard of virtue, unwarily pays to itself: " 'You're talking nonsense,' the prince said impatiently. 'I had Hsiu-hsiu beaten to death and

buried in the back garden. You yourself must have seen what
happened. How can she be there now?' " ("Artisan Ts'ui and His
Ghost Wife"). Maybe ghosts and such appear as often as they do—
two of the sections are titled "The Superhuman Maiden" and "The
Ghost Wife"—because life is so cheap that having a second chance
seems the only hope: not fairy tales of the far and wee or scary
tales of the grotesque and arabesque, but dreary tales of girl ghosts
or "fox demons" (" 'I'm not quite the same as anybody else,' she
told him. 'Don't shine any lights on me' ") who marry and have
children and go daily to the market for fish and cabbage unless
their husbands find them out, whereupon they return to the grave
or metamorphose into foxes (or vixens) and scurry off into the
woods till the next contingent of marriageable bumpkins rolls in
on the honey wagon.

Many of these stories—whether about princes, priests, peasants,
bureaucrats, or shopkeepers—suffer from a pettybourgeois stra-
bismus, squinting toward a focus at a point not much beyond the
tip of the nose. A bandit's wife keeps exhorting her husband to
take his ill-gotten gains and "start a small business that could
provide enough income to live on" ("The Jest that Leads to Disaster"). "Red Jade" begins with an "upright" old man whose wife
and daughter-in-law both die "within the span of a few years,"
a double bereavement of which the sole consequence worth mentioning is that "thereafter, he and his son had to take care of all
the housework"; but along comes a "fox spirit" disguised as an
unimaginably gorgeous girl with whom the son makes merry "every
night," and, after some vicissitudes (the son's first wife is attacked
and dies "preserving her chastity," the father dies of internal
injuries after a terrible beating, the son is imprisoned and tortured
on false charges, there are six or seven vendetta murders), all ends
happily: the son is reunited with Red Jade, is restored to the list
of scholars in good standing, passes "with honors" his examinations
for official status, and

> at thirty-six . . . already had a large piece of land and a big
> house. Red Jade looked so delicate that it seemed as if the
> wind could blow her away, yet she worked harder than a
> farmer's wife. Even in the bitterest winter, her hands were

soft and as smooth as cream. She herself told everyone that
she was thirty-eight years old, but she only looked a little
over twenty.

(It's the powdered rhinoceros horn that does it.) Anything is possible except nobility of mind. The supernatural happens every day
and night, but the heroic is almost unheard of: in "Loach Fan's
Double Mirror," a man "since childhood . . . skilled in the martial
arts" is trying to escape with his wife before a panicked and
plundering army, but because he "was no match for the routed
troops pouring in . . . he fled for his life [and] . . . soon lost
track" of her without feeling so much as a twinge of guilt or
remorse then or later. The editors cite a critic's observation that
the Chinese "nominal hero is generally a quite unheroic person
who, on finding a maiden in distress, sinks into a kind of physical
and mental decline under the strain of trying to evolve a plan of
rescue" (he's a worrier, it's the fly in his soup, the if you'll pardon
the expression chink in his armor); or, they add, he may choose
a less passive course of action—"immediately take to his heels."
Ambition is feeble, it tends to aim at nothing higher than the
hope of success in the imperial examinations and the subsequent
safe job in government service: a typical story will get started
when a young scholar married to a bride "as pretty as a flower"
travels to the capital for the exams, and it isn't to be doubted
that once there he will stumble into amorous or other diversions—
youth will be served. Sex, by the way (and that's how it usually
is: by the way), is easy, impersonal, repetitive, summed up in a
sentence or two of relentless cheeriness (and for the reader not
much more appetizing than Chao's order of cannibal dumplings):
"gave themselves over to a night of consuming passion"; this simple
connection so uniformly blissful to both parties night after night
as to outdo even the lovemakers of Boccaccio's *Decameron*, which
allows at least some of its studs—though not their fabulous
women—to turn irritable and uninterested after a few too many
simple connections. In general, physiology and the natural func-
tions aren't prudishly ignored but the treatment of them is neither
innocent nor pornographic, when it comes down to cases it gives
a first impression of matter-of-factness but why the concentration

on women? since none of the men is singled out thus—"Without waiting to finish her business, Warm Snow hurriedly pulled up her pants and dashed outside"; "the white lady rose from her seat to go to the toilet"; "since you're so poor and could not afford to get married, I tried to give you an heir. I was hoping to bear you a boy by taking you just once, but unfortunately my period came as usual afterward so I had to break my rules and do it again." Break your rules and do it again, baby. Nor will the passages of verse which freely punctuate the text, and which are often of the Chinese-poetry-for-our-time school (The apricot blossoms flap in the wind / And my heart turns sluggishly to the past), elevate the American reader much above the Sears Christmas Book: "The silken robe trails through the thin mist; / The pendant circles tinkle in the light breeze." Probably something is lost in translation.

Many of the stories are expressly cautionary, they spell out and illustrate maxims of the sort that over here are likely to be printed on brown cardboard and posted on the walls of one-man shoe-repair shops: In God We Trust, Others Pay Cash. Servants and shady ladies receive much attention; and in fact two of the best stories in the book slip out of their moralistic straitjacket to present, without simplification, not only a faithful old servant who nonetheless does a lot of hard thinking while on the job, but a snobbish and expensive young courtesan who nonetheless proves to have an honest-to-goodness heart of gold when a modest, likable, patient young workingman falls in love with her:

> Mei-niang did not wake again until daybreak. When she turned around and found Ch'in Ch'ung lying beside her, she asked, "Who are you?"
>
> "I'm Ch'in Ch'ung," he answered.
>
> Mei-niang thought about the night before but could only vaguely recall what had happened. She said, "I must have been dead drunk last night."
>
> "No, not really."
>
> "Did I throw up?" she asked again.
>
> "No," Ch'in Ch'ung replied.
>
> "That's good." But on second thought she said, "I re-

member having vomited and also drinking tea. Was I dreaming then?"

Ch'in Ch'ung then told her, "Yes, you did throw up. I thought you might so I was prepared for it. I held my tea against my body to keep it warm and when you did throw up and asked for tea, I poured you some. I'm glad you didn't refuse and drank two cups."

Mei-niang was shocked. "Oh, how filthy! Where did I throw up?"

"I was afraid you might soil the bedding, so I held it with my sleeves."

"Where is your robe now?"

"I rolled everything up inside the robe. It's over there."

"What a pity that your robe is soiled."

"I'm only too glad that my robe could be of some service to you."

When Mei-niang heard that, she thought to herself, "What a considerate man!" and already liked him quite a bit.

"The Oil Peddler Courts the Courtesan" is the longest story in the book: there are lovers' obstacles of all kinds, two distinct and intertwining plots, a pair of businesslike but not wholly corrupt madams, a prime villain too; but Ch'in is the salt of the earth and Mei-niang is a lovely girl, they win through at last, and we're delighted to learn that "They lived happily until their old age, and their two children both became famous scholars." It's the familiar Middle Kingdom of the other stories but a couple of nice kids in love make a difference.

As for Old Servant Hsü of the story of the same name, he succeeds quite like a copybook servant in mending the fortunes of the widow and children of his former master, but he's also as tough and careful an old bird as the real world could ask for:

[His wife] was afraid that when he became aware of the situation he would go over and let loose a string of words. She dragged him over to one side and told him, "Today the first master has divided the family property. Don't you go over there meddling again! You'll be only inviting trouble if you do."

When A-chi heard this, he started and said, "The old master's will instructed that they must not divide the property. How can they push the orphans and the widow aside when the third master has just passed away? How could they make a living? If I don't say it, who will be willing to speak out for them?"

No sooner had he finished speaking than he began to move. His wife stopped him again and said, "Even an honest official cannot pass judgment on family affairs. Many relatives and neighbors have come to bear witness to the occasion and not one of them has said a word. Who are you but a servant? You're certainly not a clan elder. What could you do?"

A-chi said, "What you say is true, and I'll keep my mouth shut if the division they've made is fair. But if they've played any dirty tricks, I'll certainly speak out, come what may." After a little pause, he again asked, "Do you know which household we've been given to?"

"Frankly, I don't know," she replied.

A-chi went to the front of the hall, where he saw everyone drinking. Since they were on the point of getting high, it wouldn't have been good for him to burst in and ask questions, so he stood at the side.

A next-door neighbor happened to raise his head and saw him, and said, "Old Hsü, today you've been given to the third branch. She's a widow. You must do your best to help her."

A-chi replied casually, "I'm an old man and can't work anymore." As he was saying this, he secretly thought to himself, "So, that's it. They wouldn't have given me to the third branch if they still had some respect for my usefulness. What a way to kick me out! But I swear I'll vindicate myself and I'll build a big business for the widow and orphans. See if they'll still look down on me then!"

Family dissension over an inheritance was apparently as frequent and vicious in China as anywhere else, and unsettled even the smuggest maxims. "Magistrate T'eng and the Case of Inheritance" is another good story on the same subject, this one of unusual psychological interest because it's about the tyranny that a bad son exercises over the wise and decent father whose property he is destined to inherit. In old age the father falls in love with a young girl and marries her; the bride is "of a warm and complaisant nature"; they are happy together; within a year they have a son. Meanwhile the older son and his wife carp and complain to each other about the impotent old cuckold who has let himself be conned into marriage by the artful young slut: "I don't know the origin of this half-breed boy, but he definitely isn't the blood descendant of my father. I certainly don't acknowledge him as my brother." The young wife and child are the father's hostages to his son, whom he hopes to propitiate by total surrender:

> streams of tears fell from her eyes. Pointing to her child, she said, "Do you mean to say that this little one is not your own blood? Why, you've so freely handed everything over to your older son! Tell me: what would you have the two of us live on in the future?"
>
> "There is something you don't understand," the prefect said. "Don't you see that Shan-chi is not a good person? If I were to divide my estate equally, it would be difficult even to guarantee this little one's life. There is no alternative to letting him have his way and giving him everything. Then he will have no cause for jealousy."

The strategy works for some time after the father's death, at least to the extent that the heir grudgingly allows the widow and her child to continue to live on the estate; but the day comes when the child is old and indiscreet enough to ask for "a piece of silk to make a robe": " 'A bastard like you,' said Shan-chi, 'why do you want to look respectable?' " Ultimately it takes the dead man's secret and all the sagacity of Magistrate T'eng to straighten things out.

There are numerous stories on religious subjects and none is memorable, but two of them are interesting for what they say about Chinese versions of hell. "Tu Tzu-ch'un" puts its pilgrim to a Taoist test of silence, even through the tortures of hell: "Swallowing molten bronze, being beaten with an iron cudgel, pounded in a mortar, ground in a mill, buried in a fiery pit, boiled in a cauldron; he climbed the mountain of knives and the tree of swords"; but after two lifetimes and many ordeals (e.g. he must and does remain unresponsive to his wife's screams of agony while he looks on as she is being sliced to death "inch by inch, beginning with her feet"), he fails the test and breaks his silence because in his final ordeal he is a mother forced to watch as "her" child's brains are dashed out against a stone; the result is that, having yielded to this human weakness, he loses his chance to "become an immortal." "The Great Maudgalyayana Rescues His Mother from Hell" tells of a monk so devoted to his wicked mother that he journeys through all the regions of hell to find her, and at length persuades the Buddha Himself to harrow hell and so release not only her but all the other souls imprisoned there—

> Without one's even hearing so much as a hint of water and drink, the months go by, the years pass, and the miseries of starvation must be endured. From a distance, pure, cool, refreshing waters can be seen, but up close, they turn into a pus flow. Delicious food, delectable meals, turn into blazing fire.

On the whole, one would rather be in Philadelphia.

The best story in the collection, also about the supernatural but the only one with the verve and recklessness of the best Occidental fairytales, is "The Legendary Marriage at Tung-t'ing" (T'ang: i.e. sometime between 618 and 907 A.D.). It opens unpromisingly enough with yet another of those candidates for a desk in the Bureau of Lost Scrolls, "a scholar named Liu Yi [who] went up to the capital for the examinations." Luckily for us, he flunks. On his way back home Yi befriends the beautiful "daughter of the dragon ruler of Lake Tung-t'ing," and, entrusted with a message about her mistreatment by her wicked husband, carries it faithfully to her father, "who covered his face with his sleeve and wept, saying, 'This is my fault as her father; I was not able to examine and listen. . . . You, sir, were a passerby, yet you were able to take the matter to heart. For as long as I have hair and teeth I will never dare to forget your kindness!' " The lord is, however, alarmed when the sympathetic weeping of the attendants grows noisy, because "Ch'ien-t'ang . . . our beloved younger brother" has quite a temper and, if he finds out, may do something rash in retaliation: "The nine-year flood . . . was due to one of his rages. Recently he quarreled with one of the generals of heaven and flooded the Five Mountains"; but Uncle Ch'ien has indeed overheard the weeping and wailing about his niece's plight, and is off to the rescue in glorious dragon style:

> there was all at once a great sound splitting the heavens and rending the earth. The palace buildings shook and clouds and mists rolled and rolled. Suddenly there appeared a red dragon more than a thousand feet long with eyes flashing lightning and a tongue blood-red, vermilion scales and a flaming beard. The neck bore a gold lock and from the lock dragged a jade pillar. Thousands of lightning bolts and tens of thousands of thunderclaps issued violently around its body, while sleet and snow, rain and hail all fell at the same time. Then it broke through the azure sky and flew away.
>
> In his fear, Yi had fallen prostrate to the ground. The lord personally helped him to rise, saying, "Don't be afraid, you will certainly not be harmed."
>
> For a long while Yi was fairly shaken, but then he regained his composure and asked to leave, saying, "I would like to return while I still have life, so that I will not be here when he comes again."
>
> "It won't happen again," the lord said. "His departures are thus, but his arrivals are not. We should be happy if we might slightly represent to you our feelings of fond esteem."

Having come back victorious with his niece in tow, Ch'ien-t'ang reports to his brother:

> "I left the Divine Void Hall in the early morning and by late morning I was at Ching-yang. I fought at noon there and returned here in the early afternoon. Before returning I flew up to the Ninth Heaven to report to the Lord on High. The Ruler understood the grievance and pardoned me. . . . However, in my impetuous outburst [when I blasted off this

morning] I did not stop to take my leave. I upset the inner
palace and was also rude to the guest. I am mortified and
deeply ashamed." Then he stepped back and bowed twice.

"How many did you kill?" the lord asked.

"Six hundred thousand."

"Damaged crops?"

"Eight hundred *li*."

"Where is the heartless fellow?"

"I ate him."

On the same scale are the entertainments and celebrations: "ten
thousand men danced . . . with reed whistles, horns, snares, war
drums, banners, flags, swords, and halberds"—rather like the Great
Helmsman's People's Red Army Cookbook ("Take a hundred thousand bowls of rice . . .").

Having recovered from Little Brother's dawn takeoff, Yi is the
very model of dignity and firmness while hearing him out on a
delicate matter:

> Ch'ien-t'ang . . . said to Yi haughtily, "Surely you know
> 'a hard rock can be split, but can't be rolled; a righteous man
> can be killed, but not put to shame'? I've got an idea I'd
> like to put to you. If you agree, we'll all be up in the clouds;
> if not, we'll be in a mess of shit. Now, what do you say?"
>
> "I would like to hear about it," Yi said.

Ch'ien carries on like a big bad bully of a Tung-t'ing dragon: You
marry my niece, buddy, says Uncle Ch'ien, and everything will
be just fine: "she was humiliated by a scoundrel, but now that
has come to an end" and I don't want you to think for one silly
suicidal moment that she isn't just the girl for you—

> Yi stood up solemnly and then laughed, saying, "I truly
> did not know that the Ch'ien-t'ang lord was so petty-minded
> and provoking! In the beginning I heard how you had spanned
> the nine parts of the country, held the Five Mountains close
> to you, to vent your anger. . . . If I should meet you among
> towering waves or in the darkness of mountains, your scales
> and beard bristling and clouds and rain about you, and you
> should threaten me with death, I would look upon this as

something done by a brute beast and would certainly not have any feeling of resentment. Now, as you are wearing hat and clothes, sitting down to discuss propriety and altruism with me, your character displays the five principles to the fullest and you have a thorough understanding of human relationships. Even sages and heroes in the human world cannot match you in these respects, still less the spirits of the rivers. Does it in any way seem right that you should now want to intimidate someone, with your body sprawled out rudely, your temper flaring, and your courage drawn from wine? My physical form cannot match the size of even one of Your Majesty's scales, yet I will dare to withstand resolutely Your Majesty's wayward mood! Will Your Majesty please reflect on this!"

Ch'ien-t'ang drew himself back and apologized. "We were born and raised in the palace rooms and have not heard forthright moral discourse. Just now we spoke arrogantly and rudely offended a person of quality. When we step back and consider this, we realize it was unpardonable. We should be fortunate if you do not regard this as an affront."

That evening they again feasted happily and Yi and Ch'ien-t'ang became intimate friends.

Of course after a few years it becomes honorable and convenient for Yi to marry the beautiful dragon lady: "Don't consider," she says to him, weeping tears of gratitude, "that because I am of another kind I have no feelings. I will certainly requite you. The dragon has a life-span of ten thousand years. We share this now. We shall travel freely on the land or in the waters." What a way to go.

Meanwhile Back
at the Ranch:
American Scholar
Meets a Lady

Medieval poems do go on about love but no doubt as allegorically as the Song of Songs, in which according to a Reliable Source the beloved's breasts and bellybutton are to be construed as among the fifty-seven most adorable attributes of the Almighty. An exasperated medievalist once confessed that except for *Piers Plowman* there wasn't a single fucking medieval poem which didn't go on about love, but of course beginning with the double pun in the title ("Piers" is pronounced "Pierce" in Middle English: this is the kind of inside information that distinguishes us scholars from you laymen) he had quite overlooked the allegory. Love conquers all, says the brooch worn by Chaucer's Prioress but slyly says so in Latin. Then there are romantic medievalists like D.W. Robertson, Jr. for whom love is God's word, lately obscured by the mists of modernism; in the good old days Christianity was "recognized as a religion of love rather than as a cult of righteousness," he reminds us with more righteousness than love and so proves his point (though the Romantic composer Berlioz had a friendlier view of Mother Church's adaptability: "since she has ceased to inculcate the burning of heretics, her creeds are charming"). During the Middle Ages love, God bless it, was everywhere—e.g. with Paolo and Francesca in hell—and didn't for an instant faze His undivided body of believers, who could stand so much of it because it always stood for something else. God was love but love was damn well whatever God said it was and don't you forget it. When Chaucer's aging Wife of Bath sighs for the lost pleasure of love, we moderns feel our eyes moisten; but in *A Preface to Chaucer* Robertson assembles texts from Psalms 27 and 102, the *Glossa major*, and St. Paul to show that we're wasting our water and that Chaucer, like God, is just having a good laugh at the expense of this untidy creature of his before bundling her off to death and damnation:

> St. Paul urges us (Eph. 4.22 ff.) to "put off the old man" and "be renewed" so as to "put on the new man." When the wife, therefore, having invoked "Lord Crist" [but she doesn't "invoke 'Lord Crist,'" she merely seasons her nostalgia with an oath: Robertson ought to read *The Friar's Tale*, in which even the devil can distinguish between an invocation and an oath] begins to talk about how good it feels to remember the "good things" of youth and then laments that age has bereft her of pith and "flour," leaving only bran, it is clearly and amusingly apparent that she has taken the name of Christ in vain and neglected her opportunity to "flourish again" in a true *renovatio*.

"Allas! allas! that evere love was sinne!" cries the Wife of Bath, rattling her chains in hell. Theologians see through a glass darkly, and perched on their shoulders the monkey poet rattles his tin cup and squeals at the passing faithful.

The trouble is that since the Church stopped burning heretics nobody has had much incentive to follow instructions. Eight centuries ago, in the very heyday of the Age of Faith, Chrétien de Troyes wrote his Arthurian romances, which nowadays to our uninstructed minds seem to be the first European books in praise of love: "we insist on reading it 'as a story,'" says Robertson with patient condescension toward our misreading of *The Knight of the Cart*, "so that we become vicariously involved in the hero's 'adventures' and so lose the exemplary force of the narrative." If only we could understand that what we're supposed to do is discover sermons in stones. For instance when Lancelot climbs into a cart meant for thieves and traitors because the carter informs him that otherwise he won't find out what has happened to Guinevere, we are moved by this evidence of the power of love; but it's clearly and amusingly apparent to Robertson, St. Paul, St. Augustine, and St. Bernard that love (i.e. not *love*) is a hotbed of hanky-panky, and that a lover who goes so far as to humiliate himself

in the service of love can look forward to V.I.P. treatment in the
hotbox next to the Wife of Bath's: what reasonable reader, therefore, would deny that if Chrétien knows what's good for him his
exemplary intention here has to be to ridicule love and (as Robertson canonically puts it) "emphasize the extent of the inversion
to which a submission of the reason to the [sic] sensuality may
lead"? Or nowadays we read Chaucer's *Troilus and Criseyde* under
the delusion that only a writer full of tenderness and concern for
his characters would write eight thousand verses on the earthly
dilemmas of men and women and the joys of love; but Robertson
knows better, knows it's (quite like Shakespeare's revolting cari-
cature of it) an exemplum about a libidinous young fool who gets
a crush on a loose woman and isn't even man enough to do the
job all by himself. In Book II, for instance, Chaucer presents his
heroine in a long episode alone, thinking about Pandarus's news
that Troilus is in love with her, wondering and worrying, still
in a state of anxiety and indecision going to bed and having the
dream of the terrific eagle with feathers white as bone, till at last
the poet regretfully leaves her with four words that read like a
signature of love: "Now lat hire slepe"; but only a reader susceptible
to tone, texture, meaning, and common decency would be moved
by Criseyde here and everywhere else, and if Chaucer is following
instructions his official and authorized intention is to "emphasize
the extent of the inversion to which a submission of the reason
to the sick [sic] sensuality may lead."

Lancelot, the Wife of Bath, Troilus, Criseyde may think that
what they feel is love but God knows better. The philosopher Karl
R. Popper has described (in *Conjectures and Refutations*) the differences between a scientific theory and such systems of opinion as
sometimes go by the name of theory but seem to their adherents
to explain everything, especially how people really feel rather than
how they think they feel. Out of a certain delicacy he concentrates
on systems propounded by mere mortals, spellbinders like Marx
and Freud whose persuasiveness "seemed to have the effect of an
intellectual conversion or revelation, opening your eyes to a new
truth hidden from those not yet initiated. Once your eyes were
thus opened you saw confirming instances everywhere: the world
was full of verifications of the theory. Whatever happened always

confirmed it. Thus its truth appeared manifest; and unbelievers were clearly people who did not want to see the manifest truth." Popper concludes: "A theory which is not refutable by any conceivable event is non-scientific. Irrefutability is not a virtue of a theory (as people often think) but a vice." Medievalists will swell with indignation and retort that (1) science has nothing to do with art; (2) respect for what the writer says has nothing to do with scholarship; (3) religious freedom is one of the pillars of democracy; (4) they themselves have disagreed with Robertson from the very moment he started waving his crucifix around (by "disagreement" they mean: "Professor Robertson perhaps goes too far, but he is an astute and vigorous scholar, and his method provides a salutary occasion for the rest of us to reëxamine our own blah blah blah"); and (5) at all events any irrefutable system is better than none. Love, careless love isn't irrefutable enough, anything so private and partial needs tucking and binding to the measure of a system, as when Robert Hanning and Joan Ferrante (in *The Lais of Marie de France*, which they introduce, translate, and annotate) gruesomely drape the private parts of Marie de France's "Guigemar" with yards of systematic gibberish:

> His success in war contrasts sharply with his complete indifference to women and love. This rejection of the possibility of a relationship that would offer purely private fulfillment (as opposed to the public rewards of prowess: i.e. honor and fame) and the resultant deepening of self-awareness mark Guigemar as sexually and psychologically immature. In modern terms, he is engaged in the dangerous enterprise of avoiding or repressing the passionate, instinctual side of himself, which is a form of psychic self-mutilation. . . .

One would rather listen to a Robertson or a St. Bernard or even a Doberman Pinscher. Certainly one would rather listen to what comes through of Marie herself in this version by Hanning and Ferrante:

> *"My lady," he replied, "for God's sake, have mercy!*
> *Don't be annoyed if I speak like this to you.*
> *It's appropriate for an inconstant woman*

to make some one plead with her for a long time
to enhance her worth; that way he won't think
she's used to such sport.
But a woman of good character,
sensible as well as virtuous,
if she finds a man to her liking,
oughtn't to treat him too disdainfully.
Rather she should love and enjoy him;
this way, before anyone knows or hears of it,
they'll have done a lot that's to their advantage.
Now, dear lady, let's end this discussion."
The lady realized he was telling the truth,
and immediately granted him
her love; then he kissed her.
From now on, Guigemar is at ease.
They lie down together and converse,
kissing and embracing often.
I hope they also enjoy whatever else
others do on such occasions.

True, the "translation" is a styleless and rhythmless crib, and ought to have been printed if at all as an interlinear gloss on Marie's terse and businesslike octosyllabic couplets (" 'Dame,' fet il, 'pur Deu, merci! / Ne vus ennoit si jol vus di! . . . .' "); true, there are infelicities ("It upset him to leave his beloved behind"): but nothing's perfect, not even love, which as Hanning and Ferrante observe "cannot forever remain static, secure, and untested within a womblike private world." What love needs is a womb with a view.

Early in the poem Guigemar suffers a "thigh wound" while hunting, and, though soon enough both he and it have been kissed and made well by the beautiful lady whereupon everybody forgets about it, the issue demands to be scrutinized. Marie couldn't have read *From Ritual to Romance,* which came out in the nick of time for T. S. Eliot, and she was probably unfamiliar with anthropological explanations of motifs in the oral Breton *lais* which in any case don't survive and by which if they existed she may have been influenced; but she had studied anatomy with one of the remote predecessors of Vesalius and knew that the thigh-bone was connected down there to the knee-bone (which was in turn connected to the shin-bone) and up here to the hip-bone, which was in turn . . . (H. and F.: "the thigh wound is a euphemism" by means of which Marie intends to "portray metaphysically a crisis of sexual growth and awareness in Guigemar that we associate today with adolescence").

Marie is a younger contemporary of Chrétien's and finds love as fascinating as he does, but she gets to the point quickly, a storyteller not a novelist, she's never ceremonious or reserved, she doesn't surround love with such a luxuriance of trials, quests, journeys, adventures, mysteries, emblems; she's as brisk and downright as the Wife of Bath will turn out to be two centuries later, as familiar with domestic routine and the physiology of marriage, shares the Wife's contempt for men who have outlived their maleness but not their meanness: so in "Guigemar" she describes the heroine's old husband and the precautions he takes—"(All old folk are jealous; / every one of them hates the thought of being cuckolded, / such is the perversity of age.) / The watch he kept over her was no joke. / . . . An old priest, hoary with age, / kept the gate key; / he'd lost his nether member / or he wouldn't have been trusted. / He said mass for her / and served her her food." The husband attends to all of his wife's spiritual and material appetites except one; and, though the eunuch priest saying mass and serving tea for the sequestered beautiful lady might well be a romantic medievalist's image of heaven, it's pure hell on earth for the lady. Marie is a woman who thinks of herself as speaking for women, she sees no reason why women shouldn't have a good time and even make the first move ("One summer morning, / the lady was lying beside her young lover; / she kissed his mouth and eyes"), she hasn't a doubt that sexual pleasure is the greatest pleasure in the world and worth all the risks, among which it doesn't occur to her to consider the risk of sin and judgment: the lady "having granted him her love," Guigemar "stayed with her for a year and a half. / Their life was full of pleasure." The husband isn't much of an inconvenience either, because once she escapes his durance vile he drops completely out of the action, which concludes a couple of hundred lines later when Guigemar, having stormed a

castle to rescue her from still another captor, "led away his mistress
with great rejoicing; / all his pain was now at an end."

True, Marie isn't alert to her obligations, she doesn't produce
manuals of etiquette for proper young maidens or religious alle-
gories for Jesus-freaks or pop-psych fables for motif-mongers; nor
is she drawn to the sort of wish-fulfillment fantasy for unexhausted
old wives that generates the Wife of Bath's Canterbury tale about
the lusty knight and the loathly lady. Marie's special quality,
which despite their resemblances sets her quite apart from the
Wife, isn't her interest in pleasure, it's her generosity of spirit,
her ungrudging and un-Christian charitableness that rejoices in
the pleasure of others. When Sir Lanval is conducted by the girl's
two beautiful attendants to the pavilion of the most beautiful girl
in the world, Marie couldn't be happier for him:

> *the lily and the young rose*
> *when they appear in the summer*
> *are surpassed by her beauty.*
> *She lay on a beautiful bed—*
> *the bedclothes were worth a castle—*
> *dressed only in her shift.*
> *Her body was well shaped and elegant;*
> *for the heat, she had thrown over herself*
> *a precious cloak of white ermine,*
> *covered with purple alexandrine* [a kind of embroidery],
> *but her whole side was uncovered,*
> *her face, her neck and her bosom;*
> *she was whiter than the hawthorn flower.*

In days of old when knights were customarily bold, Lanval is
on the contrary "depressed and very worried" because King Arthur
has passed him over in the distribution of largesse, and so Marie
sends him off into the countryside where all of a sudden she
accentuates the positive by giving him just everything—

> *The knight went forward*
> *and the girl addressed him.*
> *He sat before the bed.*
> *"Lanval," she said, "sweet love,*

because of you I have come from my land;
I came to seek you from far away.
If you are brave and courtly,
no emperor or count or king
will ever have known such joy or good;
for I love you more than anything."
He looked at her and saw that she was beautiful;
Love stung him with a spark
that burned and set fire to his heart.
He answered her in a suitable way.
"Lovely one," he said, "if it pleased you,
if such joy might be mine
that you would love me,
there is nothing you might command,
within my power, that I would not do,
whether foolish or wise.
I shall obey your command;
for you, I shall abandon everyone.
I want never to leave you.
That is what I most desire."
When the girl heard the words
of the man who could love her so,
she granted him her love and her body.
Now Lanval was on the right road!

Right on! exults Marie, applauding her love-struck hero who
will do anything whatever (maybe even climb into a cart meant
for thieves and traitors) at love's command. Women have never
been much into theology, but Marie is so out of it that she doesn't
take a minute to think about compatibility or morality or civic
responsibility either, and she's so *cheerful!* as if she gets a *charge*
out of her young lovers.

It goes without saying, though the fairy princess does say it
to make sure Lanval is aware of whom he's dealing with, that he
had better keep his luck to himself: "you would lose me for good
/ if this love were known"; but otherwise he's in clover: "there
is no place you can think of / where a man might have his mistress
/ without reproach or shame, / that I shall not be there with you

/ to satisfy all your desires. / No man but you will see me / or hear my words." Understandably, riding back to the city, Lanval is stunned and incredulous, he doesn't "expect ever to see her again." Equally understandably, some time later, having his mistress as often and ecstatically as promised, Lanval is in no condition for society or other women: on an excursion with a company of knights and ladies and the Queen, he stands aside as usual in a daze of love "far from the others; he was impatient / to hold his love, / to kiss and embrace and touch her"; thus, when the Queen propositions him, he rejects her so scornfully that in their ensuing exchange—why would a man not only seem quite uninterested in women but reject the Queen herself?—she insults him into giving away the secret: " 'Lanval,' she said, 'I am sure / you don't care for such pleasure; / people have often told me / that you have no interest in women. / You have fine-looking boys / with whom you enjoy yourself' ";

> *When Lanval heard her, he was quite disturbed. . . .*
> *He said something out of spite*
> *that he would later regret.*
> *"Lady," he said, "of that activity*
> *I know nothing,*
> *but I love and I am loved*
> *by one who should have the prize*
> *over all the women I know. . . .*
> *Any one of those who serve her,*
> *the poorest girl of all,*
> *is better than you, my lady queen,*
> *in body, face, and beauty,*
> *in breeding and in goodness."*

It's not as if life still doesn't have its bad patches; and Lanval soon finds himself up before the furious King, who has been told by Guinevere that she had to fight off Lanval's advances and that he thereupon compounded the outrage by declaring her inferior not only to his mistress but to the lowliest of his mistress's chambermaids. By his boasting, then, Lanval has advertised and lost his mistress, who is also the only possible body of evidence that can save him at the trial. Don't despair, though, because on the appointed day, two at a time in dazzling and stately procession, amazing and delighting the knights and the townspeople, appear her beautiful and seductively dressed attendants till at last with what amounts to a fanfare of all the trumpets of fairyland appears the paragon herself:

> *They were about to give their judgment*
> *when through the city came riding*
> *a girl on horseback:*
> *there was none more beautiful in the world.*
> *She rode a white palfrey,*
> *who carried her handsomely and smoothly. . . .*
> *She was dressed in this fashion:*
> *in a white linen shift*
> *that revealed both her sides*
> *since the lacing was along the side.*
> *Her body was elegant, her hips slim,*
> *her neck whiter than snow on a branch,*
> *her eyes bright, her face white,*
> *a beautiful mouth, a well-set nose,*
> *dark eyebrows and an elegant forehead,*
> *her hair curly and rather blond;*
> *golden wire does not shine*
> *like her hair in the light.*
> *Her cloak, which she had wrapped around her,*
> *was dark purple.*
> *On her wrist she held a sparrow hawk,*
> *a greyhound followed her.*
> *In the town, no one, small or big,*
> *old man or child,*
> *failed to come look.*
> *As they watched her pass,*
> *there was no joking about her beauty.*

"The judges who saw her / marveled at the sight; / no one who looked at her / was not warmed with joy." Lanval, true knight, rises to the occasion: " 'By my faith,' he said, 'that is my love. / Now I don't care if I am killed, / if only she forgives me. / For I am restored, now that I see her.' " It's almost incidental that

her presence ("she let her cloak fall / so they could see her better")
and her testimony cause the judges to acquit him; what matters
is that afterward and forever

> *When the girl came through the gate*
> *Lanval leapt, in one bound,*
> *onto the palfrey, behind her.*
> *With her he went to Avalun,*
> *so the Bretons tell us,*
> *to a very beautiful island;*
> *there the youth was carried off.*
> *No man heard of him again,*
> *and I have no more to tell.*

(H&F: "The superficiality, perhaps even falseness, of the court's
values, which was apparent in the mistreatment of Lanval in the
beginning, is revealed particularly in the accusation and trial of
the hero.")

"Lanval" is Marie's sunniest celebration of love; but idylls are
rare, love isn't necessarily reciprocated or desire always gratified,
circumstances are sometimes intractable, women aren't always
worthy of the love they inspire. In "Chaitivel" ("The Unfortunate
One"), a lady who has "the very best manners" trifles with four
men's affections on the pretext of not being able to choose among
them: eventually, to impress her while she looks on, they all
compete so ferociously in a tournament that three are killed and
the fourth castrated ("the tip of the lance shot through his thigh
/ into his body"—this time a thigh wound too real for such an
artificial lady to kiss and make well); she grieves with due decorum
and consoles the survivor ("I shall compose a *lai* about the four
of you / and call it *The Four Sorrows!*"), who however proposes that
a more accurate title would be *The Unfortunate One* because he
alone remains to see his love "coming and going . . . morning
and evening . . . / but I can have no joy from her, / from kisses
or embraces, / nor anything good but talk"; " 'By my faith,' she
said, 'I like that. / Let's call it *The Unfortunate One.*' " Marie's most
touching piece ("Chevrefoil") is a little anecdote about "Tristan
and the queen / and their love that was so true, / that brought
them much suffering / and caused them to die the same day":

Tristan from his exile steals back to Cornwall for a precious meeting—

> *She went a short distance from the road;*
> *and in the woods she found him*
> *whom she loved more than any living thing.*
> *They took great joy in each other.*
> *He spoke to her as much as he desired,*
> *she told him whatever she liked.*
> *Then she assured him*
> *that he would be reconciled with the king—*
> *for it weighed on him*
> *that he had sent Tristan away;*
> *he'd done it because of the accusation.*
> *Then she departed, she left her love,*
> *but when it came to the separation,*
> *they began to weep.*

And "Laüstic" ("The Nightingale") is another tribute to the power of hopeless love, which here having not so much as a fading memory of gratified desire, settles for tokens: listening to the nightingale has been the lady's excuse for spending the night at her window sharing "across a high wall of dark stone" words and looks with her lover—"she often rose from . . . [her husband's] side / and [Marie's heroines are practical as well as brave and passionate] wrapped herself in a cloak"—but her husband traps the nightingale: "She asked her lord for the bird / but he killed it out of spite, / he broke its neck in his hands— / too vicious an act— / and threw the body on the lady; / her shift was stained with blood, / a little, on her breast. / Then he left the room"; so she "took the little body; / she wept hard and cursed / those who betrayed the nightingale, / who made the traps and snares, / for they took great joy from her. / 'Alas,' she said, 'now I must suffer' "; and sends it wrapped in samite to her lover, who

> *. . . had a small vessel fashioned*
> *with no iron or steel in it;*
> *it was all pure gold and good stones,*
> *very precious and very dear;*

the cover was very carefully attached.
He placed the nightingale inside
and then he had the casket sealed—
he carried it with him always.

Except for the coy and heartless bluestocking of "Chaitivel,"
Marie's heroines have no girlish tricks, they are strong and guileless
girls who, if love strikes them, offer themselves as explicitly as
Lanval's fairy princess to the men they love. Even sight unseen:
in "Milun" a baron's daughter, "a beautiful and most refined girl
. . . / [who] had heard of Milun / . . . began to love him. / She
sent a messenger to him, / to say that, if it pleased him, she would
love him" (the good old days! before the saints came marching
in). It pleases him so well that "Outside her room, in a grove /
where she went to amuse herself, / she and Milun, very often, /
had a rendezvous. / Milun came there so often and loved her so
much / that the girl became pregnant." (Marie places "Milun" in
South Wales, and the lovers' messages are carried back and forth
by Milun's pet swan—whereon H&F's ornithological gloss: "It has
been argued that the lovers' use of a swan is a realistic touch since
swans breed in certain parts of South Wales.") "Yonec" is like
"Guigemar" in presenting a beautiful young wife imprisoned in
a tower by her jealous old husband, and like a mirror-image of
"Lanval" in providing the heroine, who prays for the blessing of
love, with an otherworldly companion. This hawk-turned-man
(once he easy as pie transforms himself into a perfect lookalike of
the lady just long enough to take communion from her unsus-
pecting chaplain and so proves to her that he's a Christian! not
a demon) becomes her lover promptly and, when she "gently
begged him / to come back often," promises that "whenever you
please, I will be here within the hour." In "Eliduc" the king's
daughter falls in love with the knight who has been called from
his own land to lead her father's army:

All night she was awake,
she couldn't rest or sleep.
The next day, in the morning, she got up
and went to a window;
she summoned her chamberlain,

> *and revealed her condition to him.*
> *"By my faith," she said, "this is terrible.*
> *I have gotten myself into a sorry mess.*
> *I love the new soldier,*
> *Eliduc, the good knight.*
> *Last night I had no rest,*
> *I couldn't close my eyes to sleep.*
> *If he wants to give me his love*
> *and promise his person to me,*
> *I shall do whatever he likes. . . .*

Still, the world takes its toll even of young lovers. Pregnancy isn't a joke for Marie any more than it turns out to be for the baron's daughter and her lover, who must give up their child for many years before the belated reunion and happy ending for all three. In "Yonec" the lovers are found out and the hawk-man impaled on spikes and killed, and it isn't till many years later that their knightly son avenges his father's death by killing his mother's husband: " 'Fair son,' she said, 'you hear / how God has led us to this spot. . . .' / Then she fainted over the tomb / and, in her faint, she died. / She never spoke again. / When her son saw that she had died, / he cut off his stepfather's head. / Thus with his father's sword / he avenged his mother's sorrow." Eliduc is a lover twice over and in sore straits, at the same time devoted to his very model of a loving wife and desperately in love with the king's daughter—

> *a storm broke out at sea . . .*
> *it broke and split their mast*
> *and tore their sail. . . .*
> *Then one of the sailors, loudly,*
> *cried: "What are we doing?*
> *Sire, you have inside with you*
> *the one who is causing our deaths.*
> *We'll never reach land.*
> *You already have a faithful wife*
> *but you're bringing another back*
> *in defiance of God and the law*
> *of right and of faith.*

Let us throw her into the sea,
so we can get home safely."

Eliduc hasn't yet told either of his ladies about the other, and
"almost went mad with anger. / 'Son of a bitch,' he said, 'rotten
/ filthy traitor, be silent! / If you had let my love go / I'd have
made you pay for it.' / But he held her in his arms / and comforted
her as well as he could / from the distress she felt from the sea
/ and from what she'd heard / of her lover's having a wife / other
than herself in his country." Marie's resolution of his problem after
many vicissitudes makes such splendid use of the institutions of
the Church Triumphant that even Robertson might approve, or
on the other hand he might say sourly that Marie can't resist
allowing her lovers to have things their own sweet way. All right,
so some of them do indeed behave badly and have to be punished:
as in "Equitan," in which the king and the seneschal's wife suffer
the horrible death they planned for the seneschal; or in "Bisclavret"
("The Werewolf"), in which the werewolf settles accounts with
his treacherous wife by biting off her nose ("a gesture of justifiable
revenge rather than of uncontrolled savagery," according to H&F,
this particular werewolf being a modest creature who won't even
"don his clothes in public" because "the cultivation of shame—
the unwillingness to fall below a certain level of behavior in the
presence of one's peers—is a mark of human social awareness, of
sensitivity to others": such language! it's enough to make any self-
respecting werewolf drop his pants in public and lope on back into
the forest).

But murderers and werewolves are exceptions, and generally
lovers—God bless them—deserve so much better than the rest of
us that for the best of them Marie reserves eternal youth and beauty
and unimpaired thighs and noses and love, love, love on the world-
lost isle of Avalun.

American Scholar Meets Japanese Stud

While engaged on his translation of *The Tale of Genji* Edward G. Seidensticker kept a diary from which he drew the extracts that make up *Genji Days*, which no doubt was published because the Japanese firm that published it wished to honor the in-every-way-meritorious translator of their thousand-year-old national treasure, and maybe they hadn't any editors fluent enough in English to recognize that his diary levels out at zilch minus eight, being less often casual and intimate (as diaries are supposed to be) than self-conscious, inert, and cheerless. During those years—the extracts run from 1970 to 1975—thinking about the job of translation gets set aside twice a day for thinking about such impenetrably collective matters as Vietnam, student militancy, Watergate or such sensational-sounding but disappointingly unexplicit personal matters as prowling the nocturnal Tokyo slums in search of kicks, sampling "porny movies," drinking too much, deploring "one's whole ugly fetid body," the usual diversions of a middle-aged American scholar who lives alone and doesn't like it in Tokyo, Honolulu, and Ann Arbor. There are at least three moments, though, that perforate the encircling torpor: a friend of his passes the open door of a classroom where Japanese are studying English and hears the question, "How much is your wife?"; a former U.S. Ambassador recalls riding to Haneda Airport with Vice-President Nixon, who turned to him and said, "Put on a hat. Only I go hatless"; and still another whizzing blivet (eleven pounds of shit in a ten-pound bag) from the Osric and Polonius of lit-crit, George Steiner—

Bob Brower brought, from the *New Yorker* of January 27, a review by George Steiner of *The Master of Go*. Mr. Steiner is puzzled by the book, and says that my introduction is uninformative. As for my translation, he calls himself incompetent to judge, but says that "it does exude a condign strangeness and ceremonial deportment." Are those not nice things to exude? Bob told me that when Laura first saw it she said, "Oh my, we mustn't show Ed"; and he replied, "Oh, go ahead and show him, but don't rub it in."

(George recently exuded yet another condign blivet in *The New Yorker* of December 8, 1980: "What," he cried anent the latest public exhibition he was making of himself, "are the sources of such scission?")

Of course, *Genji Days* also has things to say about *Genji*, and this part of the book is sparer and more professional, notably praiseworthy for not trying to paper over the translator's changes of opinion about one or another character or episode when, putting it into English, he decides it's worse or better than he had thought: "I have never much liked the Tamakazura sequence, centering upon a dry career-maker, . . . and I doubt that I am going to like it this time around either"; but, a week later, "I am beginning to like Tamakazura. I like the solidity and efficiency with which she arranges her life. I suppose the truth is that as I grow older I like the sane, businesslike ones more and more, and more and more distrust the romantics." Of whom the chief is the shining Genji himself, favorite son of the old Emperor, glory of the Court, cynosure of men, lover of women; and, though Seidensticker acknowledges that Genji is sometimes sensitive and kind, he keeps arguing not only that his hero is a trifler and a cad ("He is not a very nice guy") but that the author had too much of a schoolgirl crush on him to judge him correctly. Now nothing is clearer in the novel than that Tamakazura is equally and simultaneously "a dry career-maker" and a "sane, businesslike" woman without missing a trick of either, or that Genji is chief of the romantics and sensitive and kind and a trifler and a cad, or that the author is interested in quite everything that boys and girls are made of, sugar and spice as well as frogs and snails and puppydogs' tails.

For instance: having heard that the nurse who took care of him in his infancy and whom he hasn't seen for ages is very ill, Genji pays her a visit. As he waits to be admitted, he notices the house next door and, because of the position of the shutters and blinds (women were sequestered behind shutters, blinds, screens, curtains), "caught the outlines of pretty foreheads. . . . A pleasantly green vine was climbing a board wall. The white flowers, he thought [with a characteristic Genjian quirk of sensibility], had a rather self-satisfied look about them." He has one of his men pick a flower for him, whereupon a little girl runs out of the house with a fan and says, "Put it on this. It isn't much of a fan, but then it isn't much of a flower either." Afterward, in the room with the old nurse, there are solemn declarations ("In recent years there have been restrictions upon my movements," confides the great man, ". . . yet I become very depressed when the days go by and I do not see you. 'Would that there were on this earth no final partings' "); the old nurse sobs with joy ("Fond of the child she has reared, a nurse tends to look upon him as a paragon even if he is a half-wit. How much prouder was the old woman . . . for having been permitted to serve" her incomparable Genji); the scene would affect a heart of stone, and Genji is "deeply touched"; by the time he makes his departure, he and everybody else are weeping—"the scent of his sleeve, as he brushed away a tear, quite flooded the room" (robes of the elite of both sexes got doused with an individually blended perfume—"Cie is me"—just in advance of a formal occasion or a heavy date: once, preparing to zap his latest lovely, Genji "spent the whole day scenting his robes"):

> Genji left orders that prayers and services be resumed. As he went out he asked for a torch, and in its light examined the fan on which the "evening face" [the flower] had rested. It was permeated with a lady's perfume, elegant and alluring. On it was a poem in a disguised cursive hand that suggested breeding and taste. He was interested.
>
> > *"I think I need not ask whose face it is,*
> > *So bright, this evening face, in the shining dew."*
>
> "Who is living in the house to the west?" he asked Ko-

remitsu [his servant, the son of his old nurse]. "Have you
perhaps had occasion to inquire?"

At it again, thought Koremitsu. He spoke somewhat tartly.
"I must confess that these last few days I have been too busy
with my mother to think about her neighbors."

"You are annoyed with me. But this fan has the appearance
of something it might be interesting to look into. Make
inquiries, if you will, please, of someone who knows the
neighborhood."

At it again, grumbles Koremitsu G. Seidensticker, who can't tell
a churl from a charmer or the difference between a schoolgirl's
crush on a rock star and a novelist's alertness to the complications
of vitality.

His own translation belies him, and brings across to us a more
complicated hero than the translator seems willing to credit his
author with. (Whether his translation supersedes Arthur Waley's,
till now the only one in English, is a question I'll leave to others,
but of course Waley's translation—almost as old as this century—
is very much on Seidensticker's mind. He says that he "grew up
on it" and that he continues to admire it, but he presents evidence
to the effect that—whereas Waley omits, curtails, amplifies, and
alters—his own translation is faithful and complete. Reading Seidensticker's translation I didn't have the impression of reading a
novel unlike the one I more or less remembered from having read
Waley's translation thirty years ago. Anyhow, I was content to
enjoy Seidensticker's without checking back on Waley's: half a
million words multiplied by two are a lot of words. On his title
page Waley calls the author "Lady Murasaki," a convenience for
anybody thinking about the novel because its principal female
character is also called Murasaki; and, since the author was of an
aristocratic family and the title "Lady" sounds natural in English
for a woman of rank, I'll use it in preference to the name which
Seidensticker uses and by which she is known in Japan: Murasaki
Shikibu, which isn't her real name either. "Murasaki" isn't her
forename—which we don't know because "in Heian Japan it was
bad manners to record the names of wellborn ladies, except, cur-

iously, imperial consorts and princesses of the blood"—but means "purple" and may in fact have been given to her because she gave it to her heroine; "Shikibu" isn't her surname but designates the office her father held: so the name is a nickname or convenient tag, like "Jack the Ripper" or "Lady Murasaki.") Indebted to Seidensticker for this consistently lucid and idiomatic Englishing of a novel as long as *War and Peace* and scarcely known in the West, one doesn't like to seem ungrateful; but even the most modest translators are susceptible to proprietary delusions about the texts for the dissemination of which they've done their scrupulous and civilizing work. Keeping an eye on the words isn't the whole story, but maybe it ought to be for Seidensticker, who for instance can't help wondering whether Lady Murasaki has a "feminine" or a "masculine" point of view: a friend tells him cryptically that in Waley's translation it seems only masculine whereas in his it seems sometimes one and sometimes the other: he is perplexed (and so am I); and elsewhere he says curtly that he is "bored" by "The Broom Tree," a chapter through most of which on a rainy night four young men, including Genji and his best friend, have a meandering long-winded locker-room-and-men's-dorm-style bull-session about the peculiarities and limitations of women:

> "She was a woman of such accomplishments that I could leave everything to her. I continue to regret what I had done. I could discuss trivial things with her and important things. . . ."
>
> Tō no Chūjō nodded. ". . . it is not easy in this world to find a perfect wife. We are all pursuing the ideal and failing to find it."
>
> The guards officer talked on. "There was another one. I was seeing her at about the same time. She was more amiable than the one I have just described to you. Everything about her told of refinement. Her poems, her handwriting when she dashed off a letter, the koto she plucked a note on—everything seemed right. She was clever with her hands and clever with words. And her looks were adequate. The jealous woman's house had come to seem the place I could really call mine, and I went in secret to the other woman from time

to time and became very fond of her. The jealous one died,
I wondered what to do next. I was sad, of course, but a man
cannot go on being sad forever. I visited the other more often.
But there was something a little too aggressive, a little too
sensuous about her. As I came to know her well and to think
her a not very dependable sort, I called less often. And I
learned that I was not her only secret visitor. . . ."

They talk and listen till daybreak, and, whether the author's point
of view is masculine or feminine, she certainly seems to be in
touch with the quick of the men's fears and fantasies and to know
or guess just how such a session ebbs and flows in and out of
consciousness. The guards officer does most of the talking, and
in one of his more didactic moments he rattles off a volley of
platitudes about the risks of philandering: Tō no Chūjō, who is
not only Genji's best friend and jealous rival and envious inferior
but the brother of his neglected wife, listens carefully and hopes
tomcat Genji will take the lesson to heart; but "he was somewhat
annoyed to note that Genji was silent because he had fallen asleep."
Genji wakes up as soon as they get back to telling stories, but
it's too late for him to be edified. If only people would stay awake
during the lecture!
    Maybe what bothers Seidensticker (and Tō no Chūjō) most about
Genji is his elusiveness, his slipperiness, which seems a not very
heroic or masculine quality; but then in any conventional sense
Genji isn't a hero or even—except for his itch after women—
masculine (e.g. not a bit like Mr. Western Civilization, Shakespeare's Hamlet), he isn't explosive or ill-tempered or pugnacious,
indeed in the entire novel he is never once described as angry or
ready for a fight though he has numerous setbacks including a
several years' banishment; to get what he wants, he doesn't demand
but coaxes and cajoles and insists; he yearns and worries a lot;
when he is really caught in a corner he can be alarmed, terrified,
panicked, he can collapse in a funk; and maybe what bothers
Seidensticker most about Lady Murasaki is that dealing with Genji
she's as slippery as he is, she isn't categorical with him, she neither
condones nor condemns, far from being goggle-eyed with adoration

she is playful and ironic when he's having his way, solicitous when he's in trouble, gravely sympathetic when he's up against the final and irrevocable things and behaving no better than the rest of us.

Because, as the affair with the lady of the house of the "evening faces" demonstrates, life isn't simple for Genji, fun is fun but doesn't stop there, not only is the best none too good but the worst is yet to come and nobody's ready for it. At the outset Genji has his customary success imposing himself on the lady (what the men of the time—even Genji—had to do, according to the author, was knock down several screens and elbow a few maidservants out of the way and commit a kind of soft-shelled rape), but then discovers to his surprise that he isn't free as the breeze, he "had grown fond of her and felt that he must go on seeing her. They were of such different ranks, he tried to tell himself, and it was altogether too frivolous. Yet his visits were frequent." As with all of Genji's other women, there is no indication that he ever excites her to a frenzy, which moreover doesn't seem a prospect that occurs to him (or to her); like the guards officer he distrusts "aggressive" and "sensuous" women; what he wants is to be indulged: "Won over by his gentle warmth, she was indeed inclined to let him have his way. She seemed such a pliant little creature, likely to submit absolutely to the most outrageous demands." Besides, she lives in a working-class neighborhood and Genji is fascinated by the unfamiliar surroundings: "Toward dawn he was awakened by plebeian voices in the shabby houses down the street. . . . He could make out every word. It embarrassed the woman that, so near at hand, there should be this clamor of preparation as people set forth on their sad little enterprises. Had she been one of the stylish ladies of the world, she would have wanted to shrivel up and disappear. She was a placid sort, however, and she seemed to take nothing . . . too seriously." On a whim he carries her off out of the bustling street to an isolated and creepy villa, where during the night he has a dream of a beautiful woman who reproaches him for his infidelity and seems to threaten the sleeping lady by his side. He rouses the attendants; certainly there are evil spirits that have been provoked and must be warded off:

He reached for the girl. She was not breathing. He lifted her and she was limp in his arms. There was no sign of life. She had seemed as defenseless as a child, and no doubt some evil power had taken possession of her. He could think of nothing to do. A man came with a torch. Ukon [her servant] was not prepared to move, and Genji himself pulled up curtain frames to hide the girl.

"Bring the light closer."

It was a most unusual order. Not ordinarily permitted at Genji's side, the man hesitated to cross the threshold.

"Come, come, bring it here! There is a time and place for ceremony."

In the torchlight he had a fleeting glimpse of a figure by the girl's pillow. It was the woman in his dream. It faded away like an apparition in an old romance. In all the fright and horror, his confused thoughts centered upon the girl. There was no room for thoughts of himself.

He knelt over her and called out to her, but she was cold and had stopped breathing. It was too horrible. He had no confidant to whom he could turn for advice. It was the clergy one thought of first on such occasions. He had been so brave and confident, but he was young, and this was too much for him. He clung to the lifeless body.

"Come back, my dear, my dear. Don't do this awful thing to me." But she was cold and no longer seemed human.

The worst has come and he isn't ready for it: "All was silence, terrifying solitude. He should not have chosen such a place—but it was too late now. Trembling violently, Ukon clung to him. He held her in his arms, wondering if she might be about to follow her lady." At last the reliable Koremitsu arrives, and begins to cope with what might turn out to be a dreadful scandal that would shatter Genji's career and break his father's heart: Koremitsu will carry the body to a mountain temple where he has an acquaintance and where a discreet funeral can be held—"Since Genji seemed incapable of the task, he wrapped the body in a covering and lifted it into the carriage. It was very tiny and very pretty, and not at all repellent. The wrapping was loose and the hair

streamed forth, as if to darken the world before Genji's eyes."
Later, over Koremitsu's objections, he rides "in the bleakest despair" through the night to the temple: "The light was turned
away from the corpse. Ukon lay behind a screen. It must be terrible
for her, thought Genji. The girl's face was unchanged and very
pretty. 'Won't you let me hear your voice again?' He took her
hand. 'What was it that made me give you all my love, for so
short a time, and then made you leave me to this misery?' He
was weeping uncontrollably." On the way back to the city, "as
they came to the river Genji fell from his horse and was unable
to remount, 'So I am to die by the wayside? I doubt that I can
go on.' " But Koremitsu is there, and "Genji somehow pulled
himself together . . . and was seen back to Nijō." Eventually he
brings Ukon into his household, and often talks with her about
their dead lady:

> ". . . She seemed so weak [says Ukon], but I can see now
> that she was a source of strength."
> "The weak ones do have a power over us. The clear, forceful
> ones I can do without. I am weak and indecisive by nature
> myself, and a woman who is quiet and withdrawn and follows
> the wishes of a man even to the point of letting herself be
> used has much the greater appeal. A man can shape and mold
> her as he wishes, and becomes fonder of her all the while."

Surely this is one of the most extraordinary self-assessments by
any romantic hero in literature, all the more extraordinary for
being accurate. It also foretells Genji's decision to cheat the chan-
ciness of love, when he abducts the beautiful child Murasaki to
keep her for himself and shape and mold her as he wishes:

> Though trembling violently, the girl managed to keep from
> sobbing aloud.
> "I always sleep with Shōnagon," she said softly in childish
> accents.
> "Imagine a big girl like you still sleeping with her nurse."
> Weeping quietly, the girl lay down.
> Shōnagon sat up beside them, looking out over the garden
> as dawn came on. The buildings and grounds were magnif-

icent, and the sand in the garden was like jewels. Not used
to such affluence, she was glad there were not other women
in this west wing. It was here that Genji received occasional
callers. A few guards beyond the blinds were the only
attendants.

They were speculating on the identity of the lady he had
brought with him. "Someone worth looking at, you can bet."

But for once they are off the mark, Genji's plans this time are
long-range, and he is determined to see to the last detail of
everything:

He asked that children be sent from the east wing to play
with her. "Pretty little girls, please." Four little girls came
in, very pretty indeed.

The new girl, his Murasaki, still lay huddled under the
singlet he had thrown over her.

"You are not to sulk, now, and make me unhappy. Would
I have done all this for you if I were not a nice man? Young
ladies should do as they are told." And so the lessons
began. . . .

Staying away from court for several days, Genji worked
hard to make her feel at home. He wrote down all manner
of poems for her to copy, and drew all manner of pictures,
some of them very good. "I sigh, though I have not seen
Musashi," he wrote on a bit of lavender paper. She took it
up, and thought the hand marvelous. In a tiny hand he wrote
beside it:

> *"Thick are the dewy grasses of Musashi,*
> *Near this grass to the grass I cannot have."*

"Now you must write something."

"But I can't." She looked up at him, so completely without
affectation that he had to smile.

He steals her and brings her up and, almost as soon as she comes
to puberty, without a pang of conscience or any preparation de-
flowers her (an event that particularly vexes Seidensticker) and so
can claim her as doubly his own—

He no longer had any enthusiasm for the careless night wanderings that had once kept him busy. Murasaki was much on his mind. She seemed peerless, the nearest he could imagine to his ideal. Thinking that she was no longer too young for marriage, he had occasionally made amorous overtures; but she had not seemed to understand. They had passed their time in games of Go and *hentsugi.* She was clever and she had many delicate ways of pleasing him in the most trivial diversions. He had not seriously thought of her as a wife. Now he could not restrain himself. It would be a shock, of course.

What had happened? Her women had no way of knowing when the line had been crossed. One morning Genji was up early and Murasaki had stayed on and on in bed. It was not at all like her to sleep so late. Might she be unwell? As he left for his own rooms, Genji pushed an inkstone inside her curtains.

At length, when no one else was near, she raised herself from her pillow and saw beside it a tightly folded bit of paper. Listlessly she opened it. There was only this verse, in a casual hand:

> *"Many have been the nights we have spent together*
> *Purposelessly, these coverlets between us."*

She had not dreamed he had anything of the sort on his mind. What a fool she had been, to repose her whole confidence in so gross and unscrupulous a man.

It was almost noon when Genji returned. "They say you're not feeling well. What can be the trouble? I was hoping for a game of Go."

She pulled the covers over her head. Her women discreetly withdrew. He came up beside her.

"What a way to behave, what a very unpleasant way to behave. Try to imagine, please, what these women are thinking."

He drew back the covers. She was bathed in perspiration and the hair at her forehead was matted from weeping.

"Dear me. This does not augur well at all." He tried in

every way he could think of to comfort her, but she seemed genuinely upset and did not offer so much as a word in reply.

(Nowhere else in the book does the author present a woman's reaction to the sex act; and the reaction here, no doubt justified by the circumstances, is indignation and disgust.) Women! says Genji. Men! says Genji's author: "Genji felt like a child thief. The role amused him and the affection he now felt for the girl seemed to reduce his earlier affection to the tiniest mote. A man's heart is a very strange amalgam indeed! He now thought that he could not bear to be away from her for a single night."

But he can bear it all right. "Felt like"; "seemed"; "thought that he could not": this world of shadows and appearances which isn't to be credited except for the momentary pleasures it offers. What Genji keeps saying but till he outlives her can't imagine is that he has met his match. The child grows up into the beautiful, loving, and ironic woman who knows him as well as her namesake the author does, who by her presence and example rejoices him as none of his other women can, but for whom as for the others he has the automatic words and gestures that scarcely try to hide his need to be somewhere else with somebody else sooner rather than later:

> She [it really doesn't matter which of his various protégées this is] pleased him more and more. "There is something singularly appealing about her," he said to Murasaki. "Her mother was a little too solemn and humorless. She is very quick and bright, and somehow a person immediately wants to be friends with her. I am very sure now that she will not be an embarrassment."
>
> Familiar with his inability to let well enough alone, she had guessed what was happening. "It must be rather difficult for her not to have any secrets and to be so completely dependent on you."
>
> "And why should she not be dependent on me?"
>
> She smiled. "Can you think that I have forgotten all the sighs and pains your way of doing things produced in my own younger years?"

How quick she was! "You find very odd and foolish things to worry about. Do you think she would permit anything of the sort?" He changed the subject . . .

—and he can always turn that dazzling light on: "Genji is so handsome," says Tō no Chūjō irritably, "that a smile from him can make you think all the world's problems have been solved." When, because he can't say no to the former emperor or to his own erotic curiosity, Genji takes a royal princess for a wife and thereby demotes Murasaki to second place, he returns from a visit with his new wife and "was filled with wonder at the more familiar lady":

> They had been together for so many years, and here she was delighting him anew. She managed with no loss of dignity— and it was a noble sort of dignity—to be bright and humorous. He counted over the several aspects of beauty and found them here gathered together; and she was at her loveliest. But then she always seemed her loveliest, more beautiful each year than the year before, today than yesterday. It was her power of constant renewal that most filled him with wonder.
>
> She slipped her jottings under an inkstone. He took them up. The writing was not perhaps her very best, but it had great charm and subtlety.

> > *"I detect a change in the green upon the hills.*
> > *Is autumn coming to them? Is it coming to me?"*

He wrote beside it, as if he too were at writing practice:

> > *"No change do we see in the white of the waterfowl.*
> > *Not so constant the lower leaves of the hagi."*

> She might write of her unhappiness, but she did not let it show. He thought her splendid.
>
> Free this evening of obligations at Rokujō, he decided to hazard another secret visit to Nijō. Self-loathing was not enough to overcome temptation.

Self-loathing is something new, but along with love and beauty it too isn't enough to keep him at home nights.

"The shining Genji was dead," writes the author not much later, when *The Tale of Genji* still has a third of its way to go, "and there was no one quite like him." With such a hero, the book is necessarily episodic in its structure: Genji isn't on a quest, doesn't limit himself to the one and only peerless lady (though he knows who she is and congratulates himself for having her around), doesn't defend a citadel or win a war or face a villain and face him down; all he does, besides taking his turn at running the country, is make love over and over again, because like a god he has the will and the power and nothing much else to do. Lady Murasaki magnificently imagines a man who has everything, even a wife both Galatea and Penelope, but at last he proves to be something of a bore not only to himself but to the author and the reader. Though she may have set out to give us a model and exemplar, she ends by showing that life is resistance, that the young Genji meets enough of it to keep himself and us occupied, but that as he gets older and the barriers fall away he finds himself, though more beautiful than ever, doing what he does because not desire and adventure but habit and momentum are stronger than love and loyalty; and by the time he is merely going through the motions so is Lady Murasaki. Authors sometimes lose heart at the same instant as their protagonists.

Lady Murasaki certainly doesn't have a crush on Genji, she isn't taken in by him, but like her namesake in the novel she loves him and therefore his fall is hers and brings a twilight down on the rest of the book. It's as if, having shown against her original intention—probably she wanted to write the life of the sexiest man in the world—that even for the sexiest man in the world life is resistance, she will now show with a kind of lover's spite, Genji being gone forever, that life is sad; and, whatever its truth, this is a far less absorbing and less dramatic proposition.

Seidensticker has many favorable things to say about the so-called "Uji chapters," the post-Genji section of the book; moreover it's easy to agree with him that the episode of Ukifune's dilemma, in which, unable to choose between her two importunate lovers, she attempts suicide, is the best in the section and—tense, sustained, unsentimental—among the best in the novel: "the obvious solution was for her to disappear." Nevertheless it's a very somber episode, and leads without a break into ever darker and deeper gloom, abysses of renunciation and piety without hope or joy. Besides he not only grants but emphasizes the obnoxiousness of the protagonist of this section: Kaoru (supposed by society to be Genji's son but in fact the son of his royal wife by another man), "saying the same thing over and over again at endless length"; "next to unbearable"; "an almost comic figure, all censorious and self-righteous"; "maybe nastiness is the nearest thing to a human trait that he has": in other words, though the translator doesn't say so, Hamlet without a pretext. The other important male character is Niou, Genji's grandson and Kaoru's best friend; and the two of them together make up a cruel because rather near parody of Genji: Life is a swindle. Both of them have exactly the same line as Genji (maybe it was the only way to get next to a highborn Japanese lady): Let me come into your parlor, said the spider to the fly, I'm all heart and no hands, you can trust me if you try; Move a little closer to the blinds or curtains, I can hardly hear you; Thud! clatter! bang! (the screens, blinds, curtains lifted up and pushed aside and bouncing on the tatami mats) but goodness gracious I'd rather die than do anything improper though I notice I'm clutching your instep: Niou, high-pitched and lightweight, races through the process like a speeded-up film with a Donald-Duck voice quacking out the flagrant Genjian fibs till the deed is done, whereas Kaoru intones them all in a voice of mournful sanctimony, slowed down to sound like Smokey Bear, and then— nothing but more talk: "The dawn came on, bringing an end to nothing. . . . 'Do you know what I would like [says Kaoru]? To be as we are now. To look out at the flowers and the moon, and be with you. To spend our days together, talking of things that do not matter.' " And do you know what the author would like? Three quarters of an hour with the young Genji; but he's dead and gone.

Another difference between the Uji section and the life of Genji is that, while the former resembles a chamber opera for three voices and small chorus, the latter teems with secondary characters who take the stage with all the assurance of prima donnas and leading tenors: Tō no Chūjō, a man's man and therefore always busy and never in doubt; Yugiri, Genji's shrewd and resentful son, on whom

his father's charm doesn't make a dent because Yugiri intends to
take over the territory ("People seem a little curious about your
reasons for being so good to her," he says to Genji, who isn't
accustomed to such bluntness and has to bob and weave for a
moment); the pious old monk self-exiled to a remote island whose
sole ambition, which he pursues with the zeal and cunning of a
child movie star's mother, is to see his daughter safely installed
in a liaison with Genji (who is very conscientious about his past
ladies: keeps them comfortably pensioned off in one or another
wing of his palace and occasionally spends a night for old times'
sake); Genji's wicked stepmother, Kokiden, whose hatred of him
and influence over her son the emperor bring about Genji's banishment; the apparently trapped and abject Tamakazura, who
manages to scatter everybody else's projects in favor of her own;
Higekuro announcing to his mad wife that he'll be fetching home
another wife—

Taking up a censer, she directed the perfuming of his
robes. . . . It was rather wonderful that they had lived together for so long. He felt a little guilty that he should have
lost himself so quickly and completely in an infatuation. But
he was more and more restless as the hours went by. . . .

His attendants were nervous. "The snow seems to be letting
up a little," said one of them, as if to himself. "It is very
late."

Moku and Chūjō and the others sighed and lay down and
whispered to one another about the pity of it all. The lady
herself, apparently quite composed, was leaning against an
armrest. Suddenly she stood up, swept the cover from a large
censer, stepped behind her husband, and poured the contents
over his head. There had been no time to restrain her. The
women were stunned.

The powdery ashes bit into his eyes and nostrils. Blinded,
he tried to brush them away, but found them so clinging
and stubborn that he had to throw off even his underrobes.
If she had not had the excuse of derangement he would have
marched from her presence and vowed never to return. It was
a very perverse sort of spirit that possessed her.

The stir was enormous. He was helped into new clothes, but it was as if he had had a bath of ashes. There were ashes deep in his side whiskers. . . .

Who except a great novelist writing in the heyday of a tradition could conceive of such moments? Yet without a precedent, six centuries before Cervantes and in a feudal empire on the other side of the world, Lady Murasaki is inventing the novel—that middle-class European document—and such moments come to her as naturally and as often as in the heyday of the tradition they will come to Dickens.

This densely populated novel is also crowded with descriptions of festivals, concerts, dances, an art-judging contest, rituals, ceremonies, palaces, nunneries, the four seasons with their changing scenery—of all of which a sizable proportion seems intended for a more leisurely temperament of an earlier time. But Genji or one of the others is in the wings, and anything can happen. Maybe the next time Murasaki speaks Genji will listen. Maybe the next time Genji speaks and says nothing Murasaki will keep a speculative eye on the large censer just behind him.

The
Immoral
Hero-Worshipper

On the evidence of his journals, in which he records "nineteen attacks of urethritis, almost all of them acute, almost all following sexual exposure, and [? almost all] almost certainly gonococcal in origin (see table, pp. 40-42)," Boswell was another undiscriminating fucker: such is the professional opinion of William B. Ober, M.D. (so styled on the title page of *Boswell's Clap and Other Essays*, a piece of science-fiction in which fiction predominates). "By applying the retrospectoscope," Ober will also "show a number of ways whereby medical information and insights can illuminate and perhaps resolve certain literary problems," one of which he resolves to his own satisfaction by discriminating between godlike creation and mere slavish copying ("Boswell's virtue for the medical historian is one of his limitations as a writer: he lacked creative imagination. Adept at recreating a scene based on real events, he could not create one out of whole cloth. . . . As a corrective to those who would rate his literary gift too highly . . ."); but literary problems are less to his taste than moral ones: e.g. how to discriminate between undiscriminating and discriminating fuckers—

One might view these first two attacks as merely the price paid for the exuberance of delayed fulfillment of adolescent sexuality, and dismiss them as nothing more. It is even difficult to fault Boswell for incurring his third attack, as he took reasonable precautions. But during the two years he passed in Edinburgh studying law, he managed to have affairs with four women and to father an illegitimate child on Peggy Doig, a servant girl. . . .

By this time Ober, who obviously gets his jollies daydreaming about high performance and low chambermaids, is worked up enough to quote a "penetrating" remark by Boswell's biographer, Frederick A. Pottle: "he enjoyed confessing so much that . . . the sacrament of penance might have been only another opportunity for self-indulgence"—quite as biographers and critics so much enjoy penetrating their subjects' sex lives that, incapable of sympathy or discrimination, they will say the dumbest things, they will even play doctor, to have a pretext for doing it. "Why," asks Ober, "should a man of good family, considerable education, adequate professional status, a satisfactory wife, and prominent social connections deliberately expose himself to the risk of gonorrhea?" and of course he produces an answer, which needn't detain us.

Like William B. Ober, M.D., Donald Greene, Ph.D. (not so styled on the title page of "A Bear by the Tail: The Genesis of the Boswell Industry," *Studies in Burke and His Time*, XVIII, pp. 114-127) is very cross with, nay hard on, Boswell for his "Castle Hill prostitutes" and his "claps" (is bored and peckish with the monotony of it all, demands some color, colors it snot-Greene), erects stiff arguments against Boswell's pretensions to literary significance: "what," ejaculates Greene, "was intended to be the cause of the excitement [when Boswell's journals were first printed fifty years ago]? That of learning the details of the day-to-day existence of a neurotic and not very successful Scottish lawyer and literary dabbler?" But Johnson himself, having read extensively in Boswell's journals, said they were excellently written and continuously entertaining, that indeed they might well be printed *if they were suitable for print*—by which he meant that only their candor about living persons and their freedom of language made them unsuitable. Besides, Johnson regarded Boswell as a lovable man and a good man: "Boswell was never in any body's company who did not wish to see him again"; "If I were in distress, there is no man I would come to so soon as you." Poor Greene isn't content with setting Johnson straight, he's determined not to be taken for a prude so he compares Boswell unfavorably to another randy journal-keeper, Pepys, who (says Greene) "had an enormous and intelligent interest in music, drama, painting, architecture, and much else," but Pepys won't help: Greene is an eighteenth-century specialist and can't be expected to have read anything in the seventeenth, but the hearsay on which he bases his attitude toward Pepys is incorrect— Pepys was an enormously inquisitive man with a lot of self-serving shrewdness, little intelligence, less morality, and no taste at all, whose comments about the arts are mercifully brief and invariably imbecile: *Romeo and Juliet* is "the worst [play] that ever I heard in my life"; *The Adventures of Five Hours* is "the best play I ever saw"; *Twelfth Night* is "but a silly play and not relating at all to the name or day." Greene does, though, rather sound like Pepys when he concludes that Boswell would never have been heard of "if it had not been for his luck in making the acquaintance of Samuel Johnson"—i.e. if he hadn't written the best biography ever. (If Chaucer hadn't written *Troilus and Criseyde* and *The Canterbury Tales*, he would be far less well known today.) And if Boswell hadn't written the *Journal of a Tour of the Hebrides with Samuel Johnson, LL.D.*, one of the three best travel books (together with Lawrence's *Twilight in Italy* and *Sea and Sardinia*) in English. And the most continuously entertaining journals ever, mines of observation and discrimination and right feeling—

Alison . . . told me that he remembered to have seen my Grandfather, a big, strong, Gothick looking man; and that he was present in the General Assembly when . . . some of the young Clergy spoke very slightingly of the Common People as unfit to judge of their teachers, there being a Cause under consideration in which the People were concerned. That my Grandfather got up and said, "Moderator, I am an old Man; and I remember the time when the Gospel was not so easy as it is now. But those who wished to hear it according to their conscience were subject to persecution. Several of those I myself have seen. But amongst them were not many rich, not many noble. They were mostly Common people, whom we here have heard treated with much contempt this day." Mr. Alison said *a Vote* was immediately called, and it was carried for the people by a great majority. He said What my Grandfather spoke had a great effect. He was a man of weight. I was pleased thus accidentally to hear another good Anecdote in addition to many which I have heard of my Grandfather. (19 September 1778)

Greene, who isn't a specialist in bibliography, may be excused for not understanding that that paragraph is worth more than the contents of all the books and articles listed in the *PMLA* Bibliography of Literary Scholarship of just about any given year; but he really ought to have been told that the four preëminent English writers of the eighteenth century are Pope, Richardson, Johnson, and Boswell.

The quack doctors of literature help us recognize greatness by their instinctive hostility to any sign of it; and so they doubly detest Boswell, who is both great himself and incapable of resisting signs of greatness in others. In 1765, during his grand tour of Europe, having already sought out and interviewed Voltaire and Rousseau, Boswell learned from Rousseau that "The Corsicans have actually applied to him to give them a set of laws," and he grew interested enough to pay a visit to the island where Pasquale de Paoli was leading his people in their fight for independence from the Genoese and the French. Eventually, in 1768, Boswell published *An Account of Corsica, The Journal of a Tour to that Island, and Memoirs of Pascal Paoli*, which not only made him a famous writer ("Corsica Boswell") but Paoli a hero to the English reading public and even a force in English politics. Of the three books Boswell published during his lifetime, the first was on Paoli and the latter two on Johnson: he was a hero-worshipper, and his two paramount and lifelong heroes were Johnson, about whom we know, and Paoli, about whom Joseph Foladare's fine and necessary book, *Boswell's Paoli*, tells us what we would like to know—who he was, why he no longer occupies a visible place in the history of Europe, and (the quacks bristle all their feathers) where his place was in Boswell's life, affections, and prodigious need to admire and be acknowledged.

And in his capacity for sustaining as well as attracting the affections of the great and good, so that, when Paoli the exile arrives in London four years after the week that Boswell spent with him in Corsica, their reunion (as Foladare cites Boswell's account of it in the journals)

suggests an experience quite as memorable as the first meeting
with Johnson. The footman made difficulties; the valet, when
he heard "My name is Boswell," gave a jump, "catched hold
of my hand and kissed it . . . [and] opening the door of the
General's bedchamber, [he] called out, 'Mr. Boswell.' I heard
the General give a shout before I saw him. When I entered
he was in his night-gown and nightcap. He ran to me, took
me all in his arms, and held me there for some time. I cannot
describe my feelings on meeting him again" (22 September). . . . Boswell reflected: "As I [had] hardly hoped to meet
Paoli in this world again, I had a curious imagination as if
I had passed through death, and was really in Elysium. . . .
I was filled with admiration whenever the General spoke. I
said that after every sentence spoken by him I felt an inclination to sing *Te Deum*. Indeed, when he speaks it is a
triumph to human Nature, and to my friendship."

No doubt Paoli's gratitude for Boswell's book, which had been
published a year before, played a part; but Paoli wasn't ordinarily
a demonstrative man, and Boswell tended to have this electrifying
effect on his friends (on Johnson for instance). As for Boswell's
own transports here, he is shamelessly proud of them, and as
frantic as anybody in love, and as usual if not "a triumph to human
nature" at least a credit to it: he congratulates himself for his
intimacy with such a man, for being *capable* of intimacy with such
a man, and he is right to feel so and surrenders nothing of the
vividness of his feelings by exulting over his capacity to have them
and his need to set them down on the page.

Twenty-three years later Paoli has been back in Corsica for three
years, with every appearance of stable temporal power and immortal
glory: but it is 1793, and, though Corsica is supposed to be
virtually autonomous under the protection of the new French constitutional monarchy, Louis XVI and his family are already under
arrest; Paoli's opposition to the extreme measures of the Directory
has become unmistakable (three years earlier, "greeted . . . with
wild applause" in the National Assembly as he visited Paris on
his way back to his homeland, he had been effusively saluted by
the deputy—not yet chief executioner—Robespierre: "You de-

fended freedom when we did not even dare to hope for it"); the Buonaparte family (including the young Napoleon), once lieutenants and unbending partisans of Paoli's, are about to desert their leader and Corsica to seek their fortunes in revolutionary France; the Directory is about to issue a warrant for Paoli's arrest; and Paoli receives letters from Boswell that have been delayed for a year and more, which inform him that Boswell is understandably brimming with enthusiasm for political circumstances ("so amiable and so glorious a restoration . . . almost equal to any of the delightful stories of Romance") that have been long outmoded by the dire recent events in France, is pleased by the publication and favorable reception of the *Life of Johnson* (of which he sends a copy), is preoccupied as usual with personal doubts and fears, is stricken often with fits of melancholy (his old complaint, but aggravated by the death of his wife the year before Paoli had left England), all of which he confides to the man Foladare properly calls one of his two "surrogate fathers" (and, at that, the kindlier and more instantly forgiving one): "In such a situation, I peculiarly feel the want of your Excellency's most hospitable house in Portman Square, in which I at all times found consolation." "Boswell's appalling obtuseness," comments Foladare,

> in not even faintly imagining the desperate concerns of one in Paoli's situation, his failure to recall that Paoli in his life had one "great object" [the freedom of Corsica]—or worse yet, his implied conclusion that that object had already been achieved—these must have disappointed the General, but disappointment doubtless immediately gave way to sadness. Paoli's reply . . . displays the old warmth but quite naturally places matters in a new perspective, and not only because France had declared war on England some weeks earlier. "When I have a little time to myself I shall send for your *Magnum Opus*, to peruse it and to be in imagination with you and with so many good friends mentioned in it." He writes of the dangerous disease from which he is still convalescing, and of the renewed demonstrations of the people's loyalty and affection. "Through fatal misfortune our nations are now at war. Could they have agreed on their plans all Europe would

have become free in a short time. Providence, which rules
over the Fate of Nations, will untangle this knot. Our vision
is too limited for us to discover the means by which it will
bring peace to the poor peoples oppressed by the ambition
and pushed to the brink of ruin by the ignorance of their
leaders. . . . I embrace you and your sons, and I should like
to say a thousand things to your lovable daughters, to make
them accept my attentions." Imagine Paoli's not dropping
everything to read the *Life of Johnson*! . . .

"Appalling obtuseness" or not—and the term seems excessive for
an eternally unsettled young man (not less young or unsettled at
the age of fifty-one) pouring out his heart to his loving and beloved
"father," even if Papa is at the moment engaged in the task of
being the father of his country and the conscience of Europe—
nevertheless it didn't turn Paoli sour or distant, *he* wouldn't have
called it "appalling obtuseness," because he loved Boswell and
didn't feel the obligation to reprimand him for a tactless word or
a drinking bout or a tumble with a Castle Hill prostitute.

Foladare's tone is quite on target, however, when he dryly
summarizes Boswell's description of the first meeting between Paoli
and Johnson, in Boswell's breathless words "illustrious men such
as humanity produces a few times in the revolution of many ages"
(and the silly man was *right!*):

Boswell's record conveys nothing earthshaking; but the meeting was satisfactory enough for any admirer of Johnson or
Paoli. "They met with a manly ease, mutually conscious of
their own abilities and of the abilities one of each other. The
General spoke Italian and Dr. Johnson English, and understood one another very well with a little aid of interpretation
from me, in which I compared myself to an isthmus which
joins two great continents." Paoli, as might have been expected, paid the first gracious compliment, but Johnson
lagged scarcely a breath behind. Paoli introduced the subjects
for discussion. The first naturally arose from Johnson's reputation as a lexicographer. The second had been set up by
Boswell four years earlier in Corsica. . . . On the General's
observations concerning language Johnson commented, "Sir,

you talk of language as if you had never done anything else
but study it, instead of governing a nation." After an exchange
of compliments the General "asked him what he thought of
the spirit of infidelity which was so prevalent." Paoli now
as always showed himself a pious man—no trouble with Johnson here. . . . Johnson went home with Boswell and drank
tea till late in the night. He said "General Paoli had the
loftiest port of any man he had ever seen."

They never became intimates, but over the next fifteen years (till
Johnson's death) they often met at dinner parties and sometimes
went off toward a private corner together to worry about Boswell's
drinking (Boswell never dared tell Johnson about his whoring,
though Paoli had listened to many a tale). There is no evidence
of Johnson's ever speaking disrespectfully of Paoli, though in the
normal course of a Johnsonian riposte he could figuratively knock
him in the head; but Paoli (as Boswell notes) for all his veneration
of Johnson could make perceptive if not entirely fair qualifications:
"Johnson is like a God who is either damning you or giving his
orders with awe. He is not like Jupiter, who lets Thetis sit on
his knee and play with his chin"; "What is upright is good for
supporting a building but does not ply to other uses"; or, with
exasperation, "That damned dictionary-making. He is all definitions"; and Boswell himself, thinking of Paoli's limitless forbear-
ance and responsiveness, remarked in a journal entry that "amidst
all my admiration of . . . [Johnson's] great talents, I recollected
how Sir John Pringle objected that he had not wisdom for giving
counsel." Nobody's perfect.

On June 19, 1794 Paoli, having renounced the authority of
revolutionary France,

in the name of the Corsican people tendered the crown of
Corsica to His Majesty the King of Great Britain, represented
by Sir Gilbert Elliot as his Minister plenipotentiary. The
Assembly named Paoli President. . . . The resilience, the
stubborn endurance of Paoli's battered capacity for hope broke
forth in his final exclamation: "Blessed, blessed, O my com-
patriots, the blood which your fathers spilled, that which you
yourselves have shed for freedom; blessed the wounds, the

hardships, the persecution, all the misfortune that you have
suffered for it: here is the fulfillment of the prayers of our
forefathers, here is the end of our sighs, our wrongs: *la patria*
is free, *la patria* is independent: now there is a Corsica."

But the great peroration was only the shadow of an already lost
hope. Because his mere presence was a thorn in the side of the
fatuous and vindictive British viceroy, Paoli had to be "invited"
to resume his exile in England; the British would soon ignobly
withdraw without a battle; and, under the Corsican renegade
Napoleon, the French would retake the island. In London almost
all his old friends were dead, and he was among strangers:

> "the contempt which they show toward me here no longer
> gives me so much pain. I am old; my principal concern must
> be to leave the memory of my character. . . . I must place
> my consolation in the hope that posterity will be more just
> to me, or at least more indulgent. . . ." As for the affairs
> of the world, he knew no more of them than was reported
> in the periodicals. "If I had to form a judgment, I would
> say that there is no likelihood of peace. . . . I strongly fear
> that this war . . . will spread and endure as long as that
> which ended in the peace at Westphalia."

The war lasted eighteen more years, till Waterloo, not quite the
thirty he bitterly predicted but long enough. He died and was
buried in London; but

> One hundred years after the first Corsican delegation had gone
> to London to escort Paoli back to his island, another came,
> this time to convey his remains to Morosaglia [his birthplace].
> The *London Times* for 2 September 1889 described the cere-
> monies, which had taken place on 31 August, in detail. "The
> exhumation was conducted beneath a marquee erected over
> the tomb, the floor and sides of which were heavily draped
> in mourning. . . ." After the coffin had been closed and sealed
> it was taken from the marquee to a hearse and subsequently
> to the church of St. Louis de Gonzague, where a requiem
> mass was conducted. "The church was heavily draped in black,
> and over the coffin, which rested on the catafalque opposite

the altar, was placed a magnificent Roman pall, while at the head was deposited a wreath from the Empress Eugénie, on the ribbon of which was the following: 'Au grand Patriote Corse.' " The coffin then began its long journey home.

While the viceroy was plotting to bring about Paoli's second English exile, Boswell died in London. His editor, Edmond Malone, in a private letter wrote his own Boswell obituary fondly and with the touch of condescension it was impossible for decent but unimaginative people to avoid feeling toward Boswell:

> I suppose you know poor Boswell died on Tuesday Morning, without any pain. I don't think he at any time of his illness knew his danger. I shall miss him more and more every day. He was in the constant habit of calling on me almost daily, and I used to grumble sometimes at his turbulence, but now miss and regret his noise and his hilarity and his perpetual good humour, which had no bounds. Poor fellow, he has somehow stolen away from us, without any notice, and without my being at all prepared for it.

Boswell went quietly because, though he was always in search of heroes, he never took himself for one.

The
Moral
Hero

Johnson reacts with a bang or merely broods, he doesn't dispose his efforts for the sake of sustained effects, he's a great writer only when he hasn't time to think. His sufficient provocation is any mass of particulars that will take his mind quite off itself: the words of his Dictionary demanding their definitions and illustrative citations; the *Lives of the Poets* compelling him to produce assessments of a miscellany of poems by his subjects and make practical inquiries in search of data, recollections, gossip, anecdote, "something to say [as he observes in a letter to Mrs. Thrale] about men of whom I know nothing but their verses, and sometimes very little of them"; Shakespeare's text, for which Johnson, assembling his edition of it, has to work up his explanatory notes that from the day they were published have constituted the one readable book of Shakespeare commentary; or, best of all, conversation, in which, though the topics may be general, at all events his cronies are such specific and irresistible quarry that he can run them down ("toss and gore" them, says Boswell) without even resorting to pen and paper:

> Talking of our feeling for the distresses of others;—JOHNSON. "Why, Sir, there is much noise made about it, but it is greatly exaggerated. No, Sir, we have a certain degree of feeling to prompt us to do good: more than that, Providence does not intend. It would be misery to no purpose." BOSWELL. "But suppose now, Sir, that one of your intimate friends were apprehended for an offense for which he might be hanged." JOHNSON. "I should do what I could to bail

him, and give him any other assistance; but if he were once fairly hanged, I should not suffer." BOSWELL. "Would you eat your dinner that day, Sir?" JOHNSON. "Yes, Sir; and eat it as if he were eating with me. Why, there's Baretti, who is to be tried for his life to-morrow, friends have risen up for him on every side; yet if he should be hanged, none of them will eat a slice of plumb-pudding the less. Sir, that sympathetic feeling goes a very little way in depressing the mind."

At this moment Johnson may well be ready for a change or a tea break, but crafty Boswell has the trick of converting Johnson's full stops into semicolons:

I told him that I had dined lately at Foote's, who shewed me a letter which he had received from Tom Davies, telling him that he had not been able to sleep from the concern which he felt on account of *"This sad affair of Baretti,"* begging of him to try if he could suggest any thing that might be of service; and, at the same time, recommending to him an industrious young man who kept a pickle-shop. JOHNSON. "Ay, Sir, here you have a specimen of human sympathy; a friend hanged, and a cucumber pickled. We know not whether Baretti or the pickle-man has kept Davies from sleep; nor does he know himself. And as to his not sleeping, Sir; Tom Davies is a very great man; Tom has been upon the stage, and knows how to do those things. I have not been upon the stage, and cannot do those things." BOSWELL. "I have often blamed myself, Sir, for not feeling for others as sensibly as many say they do." JOHNSON. "Sir, don't be duped by them any more. You will find these very feeling people are not very ready to do you good. They *pay* you by *feeling.*"

"Clear your mind of cant," Johnson advises Boswell on another occasion; and Boswell's Johnson is the world's champion cant-detector, cant being the payment in full by such counterfeits of feeling as for example, when his mind has gone numb under the weight of moral responsibility, the rolling Johnsonian period that fails to conceal a total lapse of attention: "every mind, however

vigorous or abstracted, is necessitated by its present state of union
to receive its information and execute its purposes by the intervention of the body," intones the Rambler, public monitor and
scold, sicklied o'er with the pale cast of platitude, having to crank
out one more weekly essay, indulging his weakness and sickness
of spirit, the same mind abstracted and dim that in a tavern or
a drawing-room turns privately vigorous and incandescent. Nonetheless literary criticism, which seldom allows itself to be confused
by fact, not only rates Johnson's writing above his conversation
(Boswell is overrated; conversation is overrated; art is long, people
are short) but of course prefers what he writes when, revered and
uncomprehended sage of the age, he's delivering his Augustan
quota of cant or any of those desperate and tautological formulations
that struggle up *de profundis*—

> So few of the hours of life are filled with objects adequate
> to the mind of man, and so frequently are we in want of
> present pleasure or employment, that we are forced to have
> recourse every moment to the past and future for supplemental
> satisfactions, and relieve the vacuities of our being by rec-
> ollection of former passages, or anticipation of events to come.

—"an idea," asserts J. P. Hardy (in *Samuel Johnson: A Critical
Study*) with stunning disregard for Boswell's, Mrs. Thrale's, the
Club's, Shakespeare's, the Dictionary's, the Lives of the Poets'
Johnson, "that permeates the whole of Johnson's experience of
life."

Indeed *The Rambler*, as Hardy enthusiastically reminds us by
means of his altogether representative quotations, when it isn't
cant is a thesaurus of nullifying words and ideas—vacancy, vacuity,
tediousness, boredom, disappointment—that, whether or not they
spill the beans about life, whether or not they may be said to
permeate the experience of anybody we'd make a detour to seek
acquaintance with, suggest a kind of life and outlook that nobody
in his right mind would freely choose (so isn't Hardy's Great
Moralist wasting his time? because he'd be better off with a carrot
and a stick): "the completion of almost every wish is found a
disappointment"; "the vacuities of our being"; "to be idle is to
be vitious"; "We are in danger of whatever can get possession of

our thoughts"; "his heart vacant, and his desires, for want of external objects, ravaging itself"; "Irregular desires will produce licentious practices; what men allow themselves to wish they will soon believe, and will be at last incited to execute what they please themselves with contriving"; "I have often thought those happy that have been fixed from the first dawn of thought, in a determination to some state of life, by the choice of one whose authority may preclude caprice"; "the natural flights of the human mind are not from pleasure to pleasure, but from hope to hope"; "The greater part of mankind are corrupt in every condition, and differ in high and in low stations, only as they have more or fewer opportunities of gratifying their desires, or as they are more or less restrained by human censures." Such "skepticism," Hardy contends, is "bracingly astringent," no doubt like a styptic pencil for a case of hemophilia.

But it isn't *The Rambler* that (according to Hardy) is Johnson's masterpiece, it's *Rasselas*, which "has something quintessential about it. . . . Ideas found elsewhere, especially in *The Rambler*, are here assimilated and transformed; *Rasselas* is, at one and the same time, both antiromantic and yet strangely optimistic. Most often quoted is the remark that 'human life is everywhere a state in which much is to be endured and little to be enjoyed'; nevertheless, the book's overall movement is, even so, surprisingly buoyant." Maybe so, or even so. Here is Hardy's summary of the beginning of *Rasselas* (Hardy's own book is useful mainly as a set of reliable summaries of Johnson's writings): "Every year, during the visitation of the emperor, the inhabitants of the Happy Valley are 'required to propose whatever might contribute to make seclusion pleasant, to fill up the vacancies of attention, and lessen the tediousness of time,' and since all that is desired is 'immediately granted,' they are therefore deprived of the opportunity of still hoping for something. Paradoxically, in this consists the boredom. . . ." Paradoxically, life is hard cheese and full of holes.

"I can discover within me," muses Rasselas, "no power of perception which is not glutted with its proper pleasure, yet I do not feel myself delighted"; and, "resolved to escape from his confinement," he passes another "four months in resolving to lose no more time in idle resolves" ("The vocabulary of 'resolving,'" exults

Hardy, "is given in *Rasselas* a richly ironic meaning"). Education
and travel don't help: "the more we enquire, the less we can
resolve." Advice from "a wise and happy man," a Stoic philosopher
he has a session with, doesn't help: "Despite . . . the philosopher's
claim that happiness is 'in everyone's power,' Rasselas next meets
him a broken man, utterly inconsolable at the death of his only
daughter" (a presumably rich irony from which Hardy draws the
conclusion that "*Rasselas*, then, is not moral allegory in any simple
sense"). There's nothing to life except going round and round the
vicious circle: "The hope of happiness is so strongly impressed that
the longest experience is not able to efface it. Of the present state,
whatever it be, we feel, and are forced to confess, the misery, yet,
when the same state is again at a distance, imagination paints it
as desirable": misery, self-delusion, misery, self-delusion, misery,
etc. So much for Johnson's strangely optimistic and surprisingly
buoyant little book. What critics can't ever let themselves think
is that for Johnson there isn't any general or philosophical notion
at all that bears thinking about and the sooner he stops thinking
about it the better: e.g. Hardy vastly admires a characteristic line
in Johnson's poem *London*, "Slow rises worth, by poverty de-
press'd," and doesn't notice that, far from carrying its meaning
of soberly qualified hope (or rising to a pitch of triumph at its
rhyme-word as, if it were Pope's, it would surely have done), it's
a bottom line that droops funereally and declines at last into just
what it's alleged to have overcome. There's nothing good or bad
but thinking makes it worse. In the *Life of Johnson* Boswell reports
an encounter between Johnson and a retired solicitor named Oliver
Edwards, who haven't seen each other since they were at Oxford
in Pembroke College forty-nine years earlier: Edwards is a friendly
and artless soul pleased to be talking with his now renowned old
fellow-collegian, to whom at length it occurs to him to tell an
inadvertent home truth—"You are a philosopher, Dr. Johnson.
I have tried too in my time to be a philosopher; but, I don't know
how, cheerfulness was always breaking in." "A cheerful disposition," Rasselas ought to have said, "is more precious than rubies."

For Johnson philosophy is the anticipation of the void, the terror
of indiscrimination, all things confounded in their general fate.

He dreaded any talk or thought of death: he told Boswell that "he never had a moment in which death was not terrible to him," and "So much . . . [is the fear of death natural to man] that the whole of life is but keeping away thoughts of it" (when Edwards casually remarked that "we are old men now" Johnson, who "never liked to think of being old," will have none of it—"Don't let us discourage one another"). He knows at every moment the propinquity, threatening to collapse into identity, of Baretti dead and Davies alive, a hanged man and a cucumber pickled, which so long as they can be kept separate permit, if not always cheerfulness, at least a certain poise and sympathy in the act of naming and distinguishing and enumerating:

> [Pope's] stature was so low that, to bring him to a level with common tables, it was necessary to raise his seat. But his face was not displeasing, and his eyes were animated and vivid. . . .
>
> Most of what can be told concerning his petty peculiarities was communicated by a female domestick of the Earl of Oxford, who knew him perhaps after the middle of life. He was then so weak as to stand in perpetual need of female attendance; extremely sensible of cold, so that he wore a kind of fur doublet under a shirt of very coarse warm linen with fine sleeves. When he rose he was invested in a boddice made of stiff canvass, being scarce able to hold himself erect till they were laced, and he then put on a flannel waistcoat. One side was contracted. His legs were so slender that he enlarged their bulk with three pairs of stockings, which were drawn on and off by the maid; for he was not able to dress or undress himself, and neither went to bed nor rose without help. His weakness made it very difficult for him to be clean.
>
> His hair had fallen almost all away, and he used to dine sometimes with Lord Oxford, privately, in a velvet cap. His dress of ceremony was black, with a tye-wig and a little sword.

(That "little sword" strikes both ways, for Johnson was an afflicted man of uncouth manners and convulsive bodily movements, he knew as well as Pope did what it meant to be an object of pity

and an oddity. Even when in company he had a habit of talking
to himself, according to Boswell "frequently uttering pious ejac-
ulations": "His friend Mr. Thomas Davies"—of pickle fame—"of
whom Churchill says 'That Davies hath a very pretty wife,' when
Dr. Johnson muttered 'lead us not into temptation,' used with
waggish and gallant humour to whisper Mrs. Davies, 'You, my
dear, are the cause of this.' " Johnson was a man of such inspiriting
wit as to be, even when deep in his affliction, the cause of such
wit in others.)

Johnson is a great biographer and a great critic not because as
the Age of Reason's chosen exemplar he's a saltmine of lugubrious
commonplaces but because when he has the job of dealing with
particulars he faithfully attends to them, for instance he feels no
obligation to misrepresent them or play down their differences for
the sake of imputing consistency or unadulterated virtue to his
subjects. Poets are vain like other men; evidence doesn't have to
be sunk in homage; poems are more or less skilful performances,
if they can be revelations they can also be the upshot and repository
of ungenerous impulses:

> [Pope] shewed his satirical powers by publishing *The Dunciad*,
> one of his greatest and most elaborate performances, in which
> he endeavoured to sink into contempt all the writers by whom
> he had been attacked, and some others whom he thought
> unable to defend themselves.
>
> At the head of the Dunces he placed poor Theobald, whom
> he accused of ingratitude, but whose real crime was supposed
> to be that of having revised Shakespeare more happily than
> himself. . . .
>
> The prevalence of this poem was gradual and slow: the
> plan, if not wholly new, was little understood by common
> readers. Many of the allusions required illustration; the names
> were often expressed only by the initial and final letters, and,
> if they had been printed at length, were such as few had
> known or recollected. The subject itself had nothing generally
> interesting; for whom did it concern to know that one or
> another scribbler was a dunce? If therefore it had been possible
> for those who were attacked to conceal their pain and their

resentment, *The Dunciad* might have made its way very slowly in the world.

Poems aren't necessarily improved, though they may be recommended to puzzle-solving readers, by their deviations from rational discourse; poets are sometimes not only no wiser than other men but neither rational nor learned; at any rate evidence is always there to be called upon, as on another occasion when, not writing a formal biography but talking among friends, Johnson with a few touches of evidence recreates to the life in this model of rational discourse another celebrated poet:

" . . . Goldsmith had no settled notions upon any subject; so he talked always at random. It seemed to be his intention to blurt out whatever was in his mind, and see what would become of it. He was angry too, when catched in an absurdity; but it did not prevent him from falling into another the next minute. I remember Chamier, after talking with him for some time, said, 'Well, I do believe he wrote . . . [*The Traveller*] himself: and let me tell you, that is believing a great deal.' Chamier once asked him, what he meant by *slow*, the last word in the first line of *The Traveller*, 'Remote, unfriended, melancholy, slow.' Did he mean tardiness of locomotion? Goldsmith, who would say something without consideration, answered, 'Yes.' I was sitting by, and said, 'No, Sir; you do not mean tardiness of locomotion; you mean, that sluggishness of mind which comes upon a man in solitude.' Chamier believed then that I had written the line as much as if he had seen me write it. Goldsmith, however, was a man, who, whatever he wrote, did it better than any other man could do. He deserved a place in Westminster-Abbey, and every year he lived, would have deserved it better. He had, indeed, been at no pains to fill his mind with knowledge. He transplanted it from one place to another; and it did not settle in his mind; so he could not tell what was in his own books."

Johnson (in Boswell's memorandum of the conversation) is turning the evidence into one of his innumerable offhand and beautiful

models of rational discourse: his "superiority over other learned
men," as Boswell sums it up, "consisted chiefly in . . . a certain
continual power of seizing the useful substance of all that he knew,
and exhibiting it in a clear and forceful manner; so that knowledge,
which we often see to be no better than lumber in men of dull
understanding, was, in him, true, evident, and actual wisdom."
There have been many men of dull understanding who have called
Boswell foolish.

Johnson is wise, Boswell foolish; Johnson warns and abstains,
Boswell plunges; Johnson talks away, Boswell transcribes for posterity; Johnson is rather a great man writing than a great writer,
Boswell is a great writer and an ordinary man; and they are two
of a kind, abysmal melancholics and compulsive socializers, afraid
of solitude, afraid of death and dissolution, victims of themselves,
meant for each other, needing each other, needing evidence and
arguments (Boswell is a lawyer, Johnson magisterially dictates to
him some of his briefs), making beautiful models of rational discourse out of the useful substance of all they know, as when after
a dozen years of marriage Boswell confides to his journal his deliberate judgment of his wife:

> I made a good many excerpts from *Tom Jones*. My Wife
> disliked Feilding's [sic] turn for low life, as I have observed
> yesterday. But it is human nature. She has nothing of that
> english [they are both Scottish] juiciness of mind of which
> I have a great deal, which makes me delight in humour. But
> what hurts me more, she has nothing of that warmth of
> imagination which produces the pleasures of vanity and many
> others, and which is even a considerable cause of religious
> fervour. *Family*, which is a high *principle* in my mind, and
> Genealogy, which is to me an interesting amusement, have
> no effect upon her. It is impossible not to be both uneasy
> and a little angry at such defects, (or call them differences;)
> and at times they make me think that I have been unlucky
> in wasting myself with one, who, instead of cherishing my
> genius [essential spirit], is perpetually checking it. But on
> the other hand, I consider her excellent sense, her penetration,
> her knowledge of real life, her activity, her genuine affection,

her generous conduct to me during my distracted love for her and when she married me, and her total disinterestedness and freedom from every species of selfishness during all the time she has been my Wife. And then I value her and am fond of her, and am pained to the heart for having ever behaved in a manner unworthy of her merit. I also consider that a Woman of the same imagination with myself might have encouraged me in whim and adventure, and hurried me to Ridicule and perhaps ruin, whereas my excellent Spouse's prudence has kept me out of many follies, and made my life much more decent and creditable than it would have been without her.

But later the same day he makes an entry that shows that she too sees the skull beneath the skin: "She has allways a dreary terrour for death. . . . She said yesterday it was desireable to live long for one reason: because old people [though, as it happened, not Johnson in old age] come to be as little affraid of death as children are." Pope can conclude *The Dunciad* with the glorious striding verses that register the end of everything—

> *Lo! thy dread Empire, CHAOS! is restor'd;*
> *Light dies before thy uncreating word;*
> *Thy hand, great Anarch! lets the curtain fall,*
> *And universal Darkness buries All.*

—because for Pope (after the spite and dullness that have preceded and that Johnson authoritatively points out) this is, thank God! the tremendous end of the poem, and he can rejoice at having completed his performance; but for Johnson and Boswell life itself is the only performance, the function of words is to commemorate it, completing it is not to be thought of, death is the end which images of death prefigure too staringly to be borne ("I saw death so staringly awaiting for all the human race," Boswell sets down in his journal, "and had such a cloudy and dark prospect beyond it, that I was miserable as far as I had animation"); and one part of *The Dunciad* that Johnson doesn't discuss is the end.

Johnson and Boswell are never superficial or trivial, because, some events looming too large for comfort, no event is too small

or idiosyncratic to concentrate their attention. "Nothing is too
little for so little a creature as man," says Johnson, advising his
biographer-elect to take note of every particular, and Boswell gladly
complies:

> On Friday, March 31, [1775,] I supped with him and
> some friends at a tavern. One of the company attempted,
> with too much forwardness, to rally him on his late appearance
> at the theatre; but had reason to repent of his temerity.
> "Why, Sir, did you go to Mrs. Abington's benefit? Did you
> see?" JOHNSON. "No, Sir." "Did you hear?" JOHNSON.
> "No, Sir." "Why then, Sir, did you go?" JOHNSON. "Be-
> cause, Sir, she is a favourite of the publick; and when the
> publick cares the thousandth part for you that it does for her,
> I will go to your benefit too."

Or the very next paragraph in the *Life*:

> Next morning I won a small bet from Lady Diana Beau-
> clerk, by asking him as to one of his particularities, which
> her Ladyship laid I durst not do. It seems he had been
> frequently observed at the Club to put into his pocket the
> Seville oranges, after he had squeezed the juice of them into
> the drink which he made for himself. Beauclerk and Garrick
> talked of it to me, and seemed to think that he had a strange
> unwillingness to be discovered. We could not divine what
> he did with them; and this was the bold question to be put.
> I saw on his table the spoils of the preceding night, some
> fresh peels nicely scraped and cut into pieces. "O, Sir, (said
> I,) I now partly see what you do with the squeezed oranges
> which you put into your pocket at the Club." JOHNSON.
> "I have a great love for them." BOSWELL. "And pray, Sir,
> what do you do with them? You scrape them, it seems, very
> neatly, and what next?" JOHNSON. "Let them dry, Sir."
> BOSWELL. "And what next?" JOHNSON. "Nay, Sir, you
> shall know their fate no further." BOSWELL. "Then the
> world must be left in the dark. It must be said (assuming
> a mock solemnity,) he scraped them, and let them dry, but
> what he did with them next, he never could be prevailed

upon to tell." JOHNSON. "Nay, Sir, you should say it more emphatically:—he could not be prevailed upon, even by his dearest friends, to tell."

A man not to be trifled with, a good man, not a wit but a powerful mind penetrated with wit, a man with many friends and strong affections, the obstreperous hero of the comedy of life:

> [Johnson] charged Mr. Langton with what he thought want of judgement upon an interesting occasion. "When I was ill, (said he,) I desired he would tell me sincerely in what he thought my life was faulty. Sir, he brought me a sheet of paper, on which he had written down several texts of Scripture, recommending christian charity. And when I questioned him what occasion I had given for such an animadversion, all that he could say amounted to this,—that I sometimes contradicted people in conversation. Now what harm does it do to any man to be contradicted?" BOSWELL. "I suppose he meant the *manner* of doing it; roughly,—and harshly." JOHNSON. "And who is the worse for that?" BOSWELL. "It hurts people of weak nerves." JOHNSON. "I know no such weak-nerved people." Mr. Burke, to whom I related this conference, said, "It is well, if when a man comes to die, he has nothing heavier upon his conscience than having been a little rough in conversation."
>
> Johnson, at the time when the paper was presented to him, though at first pleased with the attention of his friend, whom he thanked in an earnest manner, soon exclaimed, in a loud and angry tone, "What is your drift, Sir?" Sir Joshua Reynolds pleasantly observed, that it was a scene for a comedy, to see a penitent get into a violent passion and belabour his confessor.

Cheerfulness can be the gift of the gods, or it can be a gift of love from a man whose very unreasonableness is a sign of his indispensable presence.

The Moral Hero II: Nobody's Dutch Uncle But the Brother of Us All

A century later, in July 1880, friendless and penniless in a dismal Belgian mining village, Van Gogh learned that his brother had sent some money to be given to him, and he broke a nine-months' silence, the longest of their lives, with a very long letter. He was twenty-seven, a failure at everything, a touchy misfit without vocation or prospects, unnerving to strangers, "impossible and suspect" (as he correctly observed) to his family, a problem for everybody. He accepted the money with thanks ("with reluctance" too, "but I am up against a stone wall"), and then, as comprehensive, intense, and exact as always, he went on to explain why Theo and the rest of the family were probably wrong to believe that getting a job and settling down would solve the problem: "I am a man of passions, capable of and subject to doing more or less foolish things, which I happen to repent, more or less, afterward. Now and then I speak and act too hastily, when it would have been better to wait patiently. . . . Well, this being the case, what's to be done? Must I consider myself a dangerous man, incapable of anything? I don't think so." The lunatic is reasoning with the doctor and ever so gently turning the tables and raising the stakes:

> the problem is to try every means to put those selfsame passions to good use. For instance, to name one of the passions, I have a more or less irresistible passion for books, and I continually want to instruct myself, to study if you like, just as much as I want to eat my bread. . . . When I was in other surroundings, in the surroundings of pictures and

works of art, you know how I had a violent passion for them, reaching the highest pitch of enthusiasm. And I am not sorry about it, for even now, *far from that land, I am often homesick for the land of pictures.*

The problem is in the spirit, in the soul, and has to be examined deliberately and at length before it makes sense for either of the two of them to think about what comes next:

> You remember perhaps that I knew well (and perhaps I know still) who Rembrandt was, or Millet, or Jules Dupré or Delacroix or Millais or M. Maris. Well, now I do not have those surroundings any more—yet that thing called soul, they say it never dies, but lives on and continues to search forever and ever and ever. So instead of giving way to this home-sickness, I said to myself: That land, or the fatherland, is everywhere. So instead of giving in to despair, I chose the part of active melancholy—in so far as I possessed the power of activity—in other words, I preferred the melancholy which hopes and aspires and seeks to that which despairs in stagnation and woe. So I studied somewhat seriously the books within my reach like the Bible, and the *French Revolution* by Michelet, and last winter, Shakespeare and a few by Victor Hugo and Dickens, and Beecher Stowe, and lately Aeschylus. . . .

A year earlier, in the village from which he was writing, he had worked as an evangelical missionary but his supervisors had dismissed him because, though they acknowledged his devoted service to the miners, he had soon demonstrated his unfitness for a Christian vocation by giving away his money, clothes, and bed and subsisting on crusts in a hovel (his father, a clergyman, made an emergency visit but couldn't persuade him to behave in a "less exaggerated" way). In the aftermath he had lost his Christian faith but not his eagerness and devotion: "you must not think that I disavow things—rather I am faithful in my unfaithfulness and, though changed, I am the same; my only anxiety is, How can I be of use in the world? Can't I serve some purpose and be of some good? How can I learn more and study certain subjects profoundly?

. . . And then one feels a terrible discouragement gnawing at one's very moral energy, and fate seems to put a barrier to the instincts of affection, and a choking flood of disgust envelops one." The problem is how to live, how to be worthy, how to be not only strong and serious but useful, made use of, used up: "Do our inner thoughts ever show outwardly? There may be a great fire in our soul, yet no one ever comes to warm himself at it, and the passers-by see only a wisp of smoke coming through the chimney, and go along their way. Look here, now, what must be done?"

Typically, artists don't do such shameless soul-searching unless they come to believe they've mistaken or exhausted the possibilities of art: Tolstoy in middle age and after, for example; but Van Gogh does it from his earliest youth, from long before he becomes a painter, and if he weren't Van Gogh one would be tempted to feel superior and uncomfortable—isn't he a bit pharisaical or masochistic or already quite beside himself with self-absorption? and even the philosopher who said the unexamined life isn't worth living might have conceded that nobody has to start so early. (Of course many people never examine their lives at all and, if the philosopher is right, are better off dead. Efficient and concentrated artists, for instance, as well as *idiots savants* aren't figments of the popular imagination, they really exist, they aren't exceptionally aware of themselves or others and have been known to pass their time between masterpieces doing whatever to whomever with nary a twinge of introspection or conscience: a mistress of Picasso's, asked what he had been like as a lover, replied, "Like all artists. In and out and back to work." The arts are hard work and don't necessarily leave the artist with soul to spare.) Van Gogh, however, seems a candidate for sainthood from the beginning, strong and serious, a moralist, a prophet, a believer, a porer over sacred books, an oracle and scribe, a big clear brightly lighted upper story; and the impression is ominous no doubt but it's accurate only as far as it goes, because at any moment he will notice something else, triumphantly discover another sacred book, bump up against a different truth—he's a seer not a prophet, an enthusiast not a believer, an amateur not an insider, loves artists not art ("I read books to find the artist who wrote them"; at twenty-one he admonishes seventeen-year-old Theo to "*Admire* as much as you can" and names fifty-four living painters "whom I like especially: Scheffer, Delaroche, Hébert, Hamon, Leys. . . . Then there are the old masters, and I am sure I have forgotten some of the best modern ones"), delights in the unending proliferation of sacred books (Balzac, Hugo, Zola, the Goncourts, Maupassant, Shakespeare, Whitman, Dickens, George Eliot, Tolstoy; from Arles, just released after solitary confinement in the mental ward, he writes Theo that "I took advantage of my outing to buy a book, *Ceux de la Glèbe*, by Camille Lemonnier. I have devoured two chapters of it—it has such gravity, such depth! Wait till I send it to you. This is the first time in several months that I have had a book in my hands. That means a lot to me and does a great deal toward curing me"), scatters truths not like the wind that bloweth where it listeth but like a good soul and a warm heart:

> When . . . [Mauve, a celebrated painter of the time and a relative of Van Gogh's by marriage] reads something that is deep, he does not say at once, That man means this or that. For poetry is so deep and intangible that one cannot define everything systematically. But Mauve has a fine sentiment, and, you see, I regard that sentiment as worth so much more than definitions and criticism. And when I read, and really I do not read so much, only a few authors—a few men whom I discovered by accident—I do it because they look at things in a broader, milder, and more loving way than I do, and because they know life better, so that I can learn from them; but I care so very little for all that rubbish about good and evil, morality and immorality. . . .

—and even when, heartbreakingly often, the truths turn painful, they never turn cold or cunning:

> Since I wrote Mauve: "Do you know that those two months you spoke of have long since passed? Let us shake hands, and then each go his own way, rather than have a quarrel between you and me," I repeat, since I wrote this and received no sign in reply, my grief chokes me.
> Because—and you know this—I love Mauve, and it is so hard that all the happiness he pictures to me will come to

naught. For I am afraid that the better my drawings become, the more difficulty and opposition I shall meet. Because I shall have to suffer much, especially from those peculiarities I *cannot* change. First, my appearance and my way of speaking and my clothes; and then, even later on when I earn more, I shall always move in a different sphere from most painters because my conception of things, the subjects I want to make, inexorably demand it. . . .

Look here, in my opinion all politeness is founded on goodwill toward everybody, founded on the necessity everyone who has a heart in his breast feels, to help others, to be of use to somebody, and finally, on the need to live together, and not alone. Therefore I do my best, I draw, not to annoy people, but to amuse them, or to make them see things which are worth observing and which not everybody knows.

I cannot believe, Theo, that I could be such a monster of insolence and impoliteness as to deserve to be cut off from society, or as Tersteeg says, "should not be allowed to stay in The Hague."

Do I lower myself by living with the people I draw? Do I lower myself when I go into the houses of laborers and poor people and when I receive them in my studio?

With his intractable reasonableness he challenges everything, and people respond *ad hominem*, and then he defends himself passionately (*Cet animal est très méchant, / Si on l'attaque, il se défend*: as the French say, What a naughty beast! if it's attacked it defends itself), and finally all they want is to cut him off from society, drive him back into the deep forest. He has the hope of a millennium ("How can I be of use?"): according to Theo, "whatever he sees that is wrong he must criticize"; "A quiet life is impossible for him, except alone with nature or with very simple people." Once he had revealed himself to society for the sort of man he was, they all turned Dutch uncle, as indignant and self-righteous as the mob in Arles that insisted the streets weren't safe unless the cops grabbed the crazy red-haired painter and carted him off. Tersteeg, successful art-dealer, arbiter of taste, manager of Goupil & Co.'s branch in The Hague, had approved of the "diligent, studious" boy (at sixteen Vincent had been hired there because his Uncle Vincent was one of the owners) but disapproved of the man, who was obviously a disgrace pure and simple and his work an insulting joke: he looked at a drawing Van Gogh showed him and said, "You failed before and now you will fail again—it will be the same story all over again" (because, as they all agreed, he couldn't settle down, keep a job, do anything worthwhile). Mauve was at first friendly and instructive to the novice painter but then refused to see him and wouldn't answer his letters, apparently for no other reason than the bad impression he sooner or later made on all respectable people except Theo. (From his early twenties Van Gogh was "impossible and suspect" to his whole family except Theo, to whom one of their sisters complained, "You think he's something more than ordinary but I think it would be much better if he thought he was just ordinary.") He didn't begin painting till late (he had been painting for only ten years when he shot himself at thirty-seven) and seems to have begun almost inadvertently. In July 1880, not yet having become the artist they would all find as eccentric and unacceptable as the man, he must have been as close as he ever was to believing they were right, this lost soul fallen away from religion and family, estranged even from Theo; so when Theo rematerialized to send him that unexpected gift, he took it: the money, the opportunity to describe and circumscribe the nature of the problem, the opportunity to implicate Theo forever. Through the family connection Theo was employed in Goupil & Co.'s Paris branch (to which, years before, Van Gogh himself had been transferred, and by which he had eventually been dismissed: family did everything, gave life and withdrew it, proposed and disposed), Theo had a salary and access to art, Theo was the last chance, Theo would help, and in his next letter he asked Theo for "prints by, or after, Millet, Breton, Feyen-Perrin, etc. . . . Send me what you can, and do not fear for me. If I can only continue to work, somehow or other it will set me right again. . . . I am busy drawing, and I am in a hurry to go back to it, so good night, and send me the prints as soon as possible, and believe me, Ever yours, Vincent"—it's the very moment when he decides to become a painter and plucks Theo out of the family as his indispensable accomplice.

In the act of living his life he has to keep justifying it to the one person on the other side who listens—not only its shape and momentum but its homeliest details: he writes from Arles that he "lives like a monk who goes to the brothel once a fortnight"; and, after the citizens have petitioned the mayor to lock him up, "All I would ask is that people I don't even know . . . do not meddle with me, when I am busy painting, or eating, or taking a turn at the brothel, since I haven't a wife." He is living out the family tragedy—confronted by the unbudgeable Van Goghs with their wives (as for himself, "my ugly face and shabby coat" frighten and repel the women he falls in love with and asks to marry him), their professions, connections, getting along, getting ahead, as well as by the family of man that can't tolerate this scapegoat, black sheep, stray animal that against blows and curses keeps trying to find its way back in: "My dear brother," he writes in January 1890 after a second breakdown, "Many thanks for your letter of December 22, containing a 50-fr. note. First of all I wish you and Jo a happy New Year and regret that I have perhaps, though quite unwillingly, caused you worry, because M. Peyron must have informed you that my mind has once more become deranged." ("Jo" was Theo's fiancée. "The trouble with Gauguin in Arles started," writes her son in his memoir of her, "and indeed Van Gogh's first breakdown occurred, "right after Vincent heard from Theo that he intended to marry. Other crises came about after Theo's marriage, after the announcement that a baby was expected, and after the birth. It must have passed through his mind that he would lose his support, though he never mentioned it and it never came about." On the other hand Charles S. Moffett, an associate curator at New York's Metropolitan Museum of Art, who recently published a piece called "Van Gogh's Year of Wonder," thinks that Van Gogh's troubles testify to his lifelong lack of nerve: "From the beginning, Van Gogh seems to have had a deep-rooted fear of success. Whenever he was close to achieving a goal or succeeding in an enterprise, his behavior became abnormal, and a crisis ensued. He had failed in everything he had ever done, and he evidently intended to see that painting was no exception." Van Gogh ought to have foreseen that he would ultimately become famous enough for bureaucrats to be showering him a century later with psychoanalytic debris.) By the time of this happy New Year Theo has steadily supported him, with money and otherwise, for nine years; he has wanted more than anything else to repay the "debt": "I can't help it that my pictures don't sell," he writes despairingly in letter after letter, he hopes and hopes they'll be "salable" (only one of his pictures was sold during his lifetime); "my dear boy, my debt is so great that when I have paid it, which all the same I hope to succeed in doing, the pains of producing pictures will have taken my whole life from me, and it will seem to me that I have not lived"; but his incidental repayment is this full and guileless record of a life.

"The survival of art," according to Harold Rosenberg (in "On Art and History"), "depends on the continued fabrication of the artist type. The urge to transform oneself into an artist is provided by the artist myth, with its lure of fame, women, and wealth. The difficulty is that the artist type can no longer be copied from existing models, since these have been appropriated by the mass media and reproduced in deteriorated form—e.g. the Poes, Van Goghs, and Toulouse-Lautrecs of the movies." But the point for the mass media is that Poe, Van Gogh, and Toulouse-Lautrec are spectacularly *visible*, they are public images congenial to a visual medium—not only the fact that two were painters but Poe's dank tarns and ghoul-haunted baggy eyes, Toulouse-Lautrec's half-size legs, the piece of Van Gogh's ear that he sliced off and carried as a gift to one of the girls at the brothel for whose fortnightly favors he punctuated his monkish routine: TV and the movies don't make their choices without a reason. Moreover Van Gogh is the IBM-sponsored Sunday-night Special because his life seems important by itself, it isn't merely that we gawk because he's human and an artist too (he had a father and mother, fell in love, needed money, and in his spare time did all those paintings), it isn't that his art seems inconceivable apart from his life or his life more important than his art, but he is special because—though all those paintings are a generous legacy, a kind of bonus for sweating it out with him—his life as he records it for us reminds us that the life of anybody at all is more important than all the art (and all the curators) in the museums: which is a proposition that a mass-media vice-president might guess is salable even if he

wouldn't guess it's true. Anyhow Van Gogh's life, spectacularly
deficient in fame, women, and wealth, was never likely to en-
courage careerists to jump into art; "the urge to transform oneself
into an artist" is less likely to be external than internal; it can
be argued that the artist type isn't the definitive human type
("the antennae of the race") and that its disappearance wouldn't
mean the end of the world; irrespective of the availability of the
artist type, art isn't eternally self-renewing, certain genres if not
entire arts fulfill themselves and become historical; artists aren't
heroes who resist the blandishments of the mass media (haven't
there always been distractions and alternatives?), they are workers
who feel at home among the practical conditions of their work
(artists *like* to do art and can't imagine *not* doing it); and history's
surprises may not all turn out to be unpleasant ones. Meanwhile
art, like religion, will continue to be overrated by those who
believe in it or profit by it or have a professional stake in it; but
artists like Van Gogh will go into it and stay with it because in
the lives they have to live art keeps them busier and more concerned
than anything else they know about:

> These painter's fingers of mine are growing supple, even
> though the carcass is going to pieces. And the merchant's
> head for selling—and a long job to learn it is—is getting
> more experience too. In our situation, which you may well
> say is so precarious, we must not forget our advantages, and
> let's try to hang on to our patience to do the right thing and
> see clearly. Isn't it true, for instance, that in any case it is
> better if someday they say to you, "Go to London," than
> chuck you out, your services no longer being required?
>
> I am getting older than you, and my ambition is to be
> less of a burden to you. And, if no actual obelisk of too
> pyramidal a catastrophe occurs and there's no rain of frogs
> in the meantime, I hope to achieve it sometime.
>
> I have just taken thirty painted studies from the stretchers.
> If it's only our living we're after in *business* affairs, would it
> be such a hardship to go to London, where I think there is
> more chance of selling than elsewhere? In any case, I tell
> myself that out of the thirty studies I shall send you, you

will not be able to sell one in Paris. But then, as old Prin-
senhage would say, "Everything gets sold." And in our case,
what I do is not salable like the Brocharts for instance, but
it can be sold to people who buy things because there is
nature in them.

Why, a canvas I have covered is worth more than a blank
canvas.

That—believe me my pretensions go no further—that is
my right to paint, my reason for painting, and by the Lord,
I have one!

All it has cost me is a carcass pretty well destroyed and
wits pretty well crazed, and only to lead the same life I might
and should lead if I were a philanthropist.

All it has cost you is, say, 15,000 francs, which you have
advanced to me. . . .

If I reminded you just now of what painting costs us, it
is only to emphasize what we ought to tell ourselves—that
we have gone too far to turn back, that's all I harp on. For,
material existence aside, what else shall I ever need?

(But some days he hasn't the heart for jokes: "A *wife* you cannot
give me, a *child* you cannot give me, work you cannot give me.
Money, yes. But what good is it to me if I must do without the
rest!" And some days, as when they are living together—Theo is
still a bachelor—in Paris, Theo can endure the burden only by
sharing it with somebody else, in this case their sister: "My home
life is almost unbearable. No one wants to come and see me any
more because it always ends in quarrels, and besides, he is so
untidy that the room looks far from attractive. I wish he would
go and live by himself. He sometimes mentions it, but if I were
to tell him to go away, it would just give him a reason to stay;
and it seems I do him no good. I ask only one thing of him, to
do me no harm; yet by his staying he does so, for I can hardly
bear it." And some days, soon after Vincent's arrival in Paris,
Theo blazes with brotherly pride and love: "He is in much better
spirits than before and many people here like him . . . he has
friends who send him every week a lot of beautiful flowers which
he uses for still life. He paints chiefly flowers, especially to make

the colors of his next pictures brighter and clearer. If we can
continue to live together like this, I think the most difficult period
is past, and he will find his way.")

He was mad about Japanese prints, which had been making
their way into Europe, and he collected as many as he could afford
and put them up on his walls: "I envy the Japanese the extreme
clearness which everything has in their work. It is never tedious,
and never seems to be done too hurriedly. Their work is as simple
as breathing, and they do a figure in a few sure strokes with the
same ease as if it were as simple as buttoning your coat." Even
in sunburnt Arles he kept seeing "Japanese" compositions:

> I saw a magnificent and strange effect this evening. A very
> big boat loaded with coal on the Rhone, moored on the quay.
> Seen from above it was all shining and wet with a shower;
> the water was yellowish-white and clouded pearl gray; the
> sky, lilac, with an orange streak in the west; the town, violet.
> On the boat some poor workmen in dirty blue and white
> came and went carrying the cargo on shore. It was pure
> Hokusai. It was too late to do it, but one day when that coal
> boat comes back, I must give it a try. I saw it in a railway
> coalyard, a spot I have just found, and where there will be
> plenty of other things to do.

But even more electrifying in Arles were its unrecorded native
products—people (women, mostly) and color: "There are women
like a Fragonard and like a Renoir. And some that can't be labeled
with anything that's been done yet in painting. The best thing
to do would be to make portraits, all kinds of portraits of women
and children. But I don't think that I am the man to do it":

> I shall go on working and here and there among my work
> there will be things which will last, but who will be in figure
> painting what Claude Monet is in landscape? However, you
> must feel, as I do, that such a one will come . . . the painter
> of the future will be *a colorist such as has never yet existed.*
> Manet was working toward it, but as you know the impres-
> sionists have already got a stronger color than Manet. But
> this painter who is to come—I can't imagine him living in

little cafés, working away with a lot of false teeth, and going to the Zouaves' brothels, as I do.

But he protested too much, he must have had a persistent suspicion that he was just the man to do it. He needed time, though; thus, when the worst happened, he tried to pretend that nothing had happened: "I got back home today. I do so regret that you had all that trouble for such a trifle. Forgive me, who am after all the primary cause of it all. I did not foresee that it would be important enough for you to be told of it." (Here is Theo's wife's account of the "trifle": "On December 24 a telegram arrived from Gauguin that called Theo to Arles. Vincent, in a state of terrible excitement and in a high fever, had cut off a piece of his own ear and taken it as a present to a woman in a brothel. There had been a violent scene; Roulin the postman managed to get him home, but the police intervened, found Vincent bleeding and unconscious in bed, and sent him to the hospital. Theo found him there, 'poor fighter and poor, poor sufferer,' and stayed over Christmas. Gauguin went back with Theo to Paris.") But two months later, when the police had come at the urging of his neighbors and carried him off, he was ready to state the case and admit the feelings ("I will not deny that I would rather have died than have caused and suffered such trouble"):

My dear brother,

I seemed to see so much brotherly anxiety in your kind letter that I think it my duty to break my silence. I write to you in the full possession of my faculties and not as a madman, but as the brother you know. This is the truth. A certain number of people here (there were more than 80 signatures) addressed a petition to the Mayor (I think his name is M. Tardieu), describing me as a man not fit to be at liberty, or something like that.

The commissioner of police or the chief commissioner then gave the order to shut me up again.

Anyhow, here I am, shut up in a cell all the livelong day, under lock and key and with keepers, without my guilt being proved or even open to proof.

Needless to say, in the secret tribunal of my soul I have much to reply to all that. Needless to say, I cannot be angry, and it seems to me a case of qui s'excuse s'accuse.

Only to let you know that as for setting me free—mind, I do not ask it, being persuaded that the whole accusation will be reduced to nothing—but I do say that as for getting me freed, you would find it difficult. If I did not restrain my indignation, I should at once be thought a dangerous lunatic. Let us hope and have patience. Besides, strong emotion can only aggravate my case. That is why I beg you for the present to let things be without meddling.

"Good-by, my dear boy," he concluded, "for a little while, I hope, and don't worry."

He lived a year and a half after the first breakdown, in and out of asylums, painting whenever he was allowed to, pouring out—this volcano of lucidity—letters to Theo as reflectively and lavishly as ever, passing through Paris to be seen for the first time by Theo's wife:

I had expected a sick man, but here was a sturdy, broad-shouldered man, with a healthy color, a smile on his face, and a very resolute appearance; of all the self-portraits, the one before the easel is most like him at that period. . . .

"He seems perfectly well; he looks much stronger than Theo," was my first thought.

Then Theo drew him into the room where our little boy's cradle was; he had been named after Vincent. Silently the two brothers looked at the quietly sleeping baby—both had tears in their eyes. Then Vincent turned smilingly to me and said, pointing to the simple crocheted cover on the cradle, "Do not cover him too much with lace, little sister."

He stayed with us three days, and was cheerful and lively all the time. St. Rémy [the asylum from which he had just come] was not mentioned. He went out by himself to buy olives, which he used to eat every day and which he insisted on our eating too. The first morning he was up very early and was standing in his shirt sleeves looking at his pictures, of which our apartment was full. . . .

From this visit he went immediately to board with Dr. Gachet in Auvers, returning for a last visit to Paris three weeks before his death: "Many friends came . . . among others Aurier, who had recently written his famous article about Vincent and now came again to look at the pictures with the painter himself. Toulouse-Lautrec stayed for lunch and made many jokes with Vincent about an undertaker's man they had met on the stairs. . . ."

During his last months and posthumously, Van Gogh had all the family he needed. When Theo came to the hospital in Arles, he laid his head on the pillow beside Vincent's, and Vincent whispered, "Just like Zundert" (the village where they had spent their childhood). When Vincent died Theo wrote their mother: "One cannot write how grieved one is nor find any comfort. It is a grief that will last and which I certainly shall never forget as long as I live. . . . Oh Mother! he was so much my own, own brother." Theo himself died six months later, and his widow and their baby son returned to Holland with trunkfuls of Vincent's unsalable paintings and his unsorted, mostly undated letters. (From her diary: "I am taking boarders—now I must be careful that I shouldn't be degraded to a household drudge by all the house-keeping worries, but I must keep my spirit alive. Theo taught me much about art, no let me rather say—he taught me much about life. Besides the care of the child he left me still another task, Vincent's work—to show it and let it be appreciated as much as possible." Nor was she a Pollyanna or the Great Man's Widow or Sister-in-Law, as she proved by concluding the paragraph with a bleak statement that Vincent-like tells the truth and shames the devil: "I am not without an object in life, but I feel lonely and deserted." She had made no entries in the diary during the year and a half of her marriage; when she took it up again a few months after Theo's death her first sentence was, "*Tout n'est qu'un rêve!*"— All is but a dream!) Without money or influence she succeeded in having the paintings exhibited and written about till within a decade or so they were internationally known; night after night she worked at putting the letters in order and, twenty-four years after his death, published them for the first time (the following year she started translating the letters into English for a prospective English edition, and by the time of her death in 1925 had completed 526, four-fifths of the letters to Theo). "At her burial," writes her son, "the directors of the Wereldbibliotheek, the publishers of the Dutch edition of the letters, sent a wreath with the inscription: Faithfulness, Devotion, Love." She not only deserved it; by that time she had turned it into the family motto.

Life Direct and the Indifferential Calculus: Three Modern Heroes and the Modernist Heresy

When he was editor of *The English Review* Ford Madox Hueffer printed Lawrence for the first time and amiably introduced him to everybody at parties as "a genius!" but Hueffer was himself a novelist in the Flaubertian tradition and thought every other modern novelist, even a genius, had no business being anything else; he disparaged the confessional expansiveness of Lawrence's fiction; kept enjoining him to adopt Flaubert's ironic detachment, though Lawrence found it "as tiresome as the infant's bib which . . . [Hueffer] says I wear for my mewling and puking"; kept arguing that "prose *must* be impersonal, like . . . Flaubert." But Lawrence held fast: "I say no." Even mewling and puking seemed to Lawrence better than being above and beyond it all. Later, trying to interest a publisher's reader in the manuscript of the novel whose eventual title would be *Sons and Lovers*, Lawrence felt obliged to concede that "It's not so strongly concentric as the fashionable folk under French influence—you see I suffered badly from Hueffer re Flaubert and perfection—want it. It may seem loose—and I may cut the childhood part—if you think better so—and perhaps you'll want me to spoil some of the good stuff. But," he obstinately summed up, "it is rather great." He was right: it is; nevertheless his correspondent (Walter de la Mare, who gets a double demerit because he was a good enough writer himself to have had an inkling of what he was dealing with but took the fashionable attitude toward this loose and all-too-English chronicle) didn't agree, recommended against it, and the publisher turned it down.

Lawrence, already self-exiled to Italy for the sake of love and art, began to suspect that not only literary England but the whole damned country had been appropriated by the French: "I have read *Anna of the Five Towns* today. . . . I hate Bennett's resignation. Tragedy ought really to be a great kick at misery. But *Anna* . . . seems like an acceptance—so does all the modern stuff since Flaubert. I hate it. I want to wash again quick, wash off England, the oldness and grubbiness and despair."

Six years earlier (in 1906) Joyce, self-exiled to Italy for the sake of love and art, was deciding that on the contrary it would be a good thing if England and, it goes without saying, Ireland were appropriated by the French: "Why are English novels so terribly boring? . . . Without boasting I think I have little or nothing to learn from English novelists"; he amuses himself guying one of Hardy's stories: "Servant-wife blows her nose in the letter and lawyer confronts the mistress. She confesses. Then they talk a page or so of copybook talk (as distinguished from servant's ditto). She weeps but he is stern. Is this as near as T.H. can get to life, I wonder?" and three days later he has settled down happily with Octave Mirbeau's *Sébastien Roch*—"It must be difficult to succeed in France where nearly everyone writes well." Writing well is the ticket: art is power; and the young artist has such confidence in the power of art that it's almost appalling when he experiences a moment of doubt: "Is it possible," Joyce writes to his brother, "that, after all, men of letters are no more than entertainers?" but no, it isn't possible, it had better not be, and "These discouraging reflections arise perhaps from my surroundings." He is unknown and unpublished, his book of poems has just been rejected by the same publisher who a few years later will reject *Sons and Lovers*; friendless and without enough money even to scrape along on in a remote and unfamiliar city, passing most of his day working at mind-boggling ill-paid jobs, writing letters to his brother—what would artists do without brothers!—in which he vivaciously discusses and exemplifies the power of art and irritably or ironically begs enough money to stay alive and keep from being put out on the street; awaiting the birth of their first child to the woman who has accompanied him without benefit of clergy in his voluntary flight from priest-ridden Ireland and who isn't thriving among these foreigners: "Nora seems to me to be in very poor health. All yesterday and the day before she has been laid up with neuralgia and pains and today she seems to be dropping down with weakness. It is very difficult for either of us to enjoy life in these circumstances." But England and Ireland were impossible. Twenty-five years later Joyce would dismiss with exasperation another English novelist he had nothing to learn from: "I read the first 2 pages of the usual sloppy English and . . . [Stuart Gilbert] read me a lyrical bit about nudism in a wood and the end which is a piece of propaganda in favour of something which, outside of D.H.L.'s country at any rate, makes all the propaganda for itself": the book is *Lady Chatterley's Lover*; but it would be more useful to have his comments on *Sons and Lovers* or some of the early short stories, which wouldn't make such stationary targets.

As for Flaubert himself, art isn't only power, it's the only power. He kept trying to explain to his mistress (whom the French make do with in default of brothers) that she had "a genuine love of art, but not the religion of art": "You do not admire enough, you do not respect enough." Still worse: "I must scold you about something that shocks and scandalizes me, namely how little you care about Art now. You care about fame—so be it: I approve; but Art, the only true and good thing in life! Can you compare any earthly love to it? Can you prefer the adoration of some relative beauty to the cult of the True?" "What is there worth discussing except Art?" "Only the Idea is eternal and necessary. There are no more artists as they once existed, artists whose loves and minds were the blind instruments of the appetite for the beautiful, God's organs by means of which he demonstrated to himself his own existence." The artist is the vessel of power—"Art is not interested in the personality of the artist"—and the greater the artist the more impersonal and unknowable the vessel: Flaubert even imagines that "who can tell me what Shakespeare loved, hated, or felt?" is a rhetorical question (so does Matthew Arnold in his solemn sonnet on the Bard: "Others abide our question. Thou art free"); in brief, O frabjous Shakespeare, Thou art Art, "which is a self-sufficient principle" and once it has used up the artist discards him like Kleenex: the artist for art's sake (not, as Lawrence rebelliously insists, "art for my sake"). To the artist life is trivial, a distraction (as for living, our mistresses will do that for us), "If you participate actively in life, you don't see it clearly: you suffer from it too much or enjoy it too much. The artist, to my way of thinking, is a monstrosity, something outside nature." Nature is merely the pretext for art, the great stage of fools for the ironic observer in the audience ("It's a sad thing to be the only spectator at a farce," hisses Lawrence from the wings). Indeed Flaubert's point is there isn't any nature, there's only art, only style (the point is, in short and full-blown, the modernist heresy rampant): "What seems beautiful to me, what I should like to write, is a book about nothing, a book dependent on nothing external, which would be held together by the internal strength of its style, just as the earth, suspended in the void, depends on nothing external for its support; a book which would have almost no subject, or at least in which the subject would be almost invisible, if such a thing is possible. The finest works are those that contain the least matter; the closer expression comes to thought, the closer language comes to coinciding and merging with it, the finer the result. I believe the future of Art lies in this direction." And lo! the future is here. "Prose was born yesterday," says the proud father: "you have to keep that in mind"; "the novel has only just been born: it awaits its Homer. What a man Balzac would have been, had he known how to write! But," Flaubert concludes with unexpected generosity and his own passing moment of doubt, "that was the only thing he lacked. An artist, after all, would not have done so much, would not have had that amplitude." Which is his sole acknowledgment of the possibility that art may contain and express matters more important than art.

At twenty-two he was a bed-ridden invalid, victim of epilepsy; afterward except for minor excursions to visit his mistress and a major one—his long-dreamed-of "voyage to the Orient" with his friend Maxime DuCamp, which according to Flaubert's detailed and explicit letters to friends at home was a year-and-a-half tour of all the brothels and bathhouses of Egypt and the Middle East— he remains behind the walls of his mother's house in a provincial town far from Paris, perfecting his art, fending off his mistress (who wants his presence not his letters) and the importunate DuCamp, who now lives in Paris and keeps urging him to move there and make a career for himself; but Flaubert isn't having any:

> I'll go to Paris for the winter. I'll be a man like other men. I'll lead a life given over to love affairs and scheming. I'll have to do many things that will revolt me and that I find lamentable in advance. Now: am I made for all that? . . . Often, when I am faced with doing no matter what, I am overwhelmed by weariness and am ready to die of boredom; and I grasp even the most straightforward idea only by dint of great effort. My youth (you knew only its latter phase) steeped me in an opiate of boredom, sufficient for the remainder of my days. I hate life. There: I have said it; I'll not take it back. Yes, life; and everything that reminds me that life must be borne. It bores me to eat, to dress, to stand on my feet, etc. I have dragged this hatred everywhere, wherever I have been at school, in Rouen, in Paris, on the Nile. . . .

Flaubert was thirty, and had just begun *Madame Bovary.* DuCamp made the mistake of supposing that Flaubert wanted a plain blunt bracing rejoinder (and paid for it with the end of their intimacy):

> Your way of life involves two great drawbacks:
> 1. It has tied you to your mother, hand and foot. It has given you the terrible habit of depending on others where your everyday life is concerned, and of thinking only of your *subjective* self and never of your *objective* self.
> 2. It has encased you completely within your own personality. You know how *you* live, but not how others live. Look about you as you may, you see only yourself; and in everything you have written, you have portrayed only yourself.
> Those are the two great flaws in your way of life; and the fact is that it is weighing on you, boring you, and making you think that you "hate life," whereas it is simply *your* life that you hate.

The demon writer isn't having any of *that*, thank you; and his impassive mask is a way of persuading readers that the Almighty Himself endorses every misanthropic commonplace: when Flaubert has Emma Bovary "discover in adultery all the banalities of marriage," it isn't he but God and Emma who strike a blow at adultery and marriage and incidentally at every other prospect of pleasure. One critic is enchanted by the letters of this "literary colossus" because "Here we may see the total man . . . without his impassive mask," an image which suggests a monumental figure on the Greek stage clomping toward his doom but doesn't explain why modern man when he grasps the sacred ballpoint has to dress himself up as if for Halloween: Why, for instance, shouldn't the man who writes the letters wear the impassive mask and the man who writes the novels express himself totally? "The stories in *Dubliners* seem to be indisputably well done but," worries Joyce, "after all, perhaps many people could do them as well. I am not rewarded by any feeling of having overcome difficulties." The indifferent artist paring his fingernails is cold comfort to the anxious young man who keeps biting them to the quick. If writing is mere manna from the intense inane, if it isn't done by anybody at all (Flaubert the father of prose is also godfather of the intense inanities of structuralism), then it can be done by just anybody: e.g. the anonymous "mean" style of *Dubliners* (relieved only by patches of pretty pathos filched from the Celtic twilight of AE or Yeats that in his letters Joyce can't abide). On the other hand Joyce the young man (not the young artist), away from his wife for a few weeks, misses her so painfully that he doesn't turn out neat little public epiphanies (to show the back of his elegant hand to priest-ridden Ireland and its dead capital), instead he uses his Irish blarney (and his hatred of the priests) in a series of private letters to work her up to a pitch of excitement where he can take the risk of expressing, if not the total man, at least a recognizable man with all of a man's (as Joyce in a letter to his brother calls it) "extraordinary cerebral sexualism":

> Darling, do not be offended at what I wrote. You thank
> me for the beautiful name I gave you. Yes, dear, it is a nice

name "My beautiful wild flower of the hedges! My dark-blue, rain-drenched flower!" You see I am a little of the poet still. I am giving you a lovely book for a present too: and it is a poet's present for the woman he loves. *But*, side by side and inside this spiritual love I have for you there is also a wild beast-like craving for every inch of your body, for every secret and shameful part of it, for every odour and act of it. My love for you allows me to pray to the spirit of eternal beauty and tenderness mirrored in your eyes or to fling you down under me on that soft belly of yours and fuck you up behind, like a hog riding a sow, glorying in the very stink and sweat that rises from your arse, glorying in the open shame of your upturned dress and white girlish drawers and in the confusion of your flushed cheeks and tangled hair. It allows me to burst into tears of pity and love at some slight word, to tremble with love for you at the sounding of some chord or cadence of music or to lie head and tails with you feeling your fingers fondling and tickling my ballocks or stuck up in me behind and your hot lips sucking off my cock while my head is wedged in between your fat thighs, my hands clutching the round cushions of your bum and my tongue licking ravenously up your rank red cunt. I have taught you almost to swoon at the hearing of my voice singing or murmuring to your soul the passion and sorrow and mystery of life and at the same time have taught you to make filthy signs to me with your lips and tongue, to provoke me by obscene touches and noises, and even to do in my presence the most shameful and filthy act of the body. You remember the day you pulled up your clothes and let me lie under you looking up at you while you did it? Then you were ashamed even to meet my eyes.

You are mine, darling, mine! I love you. All I have written above is only a moment or two of brutal madness. The last drop of seed has hardly been squirted up your cunt . . .

—and so on and so forth (maybe he ought to have phoned instead: Reach out and touch someone): in comparison with which Leopold

Bloom (not to mention Stephen Dedalus or the poet and novelist James Joyce) is only your average run-of-the-mill literary colossus all dressed up in his impassive mask, indifferent, paring his fingernails.

It becomes an issue of integrity. When Lawrence's mother is dying of cancer, he describes the circumstances in a letter to a woman who is barely an acquaintance:

> I did not know where you were. I am glad you wrote to me.
>
> I have been at home now ten days. My mother is very near the end. Today I have been to Leicester. I did not get home till half past nine. Then I ran upstairs. The pains had been again.
>
> "Oh my dear" I said, "is it the pains?"
>
> "Not pain now—Oh the weariness" she moaned, so that I could hardly hear her. I wish she could die tonight.
>
> My sister and I do all the nursing. My sister is only 22. I sit upstairs hours and hours, till I wonder if ever it were true that I was at London. I seem to have died since, and that is an old life, dreamy.
>
> I will tell you. My mother was a clever, ironical delicately moulded woman, of good, old burgher descent. She married below her. My father was dark, ruddy, with a fine laugh. He is a coal miner. He was one of the sanguine temperament, warm and hearty, but unstable: he lacked principle, as my mother would have said. He deceived her and lied to her. She despised him—he drank.
>
> Their marriage life has been one carnal, bloody fight. I was born hating my father: as early as ever I can remember, I shivered with horror when he touched me. He was very bad before I was born.
>
> This has been a kind of bond between me and my mother. We have loved each other, almost with a husband and wife love, as well as filial and maternal. We knew each other by instinct. She said to my aunt—about me:
>
> "But it has been different with him. He has seemed to be part of me."—and that is the real case. We have been

like one, so sensitive to each other that we never needed words. It has been rather terrible, and has made me, in some respects, abnormal. . . .

And the letter goes on to complete the telling of the same story that Lawrence dramatizes and expands to the length of a novel in *Sons and Lovers*, where his mother is the heroine and immortal beloved and moreover his father takes the opportunity that the son belatedly gives him to affirm and occupy his own blessed space (as Lawrence the novelist takes the opportunities he is given by Lawrence the son and lover):

> He always made his own breakfast. Being a man who rose early and had plenty of time he did not, as some miners do, drag his wife out of bed at six o'clock. At five, sometimes earlier, he woke, got straight out of bed, and went downstairs. When she could not sleep, his wife lay waiting for this time, as for a period of peace. The only real rest seemed to be when he was out of the house.
>
> He went downstairs in his shirt and then struggled into his pit-trousers, which were left on the hearth to warm all night. There was always a fire, because Mrs. Morel raked. And the first sound in the house was the bang, bang of the poker against the raker, as Morel smashed the remainder of the coal to make the kettle, which was filled and left on the hob, finally boil. His cup and knife and fork, all he wanted except just the food, was laid ready on the table on a newspaper. Then he got his breakfast, made the tea, packed the bottom of the doors with rugs to shut out the draught, piled a big fire, and sat down to an hour of joy. He toasted his bacon on a fork and caught the drops of fat on his bread; then he put the rasher on his thick slice of bread, and cut off chunks with a clasp-knife, poured his tea into his saucer, and was happy. . . .

Flaubert like Lawrence was exceptionally devoted to his mother, though art is so much more important than life that he doesn't for quite a while remember to reassure her in the letter in which he rather tactlessly asserts that the artist can't afford to feel a thing but has to live outside life and (doesn't his mother occupy any space?) "alone":

> If a man, whether of low or high degree, wishes to meddle with God's works, he must begin, if only as a healthy precaution, by putting himself in a position where he cannot be made a fool of. You can depict wine, love, women and glory on the condition that you're not a drunkard, a lover, a husband, or a private in the ranks. If you participate actively in life, you don't see it clearly: you suffer from it too much or enjoy it too much. The artist, to my way of thinking, is a monstrosity, something outside nature. All the misfortunes Providence inflicts on him come from his stubbornness in denying that axiom. He suffers from that denial and makes others suffer. Ask women who have loved poets, or men who have loved actresses. So (and this is my conclusion) I am resigned to living as I have lived: alone, with my throng of great men as my only cronies—a bear, with my bear-rug as company. I care nothing for the world, for the future, for what people will say, for any kind of establishment, or even for literary renown, which in the past I used to lie awake so many nights dreaming about. That is what I am like; such is my character.

Suddenly it occurs to him that he is, after all, addressing the woman in whose presumably negligible company he will be living, as he insists, "alone," all by himself, without any company save that of the gracious dead:

> The devil take me if I know why I've written you these two pages of tirade, poor dear. No, no: when I think of your sweet face, so sad and loving, and of the joy I have in living with you, who are so full of serenity and such grave charm, I know very well that I shall never love another woman as I do you. You will have no rival, never fear! The senses or a momentary fancy will not take the place of what lies locked in the fastness of a triple sanctuary . . . [Flaubert's ellipsis]

Still, the novelist never takes the opportunity that the son and lover gives him: or the senses are locked away forever from the only mystery that might shake them up: none of the women in Flaubert's fiction resembles the woman of that last paragraph; if they aren't imbecile plaster saints like Félicité in *A Simple Heart* they're sardonic or pathetic testimony to the hopelessness of marriage, adultery, and life in general—

> But it was above all at mealtimes that she could bear it no longer, in that little room on the ground floor, with the smoking stove, the creaking door, the oozing walls, the damp floor-tiles; all the bitterness of life seemed to be served to her on her plate, and, with the steam from the boiled beef, there rose from the depths of her soul other exhalations as it were of disgust. Charles was a slow eater; she would nibble a few hazel-nuts, or else, leaning on her elbow, would amuse herself making marks on the oilcloth with the point of her table-knife.

I choose this paragraph from *Madame Bovary* because it's the text for a famous exercise in admiration by Erich Auerbach in *Mimesis*; and because, just as Lawrence's description of Walter Morel's "hour of joy" demonstrates that life is always possible, so Flaubert's description of the Bovarys at table demonstrates that bourgeois routine is suffocating, the provinces are deadly, marriage is loathsome (not that some people have trouble enjoying life; not that some relationships go wrong, or are wrong from the beginning): it's a giveaway that the paragraph would present a cosy domestic scene, which Flaubert would rather have died than written, if one substitutes "loved" for "could bear it no longer, in"; "joy" for "bitterness"; "contentment" for "disgust": the point of Flaubert's paragraph is that every sensation or perception has no other purpose than to reinforce the inference that life is impossible except for the observer who imperturbably reports it. Flaubert's satisfaction in writing life off is so much greater than any satisfaction available to his characters that his only feasible subject is the satisfaction he takes in writing life off; and so he has arrived at his artistic ideal, "a book about nothing, a book dependent on nothing external."

Furthermore Flaubert's personal enthusiasm when he explains to his mother why the artist has to dispense with personality and enthusiasm produces better, fuller, richer, livelier writing than his novels; just as Joyce's personal enthusiasm in his letters does, the street-gamin cheekiness and wit, the sheer haste to get back to work at the bank or the language class or back to guileless Nora: "I really can't write. Nora is trying on a pair of drawers at the wardrobe"; "At present she is licking jam off a piece of paper. She is very well, wears a veil now and looks very pretty. Just now she came in and said 'The landlady has her hen laying out there. O, *he's* after laying a lovely egg.' Jaysus! O Jaysus!": just as Joyce's intellectual appetite trammeled by life but not for the moment by theories of art produces in his letters all sorts of bonuses, from a vigorous and affectionate defense of Tolstoy (who was still alive and kicking and probably less "genuinely spiritual" than Joyce imagined)—

> As for Tolstoy, I disagree with you altogether. Tolstoy is a magnificent writer. He is never dull, never stupid, never tired, never pedantic, never theatrical! He is head and shoulders over the others. I don't take him very seriously as a Christian saint. I think he has a very genuine spiritual nature but I suspect that he speaks the very best Russian with a St Petersburg accent and remembers the Christian name of his great-great-grandfather (this, I find, is at the bottom of the essentially feudal art of Russia). I see that he wrote a 13 column letter to *The Times* of London attacking governments. Even the English "liberal" papers are indignant. Not merely does he attack armaments, he even alludes to the Tsar as a "weak-minded Hussar officer, standing below the intellectual level of most of his subjects, grossly superstitious and of coarse tastes." The English liberals are shocked: they would call him vulgar but that they know he is a prince. . . .

—to a "cinematographic" account of his daily miseries in Rome:

> Do you imagine you are corresponding with the indifferential calculus that you object to my vituperation on Italy and Rome. What the hell else would I do? If you had to traipse about a city, accompanied by a plaintive woman with infant (also plaintive), run up stairs, ring a bell, "Chi c'è?" "Camera"

"Chi c'è?" "Camera!" ["Who's there?" "Room!"] No go: room too small or too dear: won't have children, single man only, no kitchen. "Arrivederla!" Down again. Rush off: give a lesson for 9½d, rush back to bank, etc etc. Am sending MS to John Long by same post. Didn't change anything. No pen, no ink, no table, no room, no time, no quiet, no inclination. Never mind, it will be back in a week or so. . . . The Italian imagination is like a cinematograph, observe the style of my letter. Wurruk is more dissipating than dissipation. Thanks for Whitman's poems. What long flowing lines he writes. Kick in the arse for the following. G.K.C.: G.B.S.: S.L.: H.J.: G.R. [Chesterton, Shaw, Sidney Lee, Henry James, Grant Richards (the publisher who accepted *Dubliners* but didn't publish it)]. Kicks in the arse all round, in fact.

Not only can he never learn to love the Italians, he doesn't scruple to show strong and personal feelings (none of the indifferential calculus of art) in expressing his distaste:

I have been trying to read Carducci's verses, induced by the fact that he died unfortified by the rites of R.C.C. But not only does it not interest me: it even seems to me false and exaggerated. I dislike Italian verse. I find Italian men lacking in delicacy and virility. They are intelligent as a rule and clever but babyish. Of delicacy neither their men nor their women have a scrap. I don't so much object to its absence in the latter. The day of Bruno's memorial procession I was standing among the crowd waiting for the cortege to appear. It was a murky day and, being Sunday, I had not washed. I was wearing a white felt hat, faded by reason of heavy rains. Scholz's five crown cloak hung bawways [arseways] on me. My boots, being Sunday, were coated with a week's dirt and I was in need of a shave. In fact, I was a horrible example of free thought. Near me were two good-looking young women, females, of the people, that is. They were in charge of an elderly woman and a middle-aged man. They were low-sized and quince-coloured in the face with amiable dog's eyes.

One of them had a trinket on a long chain and this she constantly raised slowly to her lips and rested it there, slowly parting them, all the time gazing tranquilly about her. I watched her do this for quite a long time until I perceived that the trinket was a miniature revolver! I tried to explain my sensation to one or two Italians, narrating the fact as best I could. They saw nothing strange in it or typical or significant. One of them told me that many Italian women wear a cazzo [prick] as a trinket and after that they talked to their heart's content about cazzo and Co—a topic which, in my opinion, it requires a great deal of talent or else a great deal of courage to render in any way interesting. When I enter the bank in the morning I wait for someone to announce something about either his cazzo, culo [arse] or coglioni [balls]. This usually happens before a quarter to nine.

A fascinating and not by any means inconsistent complaint from the R.C. apostate who would write *Ulysses* as well as those cazzo-culo-coglioni letters to Nora.

Life direct, as in this homesick outburst, is what Flaubert and Joyce have convinced themselves the man may never get quite clear of but the artist has nothing to do with. What they can't admit is that art is overrated: which artists, faking and fumbling it together out of spit and toothpicks, should know best of all. Lawrence writes his current girlfriend that he has taken *The Red and the Black* out of the library: "I shall enjoy it"; but he adds wistfully, "The worst of being a novelist, and having dreams and fancies, is that you know all this is fiction. You know the inanimate dumminess of them—and demand life direct like a blow." Even if, as Flaubert would object, it puts you in a position where you can be made a fool of.

A year later Lawrence, having eloped to the Continent with somebody else's wife, writes to a friend back home:

I love Frieda so much I don't like to talk about it. I never knew what love was before. She wanted me to write to you. I want you and her to be friends always. Some time perhaps she—perhaps we—shall need you. Then you'll be good to us, won't you?

The world is wonderful and beautiful and good beyond one's wildest imagination. Never, never, never could one conceive what love is, beforehand, never. Life *can* be great— quite god-like. It *can* be so. God be thanked I have proved it.

You might write to us here. Our week of honeymoon is over. Lord, it was lovely. But this—do I like this better?— I like it so much. Don't tell anybody. This is only for the good to know. Write to us.

It didn't last forever, but then neither does art.

Life Direct, or
A Dream of
Fair Women

"La donna è mobile": Woman is fickle, chirps the Duke of Mantua in Verdi's *Rigoletto*, taking a moment from his rakish pursuit of all the women in Mantua. In this parable the Duke is the sovereign artist, and women are his fidgety and dispensable subjects to do with as he will. In Lawrence's *Women in Love* the sovereignty of art over woman is reaffirmed by the nasty little artist Loerke (for whom as for Flaubert art isn't life, art has no subject, the artist has no responsibility to his subject, people don't matter, art doesn't mean what the artist plainly says), but it's also challenged by one of his potential subjects:

> Loerke snorted with rage.
> "A picture of myself!" he repeated in derision. "Wissen Sie, gnädige Frau, that is a Kunstwerk, a work of art. It is a work of art, it is a picture of nothing, of absolutely nothing. It has nothing to do with anything but itself. . . ."
> Ursula . . . was furious. . . .
> "It isn't a word of it true, of all this harangue you have made me," she replied flatly. "The horse is a picture of your own stock, stupid brutality, and the girl was a girl you loved and tortured and then ignored."

In Jane Austen's *Persuasion* Anne Elliot is another mutinous subject who has the temerity to raise objections:

> ". . . Well, Miss Elliot [says Captain Harville], . . . we shall never agree I suppose upon this point. No man and woman would, probably. But let me observe that all histories are

against you, all stories, prose and verse. If I had such a memory as Benwick, I could bring you fifty quotations in a moment on my side the argument, and I do not think I ever opened a book in my life which had not something to say upon woman's inconstancy. Songs and proverbs, all talk of woman's fickleness. But perhaps you will say, these were all written by men."

"Perhaps I shall.—Yes, yes, if you please, no reference to examples in books. Men have had every advantage of us in telling their own story. Education has been theirs in so much higher a degree; the pen has been in their hands. I will not allow books to prove any thing."

Men write the books, and no doubt the exigencies of art prevent them from telling the truth. Chaucer's Wife of Bath outsmarts and outlives her first four husbands because they have no books, but the fifth (before tardily succumbing in his turn) is a tartar: a scholar with a compendious book of texts (all written by men) that list and describe all the horrors committed by women—

> *Now wol I seye yow sooth, by seint Thomas,*
> *Why that I rente out of his book a leef,*
> *For which he smoot me so that I was deef. . . .*
> *. . . every nyght and day was his custume,*
> *Whan he hadde leyser and vacacioun*
> *From oother worldly occupacioun,*
> *To reden on this book of wikked wyves.*
> *He knew of hem mo legendes and lyves*
> *Than been of goode wyves in the Bible.*
> *For trusteth wel, it is an inpossible*
> *That any clerk wol speke good of wyves,*   [scholar]
> *But if it be of hooly seintes lyves,*
> *Ne of noon oother womman never the mo.*
> *Who peyntede the leon, tel me who?*

(The Wife is triumphantly reminding us of Aesop's Fable 183: "In a controversy betwixt a Lion and a Man, which was the braver and the stronger creature of the two; why look ye, says the Man, we'll appeal to that statue there; and so he showed him the figure of a man cut in stone, with a lion under his feet. Well! says the Lion, if we Lions had been brought up to painting and carving, as you Men are, where you have one Lion under the feet of a Man, we should have had twenty Men under the paw of a Lion.")

> *By God! if wommen hadde writen stories,*
> *As clerkes han withinne hire oratories,*
> *They wolde han writen of men moore wikkednesse*
> *Than al the mark of Adam may redresse.*   [all
>   in the image of Adam]

Men write the books (and preach them to women), and what's more when sweet reasonableness fails they have the heavier hand:

> *And whan I saugh he wolde nevere fyne*   [end]
> *To reden on this cursed book al nyght,*
> *Al sodeynly thre leves have I plyght*   [plucked]
> *Out of his book, right as he radde, and eke*
> *I with my fest so took hym on the cheke*
> *That in oure fyr he fil bakward adoun.*
> *And he up stirte as dooth a wood leoun,*   [mad]
> *And with his fest he smoot me on the heed,*
> *That in the floor I lay as I were deed.*

Still, in Chaucer's book at any rate, such women as the Wife of Bath even *in extremis* aren't altogether without resources:

> *And whan he saugh how stille that I lay,*
> *He was agast, and wolde han fled his way,*
> *Til atte laste out of my swogh I breyde.*   [swoon, started]
> *"O! hastow slayn me, false theef?" I seyde,*
> *"And for my land thus hastow mordred me?*
> *Er I be deed, yet wol I kisse thee."*
>   *And neer he cam, and kneled faire adoun,*
> *And seyde, "Deere suster Alisoun,*
> *As help me God! I shal thee nevere smyte.*
> *That I have doon, it is thyself to wyte.*   [to blame]
> *Foryeve it me, and that I thee biseke!"*
> *And yet eftsoones I hitte hym on the cheke,*   [immediately]
> *And seyde, "Theef, thus muchel am I wreke;*   [revenged]

Now wol I dye, I may no lenger speke."
But atte laste, with muchel care and wo,
We fille accorded by us selven two.   [fell into accord]
He yaf me al the bridel in myn hond,
To han the governance of hous and lond,
And of his tonge, and of his hond also;
And made hym brenne his book anon right tho.

Burning his book was the beginning of wisdom, and they lived happily ever after till he died.

Chaucer is one of the few male writers who feel comfortable with their female characters: the all-too-ladylike Prioress; Alisoun the Arch-Wife; the not-uncomplicatedly-patient Griselda; that other Alisoun in *The Miller's Tale*, the knockout of a young wife who incites the sudden love of the young scholar who (looking up from his book) sees a vision, all dolled up and ready to go—

A ceynt she werede, barred al of silk,   [girdle, striped]
A barmclooth eek as whit as morne milk   [apron]
Upon hir lendes, ful of many a goore.   [loins]
Whit was hir smok, and broyden al bifoore   [chemise, embroidered]
And eek bihynde, on hir coler aboute,
Of col-blak silk, withinne and eek withoute. . . .
She was ful moore blisful on to see
Than is the newe pere-jonette tree,   [blossoming, early-pear]
And softer than the wolle is of a wether.
And by hir girdel heeng a purs of lether,   [belt]
Tasseled with silk, and perled with latoun.   [ornamented with beads]

—most and best of all, Criseyde. Chaucer's women aren't daydreams or nightmares (Shakespeare's before and after), they aren't pushovers or uncontrollable sensualists, they hold off and hold out: the Wife of Bath, till she has the reins in her hand and those misogynist pages crackling up the chimney; the Miller's Alisoun, till her husband is safely stashed for the night in a tub just under the roof-beams; Criseyde, till she's ready and every barrier has fallen as if by inspiration or magic: and once they yield they have a fine time many times over. Two centuries later Shakespeare's

version of Cressida (as her name has by then evolved) holds out
not because she isn't yet ready (she muses that to begin with she's
ready! she's ready! she's as raring to go as Troilus), she holds out
till—well, would hold out indefinitely if she could because as every
woman knows a woman loses her value for a man at the very
microsecond of yielding:

> . . . *more in Troilus thousandfold I see*
> *Than in the glass of Pandar's praise may be.*
> *Yet hold I off. Women are angels, wooing.*   [when being wooed]
> *Things won are done. Joy's soul lies in the doing.*
> *That she beloved knows nought that knows not this:*
> *Men prize the thing ungained more than it is.*
> *That she was never yet that ever knew*
> *Love got so sweet as when desire did sue.*
> *Therefore this maxim out of love I teach:*
> *Achievement is command; ungained, beseech.*
> *Then though my heart's content firm love doth bear,*
> *Nothing of that shall from mine eyes appear.*

(Typical tortive and protractive Shakespeare. That indigestible
cramp of a tenth line means: When a man takes a woman he takes
command of her; untaken, she can keep him begging.) It then
must follow, as the day the night, that when blank day follows
the night of consummation, the tables are turned forever: Troilus,
having had his fun ("Enjoy'd no sooner but despised straight"),
from raring to go is now quite ready to go and Cressida, having
given her all, is left with nothing—

>   *Prithee, tarry.*
> *You men will never tarry.*
> *O foolish Cressid! I might have still held off,*
> *And then you would have tarried.*

These Shakespearean lovers, so quickly doused and enervated,
aren't a bit like Chaucer's, for whom making love makes for more
and more love not less:

> *Thise ilke two, of whom that I yow seye,*   [same]
> *Whan that hire hertes wel assured were,*

Tho gonne they to speken and to pleye,
And ek rehercen how, and whan, and where
Thei knewe hem first, and every wo and feere
That passed was; but al swich hevynesse,
I thank it God, was torned to gladnesse.

And evere mo, whan that hem fel to speke
Of any wo of swich a tyme agoon,
With kissyng al that tale sholde breke,
And fallen in a newe joye anoon;
And diden al hire myght, syn they were oon,
For to recoveren blisse and ben at eise,
And passed wo with joie contrepeise.   [past, counterbalance]

Resoun wol nought that I speke of slep,
For it acordeth nought to my matere.
God woot, they took of that ful litel kep!
But lest this nyght, that was to hem so deere,
No sholde in veyne escape in no manere,
It was byset in joie and bisynesse
Of al that souneth into gentilesse.   [conduces to]

(Notice that six hundred years ago inside the strangely spelled words and intricate stanzas and rhyme-patterns Chaucer, unlike certain other major English poets, is speaking English.) And, when morning comes, it isn't the more and more irreversibly love-struck Troilus but apprehensive Criseyde, concerned to avoid scandal, who has to rise and leave:

"Myn hertes lif, my trist, and my plesaunce,   [trust]
That I was born, allas, what me is wo,
That day of us moot make disseveraunce!
For tyme it is to ryse and hennes go,
Or ellis I am lost for evere mo!
O nyght, allas! why nyltow over us hove,
As longe as whan Almena lay by Jove? . . ."

Chaucer's primary source for his poem is Boccaccio's *Il Filostrato* (The Man Stricken by Love); but Boccaccio's Criseida (like the Duke of Mantua's passing fancies) is made from a man's fancy for

the sake of his pleasure (unlike Shakespeare's Cressida, made from
a man's funk for the sake of his total demoralization), she's a
coarse-grained projection on the locker-room wall ("every lady leads
an amorous life in her wishes," says Pandaro, "and . . . naught
but fear of shame holds her back"), a swinger in all but opportunity,
a widow and everybody knows what *they're* like, all turned on and
nowhere to turn (widows still more than other women are "desirous," says Pandaro delicately); one of those fabulous mechanisms
that, once broken in, are hotter than a smoking gun (remember
the Italian woman Joyce noticed touching the toy revolver again
and again to her lips), certainly hotter than any mere man: unlike
Criseyde, she doesn't have to be maneuvered and tricked into an
assignation but arranges it herself; unlike Criseyde, she confesses
to enjoying it even more than the man ("if thou dost eagerly desire
to return here, I desire it far more than thou"); unlike Criseyde,
she is rather like a man—except for details of appearance and
physiology—only more so; and when Troilo leaves her on their
first morning after (because it's at her place not his where they've
spent the night) "he felt clearly that love tormented him far more
than it had done in his earlier desires; so much had he found
Criseida to surpass what he had before conceived of her": apparently
she has moves he never dreamed of, even Shakespeare's Troilus
(or Shakespeare himself) might have relished another crack at her
after a brief pause for rest and refreshment.

Chaucer doesn't carry on like that about standoffish Criseyde,
whom he seems to think of as both a typical and an ideal woman.
One fact he makes clear from the outset is that she has no trouble
living without men and love, she has no interest in either tor-
menting or gratifying or enjoying any imaginable man, she cher-
ishes her freedom (now that her husband's dead and she can live
in quiet retirement)—

> "I am myn owene womman, wel at ese,
> I thank it God, as after myn estat,   [social position]
> Right yong, and stonde unteyd in lusty leese,   [pleasant pasture]
> Withouten jalousie or swich debat.
> Shal noon housbonde seyn to me 'chek mat!'

For either they ben ful of jalousie,
Or maisterfull, or loven novelrie. . . ."

—she isn't a Shakespearean slut ("Fie, fie upon her!" cries Ulysses about Cressida, this "daughter of the game" who has wiggled a hip or two while taking a stroll among the Greeks) or a Boccaccian hot number or Shakespearean cold meat on a trencher (any morning after), she'll settle for being left alone though she has a mirror and eyes to see with: "For wel woot [*know*] I myself, so God me spede, / Al wolde I that noon wiste [*knew*] of this thought, / I am oon the faireste, out of drede [*doubtless*], / And goodlieste, whoso taketh hede, / And so men seyn, in al the town of Troie." She isn't naïve or stupid, she is watchful (timid, solitary), she knows her beauty (There was never yet fair woman didn't make mouths in a glass, and why shouldn't she?), she knows the likely effect of her good looks on whoever has a good look, besides in private she's a warm and gentle soul formed for affection and love—if she weren't so fond of her uncle Pandarus there's no question that Troilus would perish unrequited—but it needs all of Pandarus's wit and improvisation and love of her and of Troilus to bring her to the point of not only falling in love with Troilus but taking him into her bed; in fact, it's (Chaucer's invention) a bed in a guest room of Pandarus's house, it's Pandarus's bed where he has tricked her into spending the night so that she'll be available to Troilus at last, and where (in a scene not only wholly invented by Chaucer but which couldn't have been conceived or even conceived of in a thousand years by Boccaccio or Shakespeare) Uncle Pandarus comes visiting his niece the morning after to rejoice in the happy outcome (for *all* of them: "so may we ben gladed alle thre," he has promised Troilus much earlier) and happily rub it in:

Pandare, o-morwe which that comen was
Unto his nece and gan hire faire grete,
Seyde, "Al this nyght so reyned it, allas,
That al my drede is that ye, nece swete,
Han litel laiser had to slepe and mete. [dream]

Al nyght," quod he, "hath reyn so do me wake,   [kept me awake]
That som of us, I trowe, hire hedes ake."

And ner he com, and seyde, "How stant it now   [nearer]
This mury morwe? Nece, how kan ye fare?"   [how are you doing]
Criseyde answerde, "Nevere the bet for yow,   [better]
Fox that ye ben! God yeve youre herte kare!
God help me so, ye caused al this fare,
Trowe I," quod she, "for al youre wordes white.
O, whoso seeth yow, knoweth yow ful lite."   [little]

With that she gan hire face for to wrye   [cover]
With the shete, and wax for shame al reed;
And Pandarus gan under for to prie,
And seyde, "Nece, if that I shal be ded,
Have here a swerd and smyteth of myn hed!"
With that his arm al sodeynly he thriste
Under hire nekke, and at the laste hire kyste.

"I passe al that which chargeth nought [*is of no importance*] to seye,"
adds Chaucer; "What! God foryaf his deth, and she al so / Foryaf,
and with here uncle gan to pleye [*kid around*]": maybe Jesus' God
doesn't have a sense of humor, but Chaucer's does, and won't mind
being compared with a living goddess who shares His power to
bestow grace on undeserving men. Criseyde is a sweet and rather
bashful girl, a classy dame, a gracious lady, a goddess with a sense
of humor and a sense of reality; she knows that Troilus loves her
the other side idolatry, and for all her eventual passionate love of
him she doesn't deceive herself that she's as crazy about him in
return: when the Trojan bigwigs have decided to turn her over
to the Greeks, the weeping lovers meet and this time Criseyde
takes Troilus into her bed so he can listen in as much comfort
as possible while she tries to reason him (and herself) into believing
that the situation isn't as desperate as it undeniably is—"I am a
womman," she begins defensively, shyly, knowing that even idol-
aters like Troilus can't help regarding women as, if surely mistresses
and companions, not possibly counselors and can't help deprecating
their arguments; and suddenly the second and more important
meaning of what she has said flashes on her consciousness and she

completes the line with a sort of self-deprecating shrug: "as ful
wel ye woot [*know*]" (Chaucer's and nobody else's heartbreakingly
attentive Criseyde): Troilus knows maybe better than she does how
specifically she's a woman, better than he knows his own maleness:
like Joyce with Nora he can taste and smell every inch of her
body. And not just her body: Trollope, most truthful of Victorian
novelists, in one of his late novels has a new husband tell his wife,
"When a man loves a woman he falls in love with everything
belonging to her": idolatry and fetishism: not only gorgeous Alisoun's bare ass with its unexpected and kissable beard out over
the window sill on a dark night in *The Miller's Tale* but what in
common daylight she merely wears, what she owns, her embroi-
dered chemise, the leather purse with silk tassels hanging at her
belt; not only Criseyde's self but her spit and image. (As a token
of his esteem Joyce kept in his trousers pocket a miniature pair
of ladies' drawers. In a letter to a friend he noted that in the work
which ended as *Finnegans Wake* he identifies Isolde's all-powerful
love-philter as nothing more than the age-old male obsession to
which the lady addresses her siren-song: "Love me, love my drawers"—though as usual in the *Wake* he spoils it with cheerless, and
in this instance unpronounceable, pedantic punning: "Love me,
love my drugrs": do you get it? do you get it?) Criseyde knows
she's less the one who loves than the one who is loved, because
when a man as pure as Troilus falls as hard as Troilus does he is
stuck for good and all as perhaps a woman however loving and
passionate, lacking a man's idolatry and fetishism, lacking his
extraordinary cerebral sexualism, will never be.

It's a man's world, and Criseyde is too spectacular a prize not
to be picked off sooner or later without her connivance, and then
as it happens packed off against her will from her cosy home in
Troy to the besieging army's encampment, which will allow her
no chance of escape and no choice except submission or heroic
defiance, but which she keeps earnestly assuring herself as well
as Troilus she will talk herself out of just like that right back to
Troilus (who would rather run off with her into the boondocks
far from cities and armies, but whom she can talk out of anything).
The fact is that, though she loves Troilus, she isn't prepared to
risk death or permanent exile with him; and so she keeps hoping

and believing that risks won't be necessary, that delay and postponement are best (Sufficient unto the day the evil thereof), that sooner or later all will be well. Men write the books, men pull the strings, and women are fickle, fearful, coy, calculating. How can a man trust them? or even trust what they say, especially when they say what he's dying to hear, as when Shakespeare's lovers are brought together by that vile and mincing Shakespearean Cupid, Pandarus ("She's making her ready. She'll come straight. You must be witty now. She does so blush, and fetches her wind so short as if she were frayed with a spirit. I'll fetch her. It is the prettiest villain. She fetches her breath as short as a new-ta'en sparrow"):

> CRESSIDA: *Boldness comes to me now and brings me heart.*
> *Prince Troilus, I have loved you night and day*
> *For many weary months.*
> TROILUS: *Why was my Cressid then so hard to win?*
> CRESSIDA: *Hard to seem won, but I was won, my lord,*
> *With the first glance that ever—pardon me,*
> *If I confess much you will play the tyrant.*
> *I love you now, but till now not so much*
> *But I might master it. In faith, I lie.*
> *My thoughts were like unbridled children grown*
> *Too headstrong for their mother. See, we fools!*
> *Why have I blabbed? Who shall be true to us*
> *When we are so unsecret to ourselves?*
> *But, though I loved you well, I wooed you not,*
> *And yet, good faith, I wished myself a man,*
> *Or that we women had men's privilege*
> *O speaking first. Sweet, bid me hold my tongue,*
> *For in this rapture I shall surely speak*
> *The thing I shall repent. See, see, your silence,*
> *Cunning in dumbness, from my weakness draws*
> *My very soul of counsel. Stop my mouth.*
> TROILUS: *And shall, albeit sweet music issues thence.*
> PANDARUS: *Pretty, i' faith.*

—another blathering and emetic Shakespearean travesty of love. (I know! I know! Shakespeare is writing about *bad* women—who

talk very much like his good women—or about good women who
are cursed, struck, murdered by husbands not easily jealous but
instantaneously driven bonkers by this or that. It's a lesson to us
all.) Chaucer has the advantage, in a narrative rather than dramatic
poem, of allowing his lovers to exchange their vows in bed; and
he has additional advantages of richness, economy, variety, tone,
taste, tact, feeling, delicacy, subtlety, discrimination, sympathy,
grace, and love:

> *Criseyde, which that felte hire thus itake,*
> *As writen clerkes in hire bokes olde,*
> *Right as an aspes leef she gan to quake,*   [aspen]
> *Whan she hym felte hire in his armes folde.*
> *But Troilus, al hool of cares colde,*   [whole]
> *Gan thanken tho the blisful goddes sevene.*   [the seven planets]
> *Thus sondry peynes bryngen folk to hevene.*

> *This Troilus in armes gan hire streyne,*
> *And seyde, "O swete, as evere mot I gon,*   [as I hope to live]
> *Now be ye kaught, now is ther but we tweyne!*
> *Now yeldeth yow, for other bote is non!"*   [help]
> *To that Criseyde answerde thus anon,*
> *"Ne hadde I er now, my swete herte deere,*
> *Ben yold, ywis, I were now nought heere!"* . . .

> *Criseyde, al quyt from every drede and tene,*   [sorrow]
> *As she that juste cause hadde hym to triste,*
> *Made hym swich feste, it joye was to seene,*   [such a celebration]
> *Whan she his trouthe and clene entente wiste;*   [intention, knew]
> *And as aboute a tree, with many a twiste,*
> *Bytrent and writh the swote wodebynde,*   [encircles, entwines]
> *Gan eche of hem in armes other wynde.*

> *And as the newe abaysed nyghtyngale,*   [at first abashed]
> *That stynteth first whan she bygynneth to synge,*   [stops at once]
> *Whan that she hereth any herde tale,*   [any shepherd speak]
> *And after siker doth hire vois out rynge,*   [confidently]
> *Right so Criseyde, whan hire drede stente,*   [stopped]
> *Opned hire herte, and tolde hym hire entente.*   [all her feelings]

(Compare Chaucer's entwining woodbine to Shakespeare's beast with two backs. Chaucer is cheerful enough to imagine coitus as not only an occasionally agreeable activity but a handsome one, whereas Shakespeare is glum enough to imagine nothing happier than that double-humped carnal monster.)

According to Shakespeare and Boccaccio women are "desirous" (Boccaccio approves; Shakespeare disapproves and despairs—"The fitchew nor the soilèd horse / Goes to 't with a more riotous appetite"); women, according to the two men, aren't nearly so hesitant and skittish about sex as they pretend to be and like to seem (or, presumably, as Chaucer's Criseyde seems to be till the long courtship ends in her full assurance and ease with Troilus). Hence it isn't surprising that Boccaccio's Criseida might well be Joyce's Italian woman "tranquilly" touching the toy revolver or cazzo-emblem to her lips—when Pandaro comes to Criseida with Troilo's first letter, Criseida "stood timidly and took it not":

> "My Pandaro, do thou have some regard for me and not only for the youth, so may love bring thee to a state of peace. Consider whether that which thou askest now is seemly—judge thyself thereof—and think whether I do well to take the letter and whether thy request is very honorable, and whether it is good to do a deed, in itself wanton, to lessen the sufferings of another. Ah, my Pandaro, leave it not with me; carry it back, for the love of God."
>
> Somewhat troubled by this, Pandaro said: "A wondrous thing is this to think of—that each woman, when others are by to see, should appear coy and angry about what is most desired by ladies. I have spoken to thee so much of this, thou shouldst not now be over-nice with me. I pray thee, do not deny me this now."
>
> Criseida smiled as she heard him, and took the letter and put it in her bosom. Then she said to him: "When I find time I shall read it as best I can. If in this I do ill, my reason is that I can do no less than please thee. May God look down from heaven and have regard to my lack of cunning."

If Criseida is lucky God will be looking elsewhere at the moment because she's lying in her teeth: she smiles at Pandaro's statement because, dear man! he has found her out (and women in general); she accepts the letter—and deposits it in her bosom to keep it appropriately warm—because there's no further reason for dissembling.

Chaucer wrote *Troilus and Criseyde* with *Il Filostrato* open on his writing table next to his manuscript as he went along: again and again he merely translates lengthy passages of the Italian into lovely supple colloquial English flowing into his rhymes and stanzas all of it as pristine as if from the very headwaters of English; he amplifies, invents, and changes as little as necessary, and only in order to sustain and clarify a gallery of characters who differ as absolutely from Boccaccio's (and Shakespeare's) as Chaucer himself differs from Shakespeare and Boccaccio. In the parallel passage in Chaucer, Pandarus comes with the letter, Criseyde is (or appears to be?) shocked and refuses it, Pandarus remonstrates, and then (because Chaucer's Criseyde wouldn't under any circumstances take it herself) he finds the only possible way of delivering it to the same depository:

Ful dredfully tho gan she stonden stylle,
And took it naught, but al hire humble chere
Gan for to chaunge, and seyde, "Scrit ne bille,   [writing, letter]
For love of God, that toucheth swich matere,
Ne brynge me noon; and also, uncle deere,
To myn estat have more rewarde, I preye,   [dignity, regard]
Than to his lust! What sholde I more seye?   [desire]

"And loketh now if this be resonable,
And letteth nought, for favour ne for slouthe,   [don't fail]
To seyn a sooth; now were it covenable   [convenient]
To myn estat, by God and by youre trouthe,
To taken it, or to han of hym routhe,
In harmyng of myself, or in repreve?   [reproach]
Ber it ayein, for hym that ye on leve!"   [Take it back,
     you believe in]

This Pandarus gan on hire for to stare,
And seyde, "Now is this the grettest wondre
That evere I seigh! Lat be this nyce fare!   [silly behavior]

To dethe mot I smyten be with thondre,
If for the citee which that stondeth yondre,
Wold I a lettre unto yow brynge or take
To harm of yow! What list yow thus it make?"   [Why do you please to take it so?]

So far no change in meaning from Boccaccio except that Pandarus omits the Boccaccian truth about women (they're all sex-maniacs) because it doesn't happen to apply to Criseyde; and then Pandarus finds the only way to do the job:

"But thus ye faren, wel neigh alle and some,   [in all respects]
That he that most desireth yow to serve,
Of hym ye recche leest wher he bycome,   [care, what becomes of him]
And whethir that he lyve or elles sterve.   [dies]
But for al that that ever I may deserve,
Refuse it naught," quod he, and hente hire faste,   [held her tight]
And in hire bosom the lettre down he thraste,   [thrust]

And seyde hire, "Now caste it awey anon,
That folk may seen and gauren on us tweye."   [gape]
Quod she, "I kan abyde til they be gon";
And gan to smyle, and seyde hym, "Em, I preye,   [Uncle]
Swich answere as yow list youreself purveye,   [as pleases you]
For trewely I nyl no lettre write."
"No? than wol I," quod he, "so ye endite."   [dictate]

Criseyde wouldn't under any circumstances take the letter voluntarily, and Pandarus has to find a way of getting her to take it that will neither implicate her nor preclude her consent. It isn't a game she's playing, it isn't even necessarily conscious or explicit, the world is full of risks she has no interest in taking, it's her nature to refuse risks or at least refuse responsibility for risks: she isn't a heroine of melodrama, but she isn't a liar or dissembler either, she won't pretend to feelings or intensities of feeling she doesn't have, and if others have intense feelings of which she happens to be the subject all they need to do is pass a miracle. Boccaccio requires no miracle, only Pandaro's shrewdness: Pandaro comes with the letter, Criseida makes her *pro forma* refusal which he invalidates by revealing his knowledge of woman's perpetual horniness, she smiles in good-natured acknowledgment of his victory—women play games: win a few, lose a few—and matter-of-factly accepting the letter stuffs it without further ado into what for Boccaccio is the obvious receptacle. Chaucer must have considered Boccaccio's simple solution with special delight because it suggested the miracle that his own Pandarus could pass: Criseyde is fond of Pandarus, she loves his wit and playfulness, she can even be playful in return, she trusts him as far as she trusts anybody, what will he think of next? and what he thinks of is to grab her with one hand and with the other put the letter where it belongs, so that in a single action he relieves her of the burden of her dignity and takes the burden of responsibility altogether upon himself. Now she can smile indulgently at his victory and even exchange wisecracks with him: "Uncle, if you want an answer to his letter, you'll have to do it yourself, because definitely I am not going to write one"; "No?" says Pandarus, on top of the world, "then I'll write it myself, provided you dictate." "Therwith she lough, and seyde, 'Go we dyne.' " Love, with the help of an occasional miracle, conquers all, and heroes walk in to dinner arm in arm with fair women.